ROSARIO
JOSÉ MARÍA DE MENA

VISIT SEVILLE

EDITORIAL EVEREST, S. A.
MADRID • LEON • BARCELONA • SEVILLA • GRANADA • VALENCIA
ZARAGOZA • LAS PALMAS DE GRAN CANARIA • LA CORUÑA
PALMA DE MALLORCA • ALICANTE – MEXICO • BUENOS AIRES

Written by: *Professor Rosario Gil Ferrer*

Documentation and revision: *José María de Mena*

Photography: *Justino Díez, Archivo Oronoz, G. M. Pou Riesco, Francisco Zubillaga, J. M. Ruiz, J. L. Rodríguez, Mariano Moreno, Palau, Paisajes Españoles, Expo'92, Archivo Everest.*

Cartography: *Everest*

Cover design: *Alfredo Anievas*

Lay Out: *María Casas*

Translation: *Impact Traducciones*

Carretera León-La Coruña, km 5 - LEÓN
ISBN: 84-241-3917-8
Legal deposit: LE. 994 - 1992
Printed in Spain

EDITORIAL EVERGRÁFICAS, S. A.
Ctra. León-La Coruña, km 5,
LEÓN (Spain)

INTRODUCTION

The historic center of old Seville is so extense and the wealth of its religious and civil monuments, museums and places of interest so vast that it would be impossible to visit the city in a single day. We have therefore divided Seville into eight sectors for sightseeing purposes, plus an additional one for a visit to Expo '92.

We have carefully assessed the interest of each sector so that, according to the time available, the visitor may see the most interesting sights. Visitors with only one day may satisfactorily take in the first one or two sectors. If there is more time available, other sectors may be added in order to obtain more thorough knowledge.

We have followed the same criteria with the six side trips within the province, which are included after the visits to the city. These include such interesting sites as the ruins of Itálica, the walls and castles of Alcalá and Carmona, the historical site of General Riego's uprising at Cabezas de San Juan, and the splendid pantheon of the Dukes in the city of Osuna.

The sectors for the city of Seville are the following:

ROUTE 1. THE GREAT MONUMENTS. The Cathedral, the Alcázar, the Palacio Arzobispal (Archbishop's Palace), and the Archivo General de Indias (Archives of the Indies).

ROUTE 2. BARRIO DE SANTA CRUZ (Santa Cruz Quarter). La Judería (the Jewish Quarter), Hospicio de los Venerables and the church, formerly a synagogue, of Santa María la Blanca.

ROUTE 3. FROM CITY HALL TO CASA DE PILATOS (PILATE'S HOUSE). This includes the great Mudéjar and Baroque churches, such as the Colegiata del Salvador, the Hospital de San Juan de Dios, the churches of San Esteban , Santa Catalina, and la Anunciación, plus the historical and picturesque calle Sierpes.

ROUTE 4. BARRIO DE LA MACARENA (Quarter). The Basílica de Nuestra Señora de la Macarena, the Hospital de las Cinco Llagas, the cemetery, the Alameda de Hércules, and the Churches of San Luis, San Juan de la Palma and the convent of Santa Inés.

ROUTE 5. FROM THE MUSEO MURILLO TO THE MYTH OF DON JUAN TENORIO. This route includes the monasteries of Santa Clara and San Clemente, the chapel with the image of Señor del Gran Poder and the dying place of Don Juan , protagonist of famous operas.

ROUTE 6. From the Hospital de la Caridad to the Real Maestranza bullring, visiting the Torre del Oro (The Golden Tower) and the church of La Magdalena . ROUTE 7. Parque de María Luisa (park), with a visit to the Archaeological Museum, the Museum of Folklore and Arts, and the palaces of the Iberoamerican Exhibition of 1929.

ROUTE 8. The Barrio de Triana , the wharf that saw the departure and safe return of the first navigators to sail around the globe in the 16th century, the church of Santa Ana, Callejón de la Inquisición (Inquisition Alley) and the Chapel of el Cristo del Cachorro.

ROUTE 9. Expo'92 with the Pavilion of Discoveries, the Pavilion of the Future, the pavilions of the one hundred countries participating and the Amusement Park.

Excursions within the province

ROUTE 1. Roman ruins of the city of Itálica, the Monastery of San Isidoro del Campo.

ROUTE 2. Carmona: walls and the alcázares (fortresses). The Roman necropolis. Medieval and Baroque buildings, churches and monasteries. Ecija: Noble palaces, Museum. The artistic treasure of its churches.

ROUTE 3. Alcalá de Guadaira: The Medieval castle. The Arahal: civil and religious architecture. Marchena: city of the Dukes of Arcos. Two cathedral churches.

ROUTE 4. Villafranca and Los Palacios, Baroque churches. Cabezas de San Juan: site of General Riego's revolt proclaiming the Constitution in 1820. Lebrija: the great altarpiece by Alonso Cano.

ROUTE 5. The city of Utrera: noble houses. The church of Santa María de la Mesa. The Sanctuary of Virgen de Consolación, Palmar de Troya, see of the schismatic church of the so-called pope Clement.

ROUTE 6. The city of Osuna. Palaces. The collegiate church and the pantheon of the Dukes of Osuna. The 16th century university.

IMPORTANT NOTES: To visit the city of Seville, it is not advisable to use private automobiles, since all the monuments to be visited are in the heart of the old town, full of narrow Medieval streets, where it is impossible to park. Besides, many of these are strictly closed to traffic, and in others, traffic is limited to public transport vehicles.

It is not worthwhile to use city buses since these do not go through the streets we are interested in, and the distance from one sight to another is quite short.

Regarding trips to towns within the province, special care has been taken to point out the roads to be used, but nonetheless, due to Expo'92, the province of Seville is undergoing extensive road renovation, so that some of these may be closed, with detours or modifications, and thus maximum attention to road signs is advised, and if possible, traffic officers sholud be consulted about each route to be followed.

In all the towns included in these provincial itineraries, the visitor will find commercial establishments, photo shops, restaurants and cafeterias, pharmacies, medical assistance, hotels, inns and service stations, since the towns are important and located on national roads.

We trust that this book, into which a great deal of work and care has gone, will help visitors to enjoy and make the most of their stay in Seville.

BY WAY OF A FOREWORD
(A very brief historical introduction)

Seville is one of the wealthiest cities in all of Western Europe as far as history and art are concerned. Founded over three thousand years ago, the most varied civilizations have passed through this city. It was the capital of the Tartessians and a Phoenician commercial emporium. Romanized after being taken by the Carthaginians, it shared the splendor of the Roman Empire, and three emperors, Trajan, Hadrian and Theodosius, are alleged to have been born in this city.

It was twice the capital in Visigoth times, in the 5th century, during the reigns of Amalaric to Theudigiseland, and at the end of the 6th century, during the short-lived reign of Saint Hemenegild. At the same time, the famous Bishop Saint Isidore, was compiling his monumental work Las Etimologías, which saved the ancient Roman culture from falling into complete oblivion.

Invaded by the Arabs in 711, Seville later became the brilliant Moslem court of King Almotamid and the poetess Queen Itimad called «La Romaiquía». The Almohads left a superb mosque, rivaling that of Córdoba, the Patio de los Naranjos (Court of the Orange Trees) and the marvelous Giralda tower can still be admired.

After being reconquered by the Christians in 1248, Seville became the capital of Castile from King Ferdinand on, and it was here that King Alfonso X the Wise wrote his famous books on astronomy and his poems Cantigas de Santa María (Songs to the Virgin). It continued to be the capital until the reign of Pedro I, who enriched the city with the construction of the incomparable Alcázar (Fortress).

During the following century, it was once again for sometime the capital of the Catholic kings, Ferdinand and Isabel, and here the unfortunate prince Don Juan was born, whose early death changed the course of Spanish history. Christopher Columbus set up his headquarters here to prepare his voyage to the New World.

For over two hundred years, Seville was the economic capital of the New World through its Casa de Contratación (Exchange) and its port, the only one where ships sailed to the Indies and where the famous Silver Fleet arrived laden with treasures.

Thus, if in earlier times the city was enriched with Roman, Arab and Renaissance monuments, at the height of its trade with the Indies, it increased its splendor with magnificent buildings and jewels of Baroque art, convents and stately palaces, of which a large number still remain, whose walls guard incredible gems of sculpture by masters such as Martínez Montañés, «La Roldana», Duque Cornejo and Ruiz Gijón; and paintings from the School of Seville, famous throughout the world, for its Velazquez, Zurbaráns and Murillos.

Seville became once more the capital of Spain for five years from 1729 to 1733, when Philip V moved his court to the Alcázar of Seville, a period which is known as the «Royal Lustrum» in the chronicles of the times.

During the 19th century, Seville supplied inspiration for authors and composers, who wrote operas such as Don Juan, Carmen, The Power of destiny, and Fidelio.

And at the dawn of the 20th century the city was enhanced by the beautiful buildings erected for the Iberoamerican Exhibition, still still revealing their fine architecture in the gardens of Park.

Seville has three incomparable feasts in the calendar of universal festivals: Holy Week, the April Fair and the pilgrimage to El Rocío, and now it offers a new event of international rank, the Universal Exposition (Expo '92) to welcome as many lovers of culture and tourism as wish to come to visit Seville.

JOSE M. DE MENA
Member of the Provincial Commission
for Historical and Artistic Monuments of Seville.

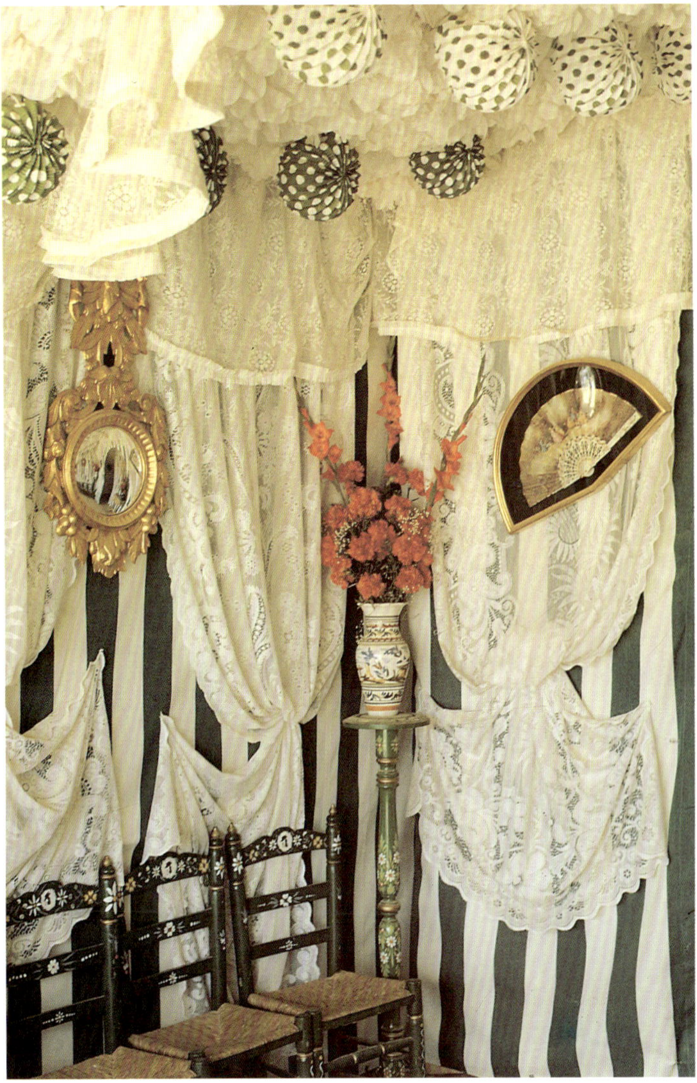

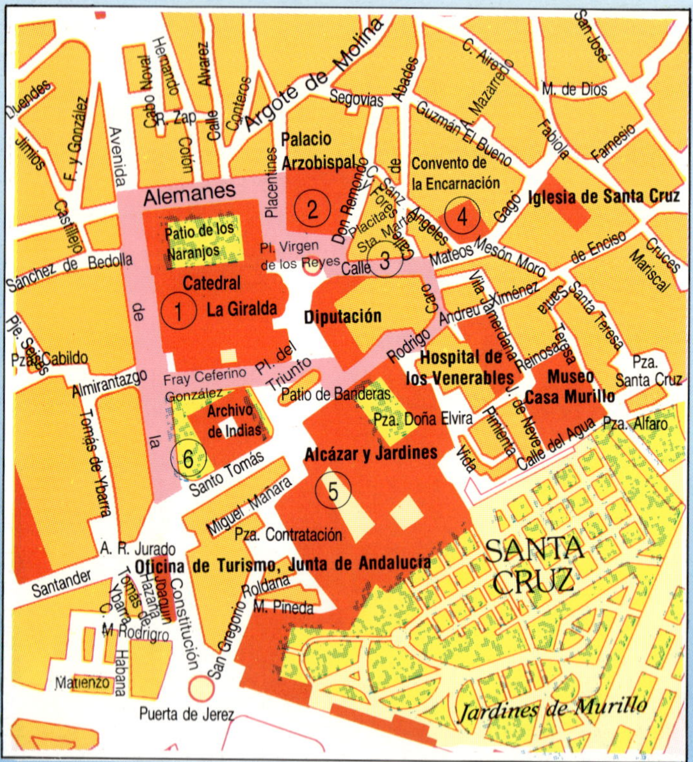

ROUTE 1
THE GREAT MONUMENTS

PLACES OF INTEREST

① **The Cathedral**

Patio de los Naranjos (Court) and tower of la Giralda, 12th century arab style. Rest of the Cathedral, gothic style of the 15th and 16th centuries.

② **Archbishop's Palace**

Baroque façade; interior of different earlier styles. Very important archive.

③ **Placita de Santa Marta**

Little square with a medieval stone cross.

④ **Convent of La Encarnación**

Its outside walls are the remains of the Mosque of the Bears of arab times.

⑤ **The Alcázar**

Fortified site from the times of the Almorávides. Contains rey don Pedro Palace, mudéjar style. Gardens.

⑥ **The Archives of the Indies**

Important documentary collection.

STARTING POINT	Avenida de la Constitución
EXIT TO NEXT ROUTE	By calle Ceferino González until plaza del Triunfo.

USEFUL ADDRESSES NEARBY

Post Office:	Avenida de la Constitución
Public telephone:	Close to Plaza Nueva
Chemists:	Avenida de la Constitución, 27 Calle Mateos Gago, 14
Photo Service:	Avenida de la Constitución, 2 Souvenir shops all along the route.
Restaurante El Giraldillo:	Plaza Virgen de los Reyes, 2
Restaurante Punta del Diamante:	Avda. de la Constitución at Alemanes
Restaurante Figón del Cabildo:	Plaza del Cabildo opposite the Cathedral
Restaurante Casa Robles:	Alvarez Quintero, 58
Restaurante Las Escobas:	Alvarez Quintero, 62. Former inn of the Escobas, established in 1386, probably the oldest in Europe. This place hosted such important guests as Cervantes, Lope de Vega, Alejandro Dumas, Lord Byron, Bécquer and the Alvarez Quintero brothers.
Restaurante Don Raimundo:	Argote Molina, 26. Placed in an old noble house with a patio.

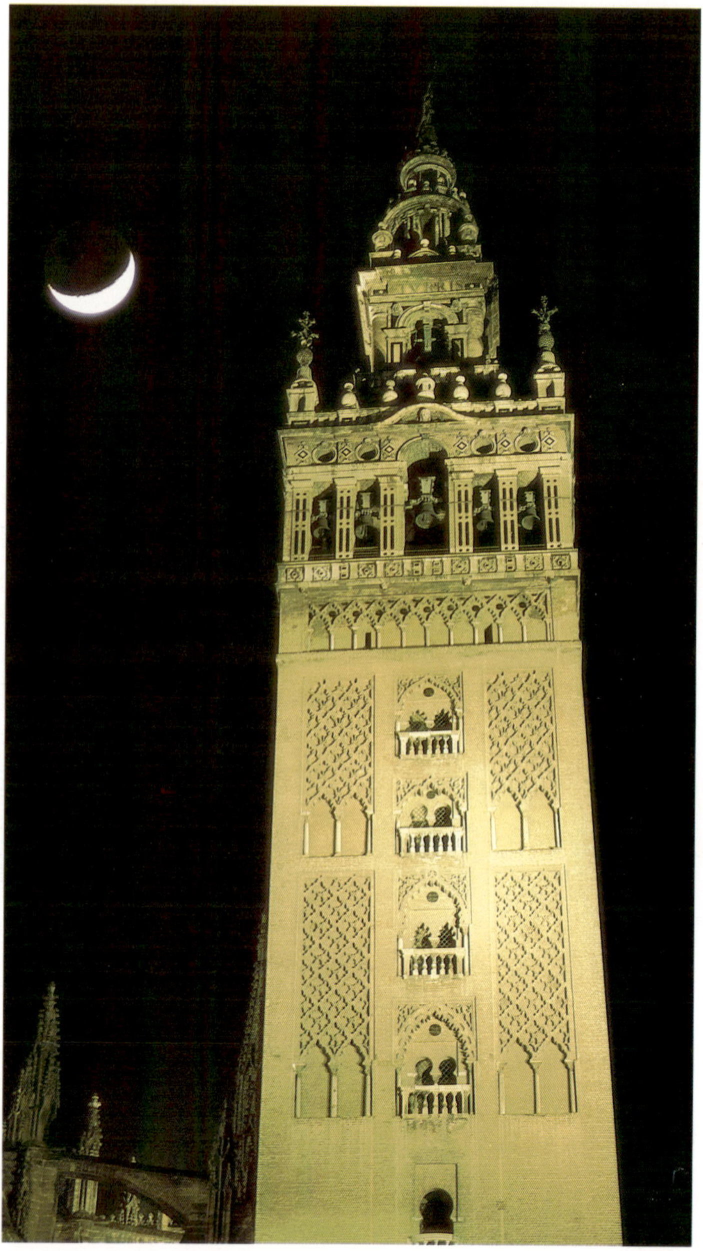

La Giralda by night

ROUTE 1: THE GREAT MONUMENTS

This route leads through the most splendid part of Seville since here, within a small area, its most important monuments are to be found: the Cathedral, the Alcázar, the Archivo de Indias.... But at the time of the Empire, it also concentrated here the richest products from the Indies, together with others brought by Italian, Flemish, French and German merchants to sell or barter for these. So much so that on the steps to the Cathedral and the building that now houses the Archivo de Indias, which was then the lonja (market), one could buy pearls from Darien wholesale, emeralds from Chocó and Muzú, silk from China and the Philippines, as well as lace from Brussels and Ghent, linen cloth from Holland, browned arms with niello work from Milan, velvet cloth from Rouen and fabulous pieces of Florentine gold and silver work.

The Steps

From avenida de la Constitución we walk up calle Alemanes, so called because this is where the German merchants set themselves up to trade their wares on the Cathedral steps. These steps were praised by the Renaissance poet Torres Naharro in a poem he wrote on the wealth of Seville:

Un templo de majestad
sin segundo;
un Guadalquivir jocundo,
y unas Gradas, que una grada
vale más que todo el Mundo.

(A temple so majestic
second to none;
a jovial Guadalquivir,
and the Steps,
of which one step is worth
more than the whole World.)

On the left sidewalk, we can still find remains of the porticoes used by these merchants.

At the end of the street, we go around the Cathedral to find the Plaza de la Virgen de los Reyes. If we walk a few yards up Mateos Gago street and look back, we can admire the grandeur of the Giralda, the roofing of the Gothic Cathedral, with its flying buttresses supporting the weight of the cupola and transferring it to the walls and buttresses, in a living lesson in architectural techniques.

The Giralda

The tower of La Giralda, as we see it today, is composed of three perfectly distinct parts: the «alminar» or minaret, the belfry, and the cupulino or small cupola, with the statue of the Giraldillo.

The alminar, or Arab part, was the tower of the Grand Mosque and was built by order of the emperor of Morocco, Abu Yacub Yusuf, when Seville was under Moroccan rule in the year 1184. The architecture of the Moslem tower closely resembles the Kutubia tower of Marrakesh. It was designed by the engineer Gever, built by the architect Aben Baso, and decorated with delicate filigree in brick by the master mason Alí de Gomara.

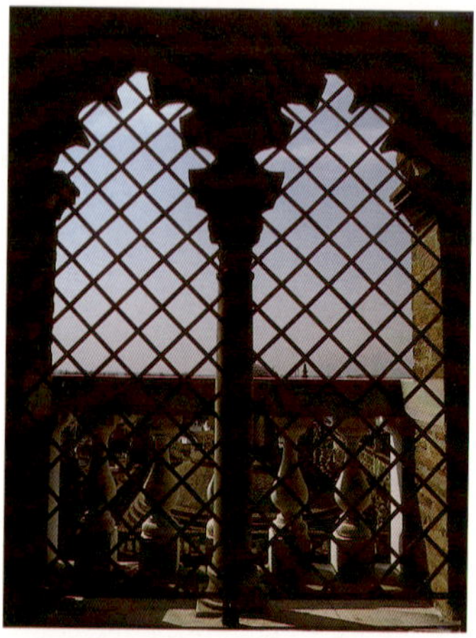

On top of the Arab minaret we can see the belfry, composed of several parts: the Bells, with twenty four bells presided by the Big Bell; the Lilies stage, which has a terrace open to the four sides with four vases full of bronze lilies on the corners; the Stars stage, so called for its decoration; the Carambolas stage; cupola; and on top, the small

◁ *Balcony of the Giralda.*

The Giralda and the Cathedral.

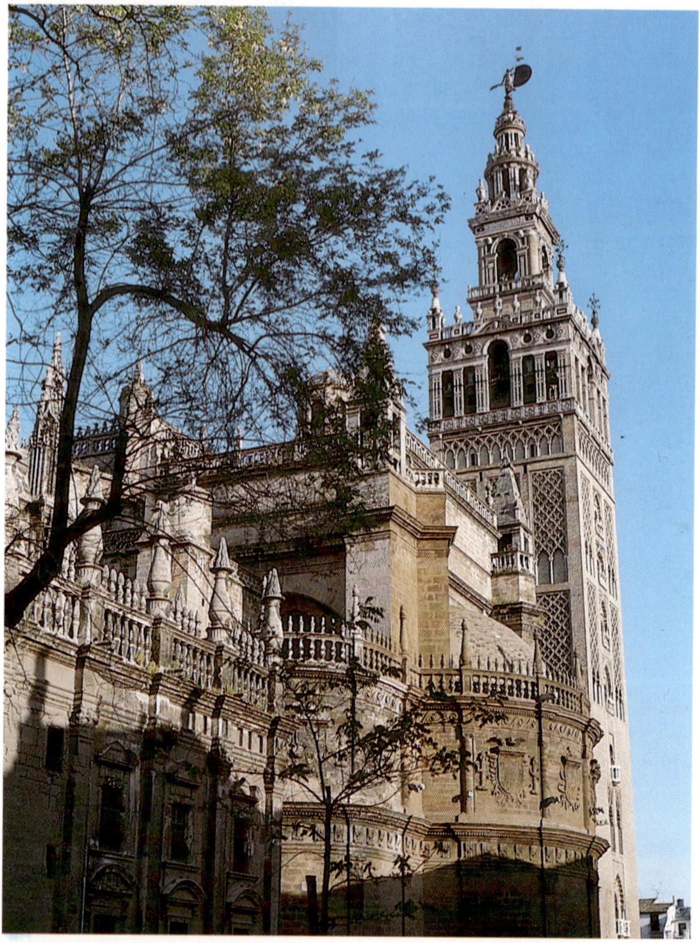

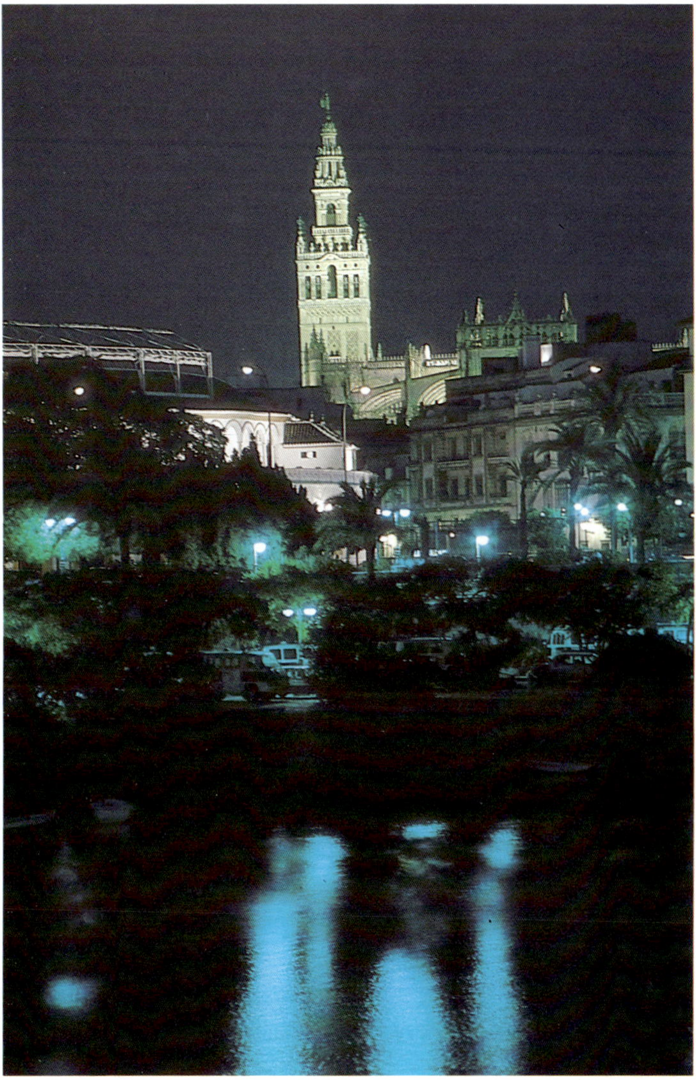

The Giralda stands out in the Sevillian evening.

cupola with the figure of a woman in Roman dress holding a shield in one hand and a palm frond in the other. Because this figure gyrates, it is called the Giraldillo, or Giralda, by extension the name of the tower. The belfry and its successive stages are the work of architect Hernán Ruiz in the 16th century and the figure of the Giralda was designed by Luis de Vargas, modeled by the sculptor Juan Bautista Vázquez the Elder, and cast in bronze by the famous caster of artillery cannons Bartolomé Morel.

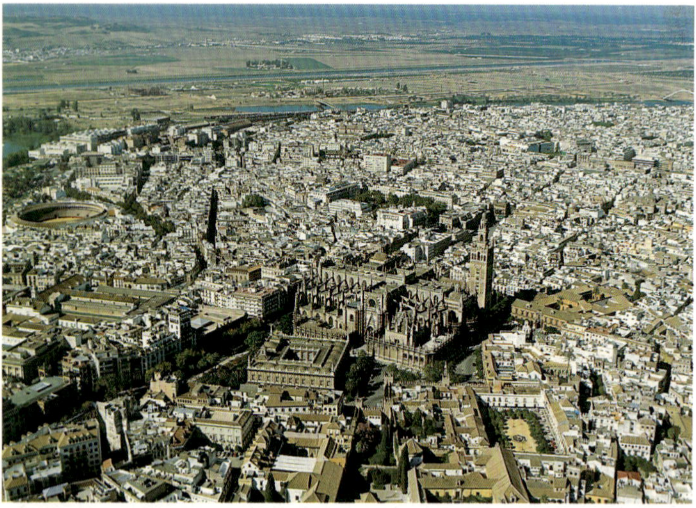

Seville surrounds its Cathedral.

The Cathedral

The Cathedral is divided into two perfectly distinct parts. The one remaining from the old Great Mosque comprises the Patio de los Naranjos (Court of the Orange Trees) and the gallery housing the Biblioteca Capitular or Biblioteca Colombina (Chapter Library or Columbian Library), so called because it holds the books of Hernando Colón, son of the Discoverer of the New World.

The Patio de los Naranjos opens on to the calle Alemanes by the puerta del Perdón. Here we can admire the two leaves of the door covered with bronze plates in exquisite Almohad work. Also in Islamic style are the arches and gallery leading onto calle Placentines.

In the center of the court there is a fountain with a large Visigothic basin where, according to tradition, Saint Hermenegild was baptized when he was converted to Catholicism, which caused the war against his father Leovigild. Also on the court floor are the tombstones of two Sevillian heroes, González Cuadrado and Palacios Malaver, who gave up their lives on the gallows rather than accuse their companions of plotting against the Napoleonic troops. This court also has a stone pulpit, in which a stone slab reminds us that from here eminent speakers preached as well as saints such as Saint John of Avila and Saint Vicent Ferrer.

The Cathedral is huge, the second in the world in size. The length of the central nave is 116 meters (380 ft.). As to the aisles, only the Milan Cathedral is wider, by 11 centimeters.

The Cathedral was designed by the Chapter Architect Alonso Martínez in 1402, and for over 100 years architects, sculptors, carvers and stonemasons

Seville, Cathedral of Santa María:
1. Main entrance. **2.** Baptism Door. **3.** Nativity or Saint Michael's Door. **4.** Door of Pardon. **5.** Court of the Orange Trees. **6.** Door of the Orange Trees. **7.** Lizard Door. **8.** Granada Chapel. **9.** Columbian and Chapter Library. **10.** Sagrario Parish Church. **11.** Easter Door. **12.** The Giralda. **13.** Palos Door. **14.** Apse of the Royal Chapel. **15.** Campanillas Door. **16.** Saint Cristóbal de la Lonja Door. **17.** Choir. **18 and 19.** Alabaster Chapels. **20.**Retrochoir. **21.** Chancel. **22.** High Sacristy. **23.** Royal Chapel. **24.** Altar of the Holy Angel. **25.** Tomb of Fernán Colón. **26.** Nativity Altar. **27.** Chapel of San Laureano. **28.** Chapel of Saint Anne or of the Christ of Maracaibo. **29.** Chapel of Saint Joseph. **30.** Chapel of Saint Hermenegildo. **31.** Antigua Chapel. **32.** Altar of the Inmaculate Conception. **33.** Tomb of Cristopher Columbus. **34.** Altar of the Pietá. **35.** Chapel of the Sorrows. **36.** Virgin of the Chalices. **37.** Chapel of Saint Andrew. **38.** Main Sacristy. **39.** Chapel of the Marshal. **40.** Vestry. **41.** Antechapter. **42.** Chapter Room. **43.** Saint Peter's Chapel. **44.** Chapel of our Lady of the Pillar. **45.** Chapel of the Evangelists. **46.** Chapel of the Maidens. **47.** Altar of our Lady of Bethlehem. **48.** Chapel of Saint Francis. **49.** Chapel of Saint James. **50.**Chapel of the Steps. **51.** Chapel of Saint Anthony or Baptismal Chapel. **52.** Chapel of Saint Leandro.

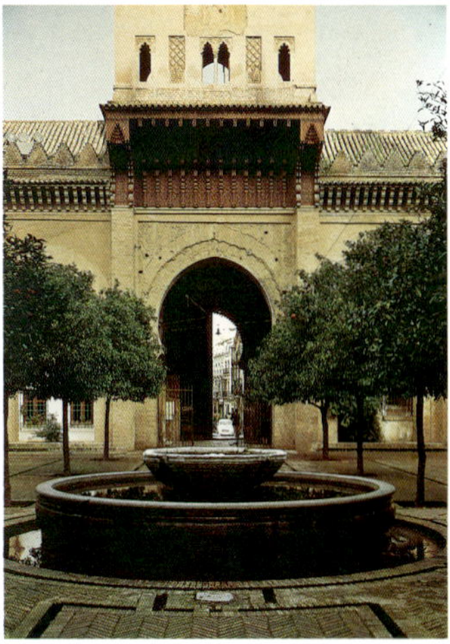

Court of the Orange Trees.

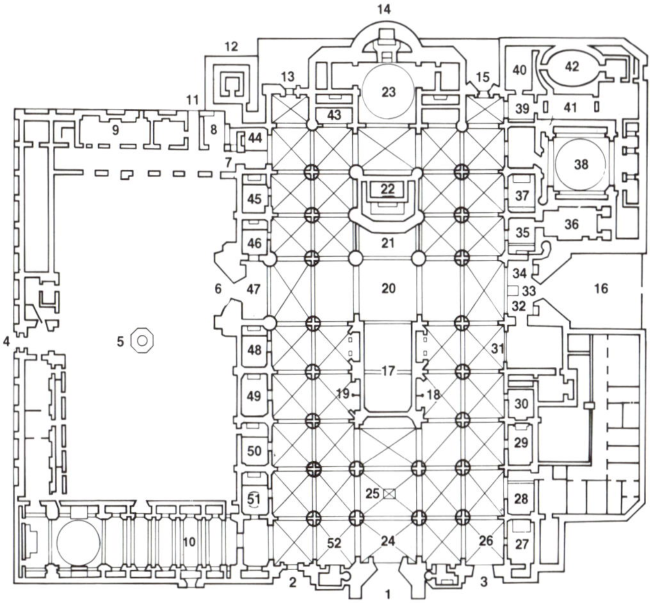

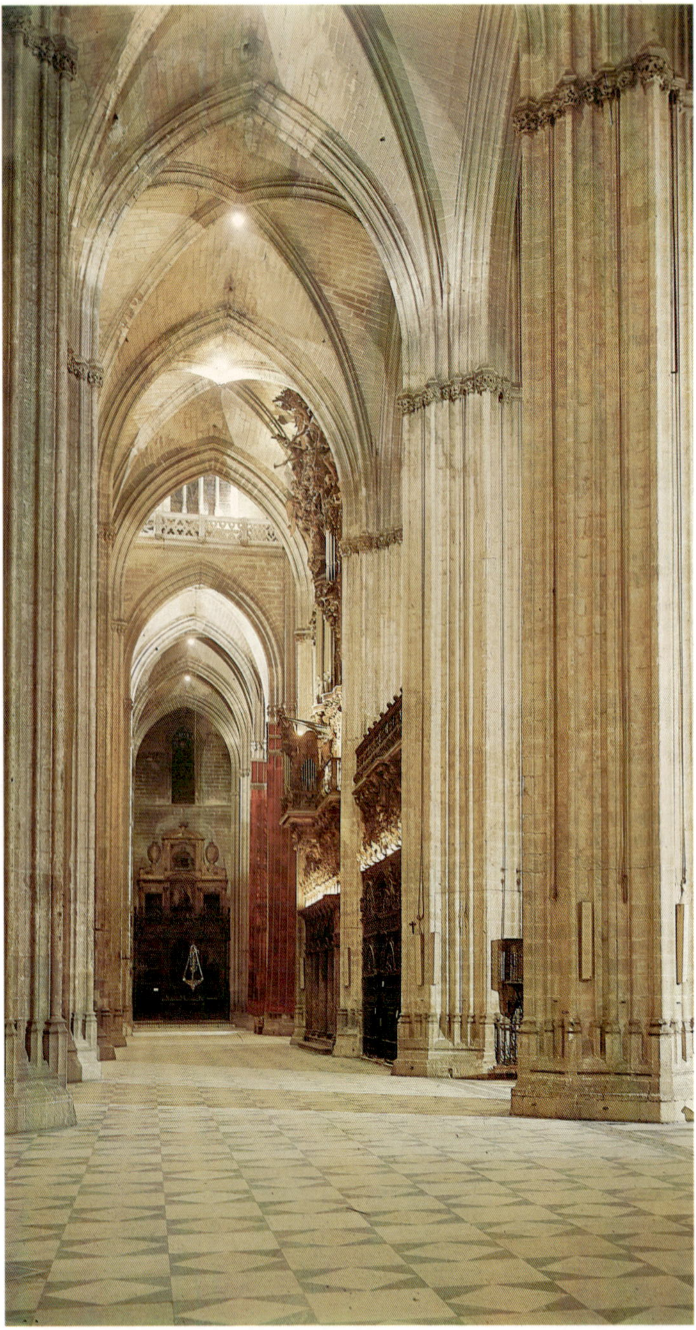

Cathedral Aisles.

from all over Europe worked in it.

The main altarpiece is the work of the Flemish artist Pierre Dankarty, and it was started in 1482 and finished in 1564. It is 20 meters (66 ft.) high and its amazing workmanship represents the life of Christ and scenes from the Bible and the lives of saints with almost a thousand figures. It is in the Gothic style, richly gilded and polychromed.

The choir is in the central nave, with valuable choirstalls, and in the center is the exquisitely worked great lectern.

There are 117 choirstalls, with a seat for the king bearing the royal coat of arms of Castile. The whole choir was carved by a single craftsman, the famous Nufro Sánchez.

The tomb of Hernando Colón is in the retrochoir.

There are five aisles, and the two lateral ones are divided into chapels, all of them with handsome gilded iron gates. In different chapels we can see paintings by masters, such as the Immaculate Conception by Zurbarán in Saint Peter's Chapel; the Allegory of the Inmaculate Conception, by Luis de Vargas, which aroused the envy of Alesio; the Vision of St. Anthony of Padua, painted by Murillo, in the Baptism Chapel.

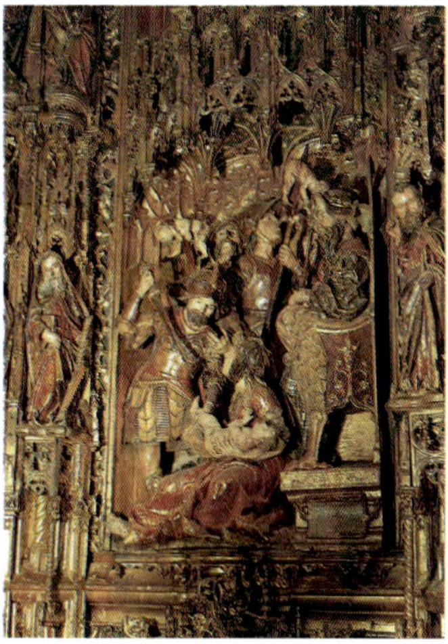
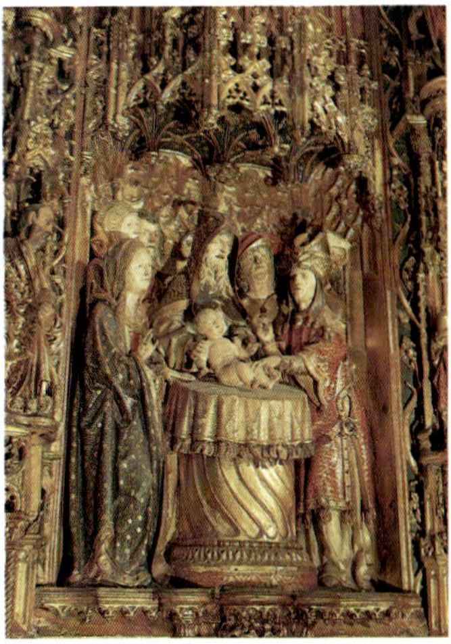

Main Altarpiece: Details of the Beheading and The Circumcision.

Next to Saint Christopher's door is a huge painting of Saint Christopher, painted by Mateo Pérez de Alesio, and in front of the door is the funeral monument where Christopher Columbus is buried, whose remains were brought from Havana when the colonies were lost in 1898. The monument is composed of four statues carrying on their shoulders Columbus' coffin, work of the famous sculptor Mélida.

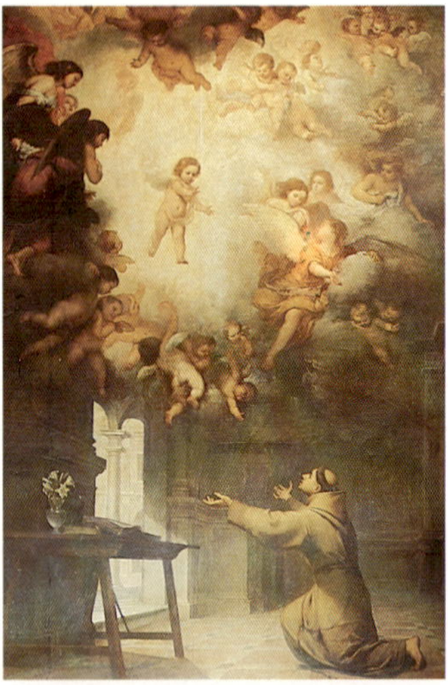

Vision of Saint Anthony of Padua.

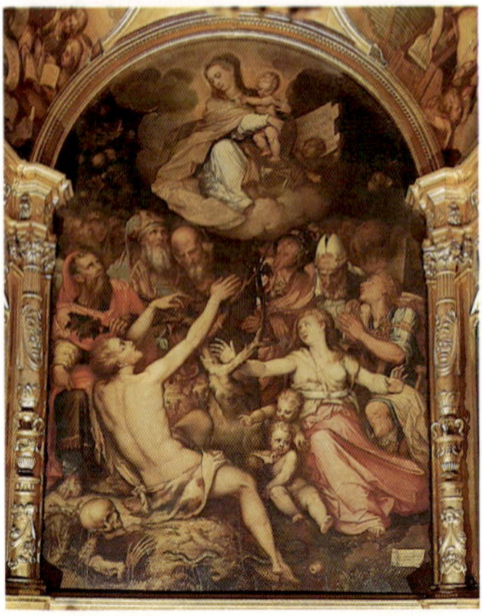

Allegory of the Inmaculate Conception.

In the Cathedral we can also see outstanding tombs, such as that of Cardinal Cervantes, with a coat of arms of deer representing his surname; the tomb of Archbishop Gonzalo de Mena, and others. The small chapels to both sides of the main altar contain fine sculptures, among these the Inmaculada known as the «Little Blind Girl», by Martínez Montañés.

The stained glass windows of the Cathedral all of them from the 15th and 16th centuries are extremely beautiful, especially the one representing the Adoration of the Shepherds before the newborn Jesus Christ.

The Chapter Room is quite

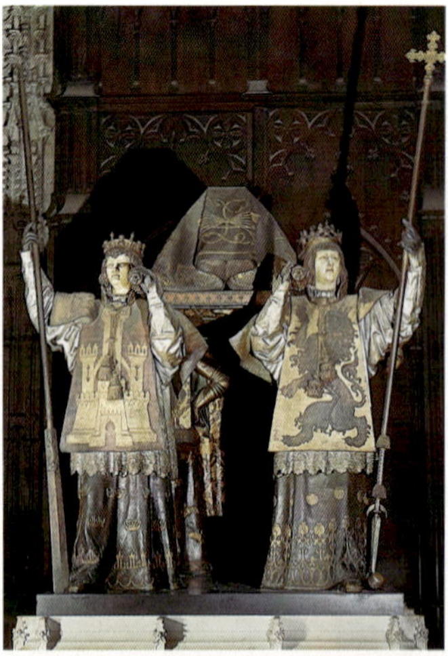

Tomb of Columbus.

outstanding, with its circular architecture covered by a vault painted by Bartolomé Esteban Murillo. It contains portraits of Sevillian prelates.

The Cathedral museum is in the Main Sacristy, where the processional monstrance by the silversmith Juan de Arfe can be admired, together with religious objects in gold and silver, embroidered chasubles, as well as other liturgical treasures from the 15th century to the 18th century, and paintings from the Flemish, Italian and Sevillian schools.

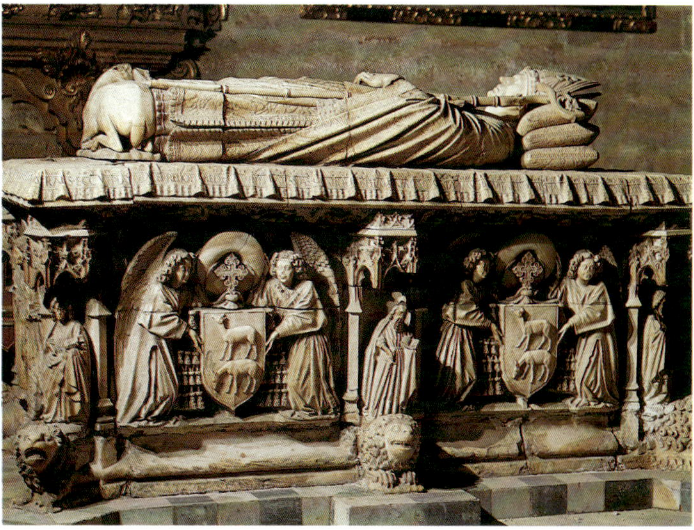

Tomb of Cardinal Cervantes.

At the head of the Cathedral is the Royal Chapel, also known as the Chapel of the Virgen de los Reyes, a genuine jewel of Renaissance architecture. On its

Stained glass window.

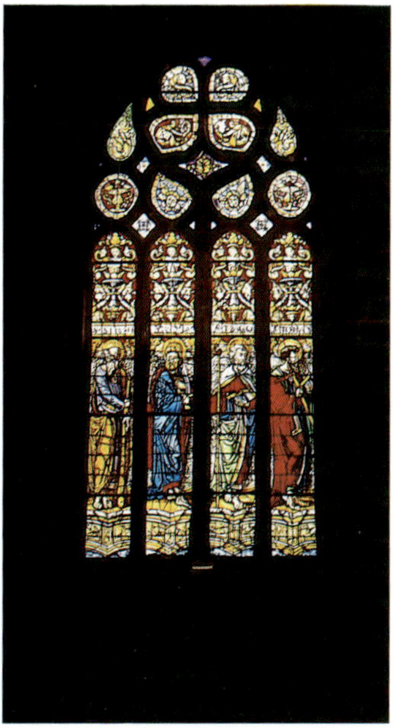

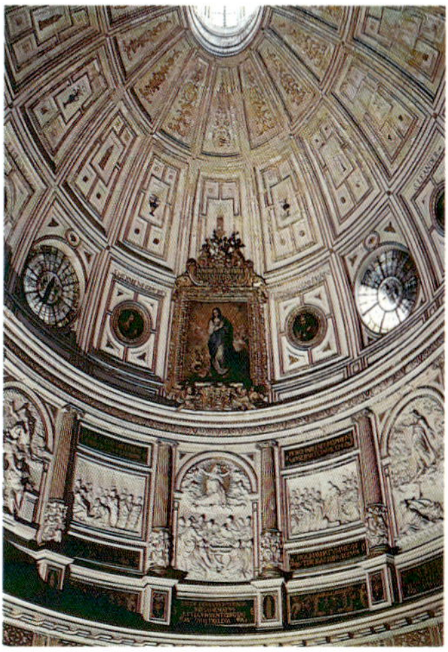

Vault of the Chapter Room.

main altar is the image of Our Lady of the Kings, patron saint of the Archdiocese of Seville, and at her feet, in a glass and silver case, the body of King Ferdinand II the Saint is kept. In extremely rich tombs placed in the lateral walls of the chapel, Queen Beatrice of Swabia,

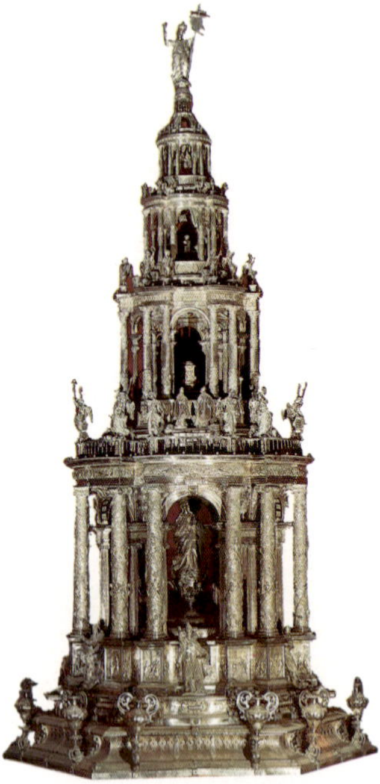

Monstrance by Juan de Arfe.

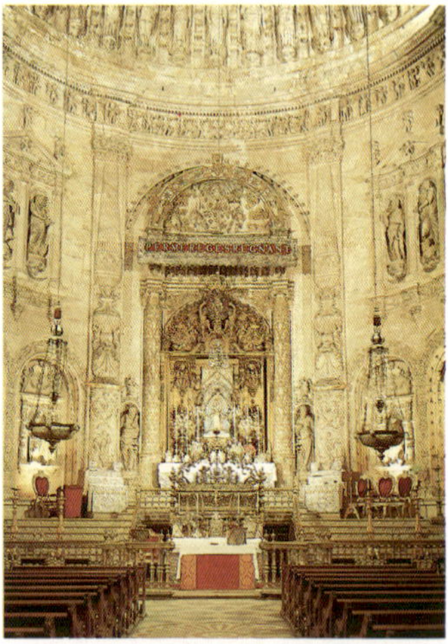

Chapel of the Kings.

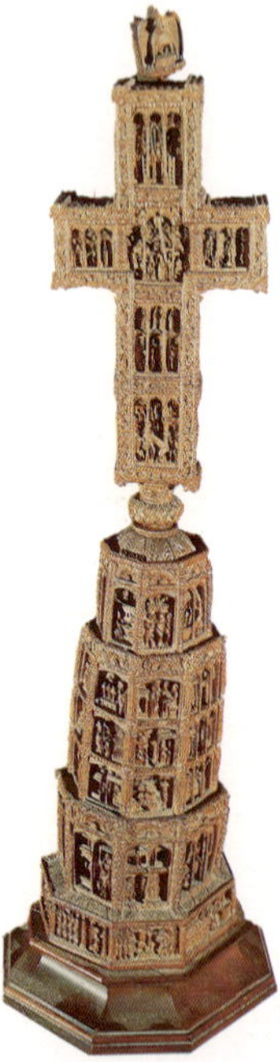

Cross of Saint Pius V.

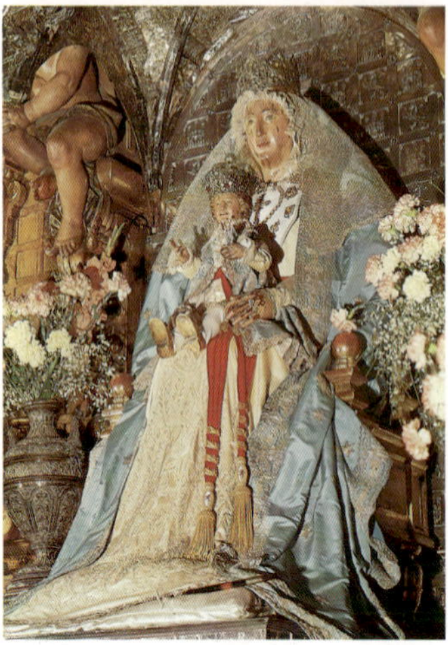

Our Lady of the Kings.

wife of Saint Ferdinand, and Alfonso X the Wise, their son, are buried. Under the altar is the Royal Mausoleum, where all the kings of Castile from Alfonso X to Pedro I are buried, as well as the queens and Infantes from the 13th and 14th centuries.

Outside the Cathedral we can see exquisite reliefs above

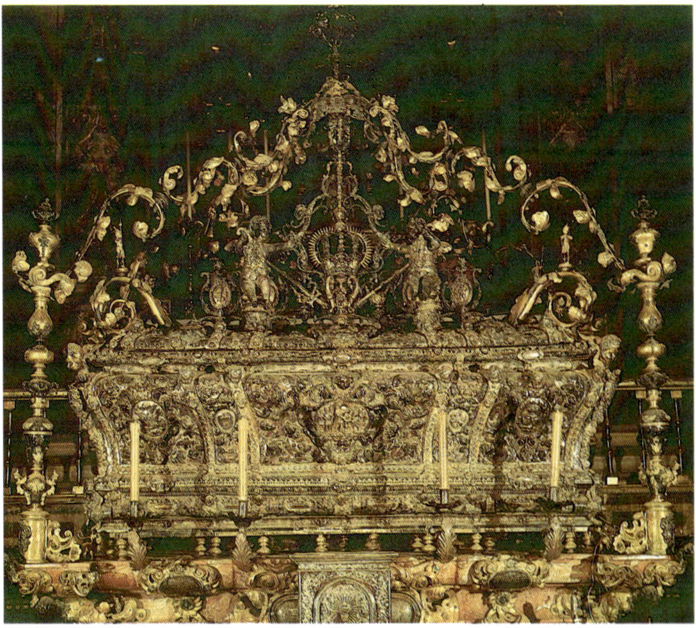

Urne with the relics of Saint Ferdinand.

each door. They are the work of Miguel Florentín and other masters. The façade facing avenida de la Constitución has two monumental frontispieces embellished with statues of the Evangelists and other saints, the work of Lorenzo Mercadante and Pedro Millán.

The iron chain completely surrounding the Cathedral determined the space which had

Tomb of Alfonso X.

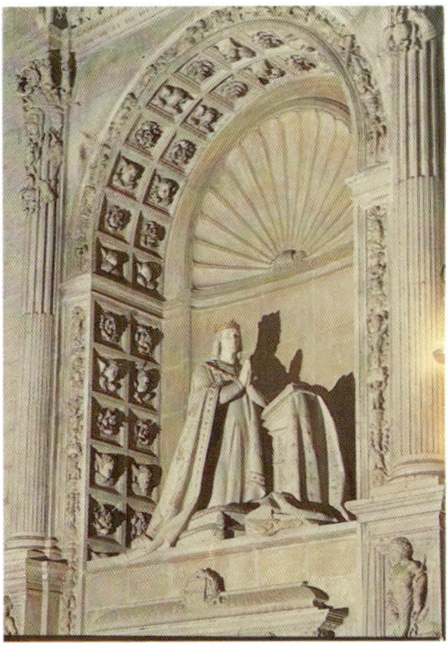

Parish Church of El Sagrario.

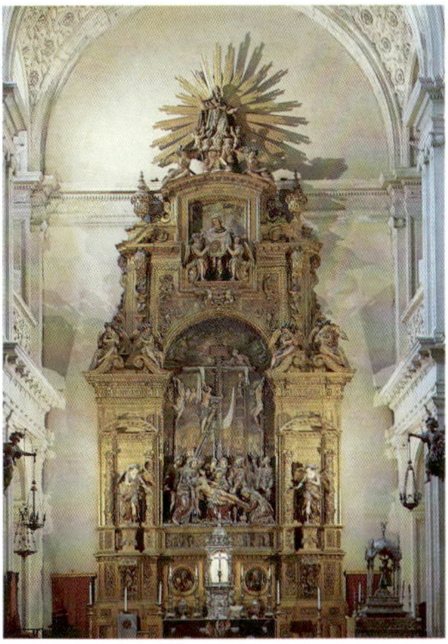

«asylum privileges» in past times.

Next to the Cathedral, with an entrance through it and with its own door onto avenida de la Constitución is the Church of El Sagrario, whose main altar was brought from the Chapel of the Biscayan Brotherhood in the now disappeared convent of Saint Francis. Its sculptures were made by famous artist Pedro Roldán in the 17th century.

The Palacio Arzobispal

Coming out of the Cathedral onto the plaza de la Virgen de los Reyes, decorated with a magnificent marble and jasper fountain in the center, we find to the left of the square, the noble building of the Archbishop's Palace. This was commenced by Remondo in the 13th century, continued by Gonzalo de Mena in the 14th century, and concluded by Manuel Arias in 1717. The coats of arms of the prelates can be seen on different parts of the building, with that of Bishop Arias on the portal of the main façade. The façade is superb, Baroque in style, the work of the architect Fray Manuel Ramos. Inside the Palace, the first court is admirable, with a magnificent marble staircase, as well as the second court, with a Renaissance fountain topped by a statue of Neptune. The Palace houses a rich collection of paintings signed by the best artists, in the manner of an ecclesiastical museum. There are also the Archidiocesan Archives containing priceless documents dating back to the 12th century.

The Archbishop's Palace.

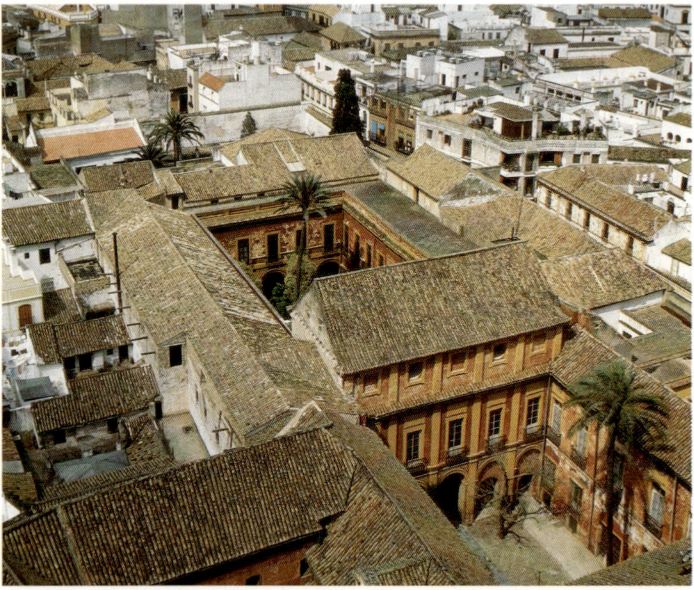

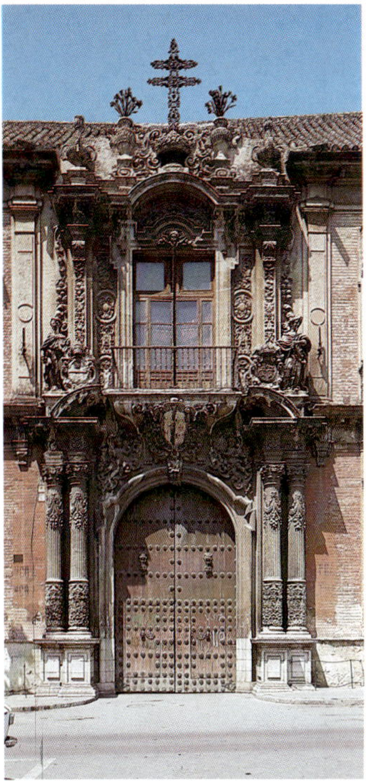

Façade of the Archbishop's Palace.

Placita de Santa Marta

Next to the plaza de la Virgen de los Reyes at the entrance to calle Mateos Gago to the right, there is an alley leading to the little square of Santa Marta, a suggestive corner surrounded by convent walls. In the center, there is an interesting ancient stone cross, which according to tradition comes from the Saint Lazarus Hospital outside the city walls.

Convento de la Encarnación

Between the plaza Virgen de los Reyes and the plaza del Triunfo, there is, facing the Cathedral, the convent of the nuns of the Encarnación, founded on the site of the former Mosque of the Bears, of which remains are still visible from the outside. The church has good images by Dionisio Rivas and other Baroque masters.

Plaza de Santa Marta.

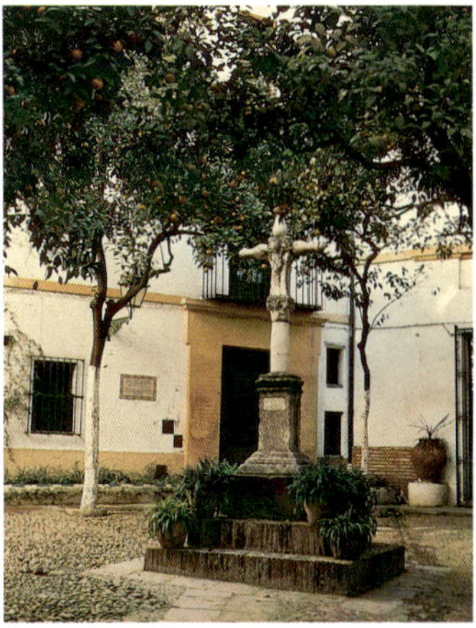

The Alcázar

The plaza del Triunfo faces the walls of the Alcázar, a splendid piece of military architecture from the times of the Almorávides, when the sultans of Morocco, after incorporating Seville into their Magreb empire, built this wall facing the city to protect themselves for fear of an uprising of the people of Seville against their oppression.

The wall has two doors leading onto this plaza, one onto the Patio de Banderas or Court of the Banners, which we will visit later, and the other, the Puerta del León (Lion's Gate), so called because it has a heral-

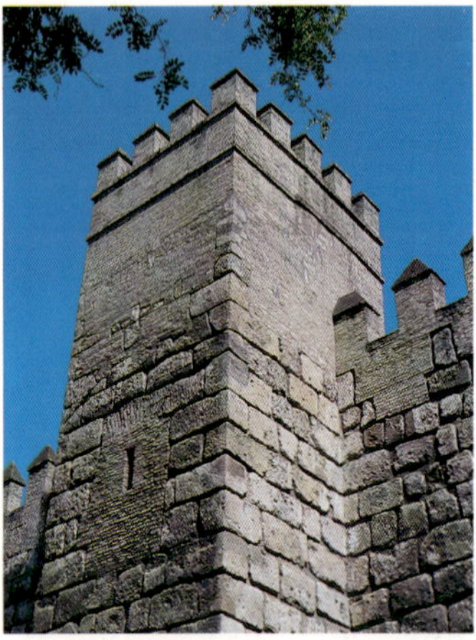

Walls of the Alcázar.

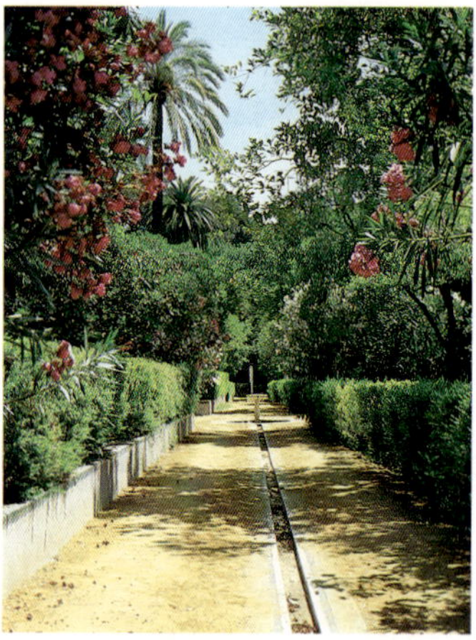

Gardens of the Alcázar.

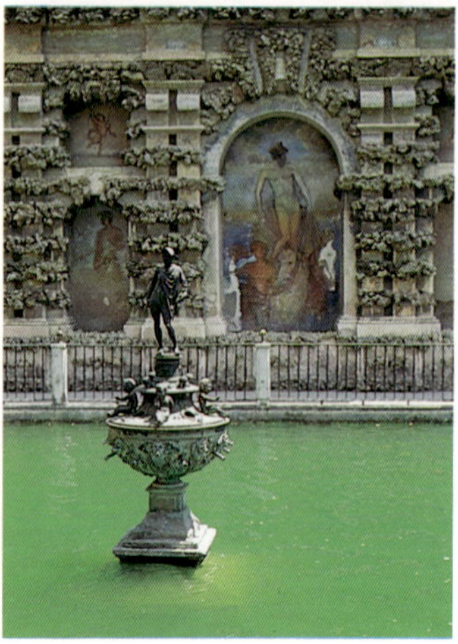

Fountain of Mercury.

dic lion painted on tiles over the arch. This is the one we will use to enter the Alcázar.

The Alcázar was not however built by the Arabs, but by the Christian King Pedro I about 1360. Certainly this site was used since Roman times as an acropolis or military fortress and governor's residence, but only some ruins remain from the Visigoth and Moslem eras. The sections of the complete building as we see them today date back to King Pedro, to the reign of the Catholic Kings and Emperor Charles I.

Entering through the Puerta del León and walking through a small open corridor, we reach the Patio de la Montería (Hunting Courtyard) where according to tradition, King Pedro gathered with his huntsmen before starting out on the hunt.

At the end of the courtyard we see the main façade of the building called the palace of King Pedro, with attractive decorations in arches and a panel of white and blue glazed tiles with the Arab inscription: «There is no conqueror but Allah», and around it a sign in Gothic script saying: «This citadel and these palaces and these portals were built in the Era of one thousand four hundred and two» (Year 1364).

Inside there are spacious galleries and tiled rooms with alternating Arabic and Gothic inscriptions and decorations of Medieval Christian coats of

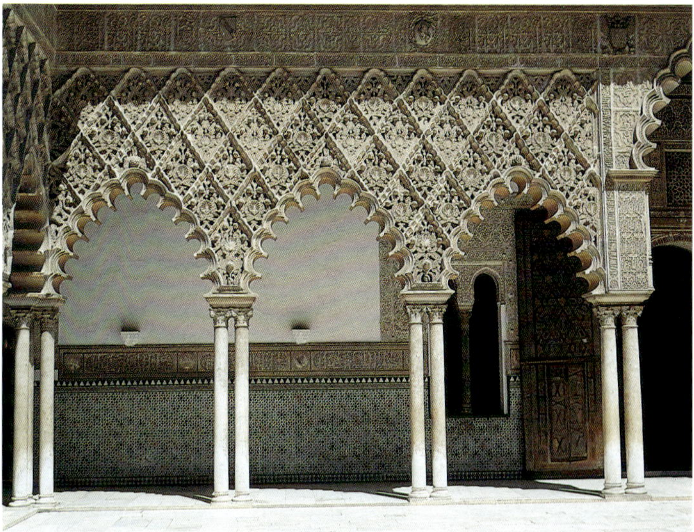

Courtyard of the Damsels.

Seville, Alcázar: **1.** Justice Hall. **2.** Plaster Court. **3.** Hunting Courtyard. **4.** Façade of the Palace of Pedro I. **5.** Vestibule. **6.** Courtyard of the Damsels. **7.** Room of Charles V's Ceiling. **8.** Bedroom of the Moorish Kings. **9.** María de Padilla's Apartments. **10.** Ambassadors Hall. **11.** Room of Philip II's Ceiling. **12.** Room of the Catholic Kings Ceiling. **13.** Doll's Courtyard. **14.** The Prince's Room. **15.** Staircase to the first floor. **16.** Chapel.

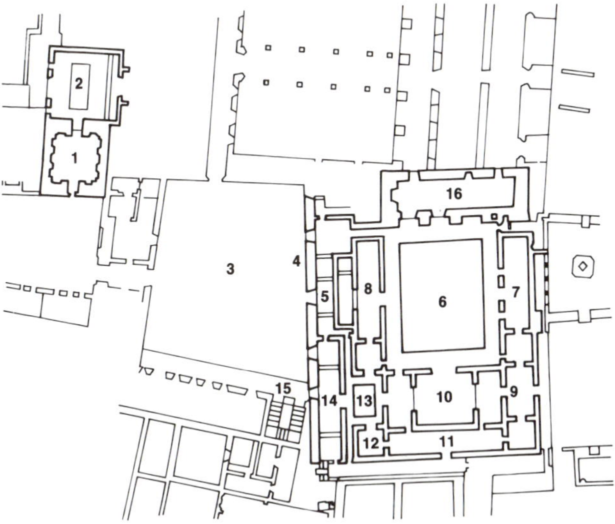

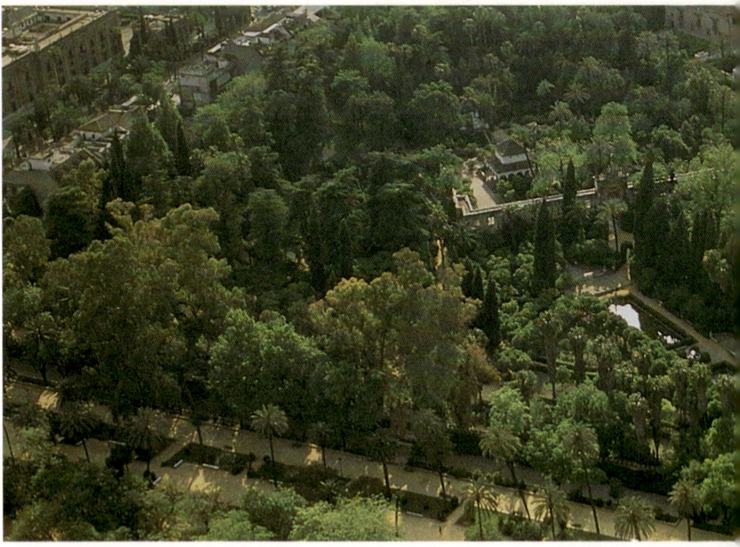

The Gardens of the Alcázar.

arms. In one of the lower galleries, there is the Master's Room, where King Pedro had his bastard brother Fadrique, Master of Santiago (Saint James) killed. In another room, Queen Isabella gave birth to her eldest son, Prince Juan, who died when he was eighteen years old, and who according to the chronicles, died from «loving his wife too much», whom he had married a year before.

In the palace we can admire the Courtyard of the Damsels, with its superb Mudéjar architecture, and the Dolls Courtyard, so called for its small size, like a jewelry box. But the best of the palace is the Ambassadors' Hall, with a cupola in Islamic style considered one of the finest works of Islamic art in the world, although it was executed by the Sevillian artist Diego Ruiz in 1389.

Another sector of the palace is the private quarters of King Pedro and his wife María de Padilla. The upper floor of the palace was built to lodge the guests who came to the wedding of Emperor Charles I and Isabel of Portugal.

Also remarkable are the two rooms on the ground floor: the Admiral's Room, where projects for expeditions were studied, and where Christopher Columbus had his office when preparing his Discovery voyage; and the Tapestry Room with a collection of tapestries made in Flanders, representing scenes of the conquest of Tunis by Charles I. On the top floor, Queen Isabella's chapel is very interesting, with a beautiful altarpiece in ceramic representing the Visit of Our Lady to Saint Isabel by the Italian ceramist Niculoso Pisano in 1502.

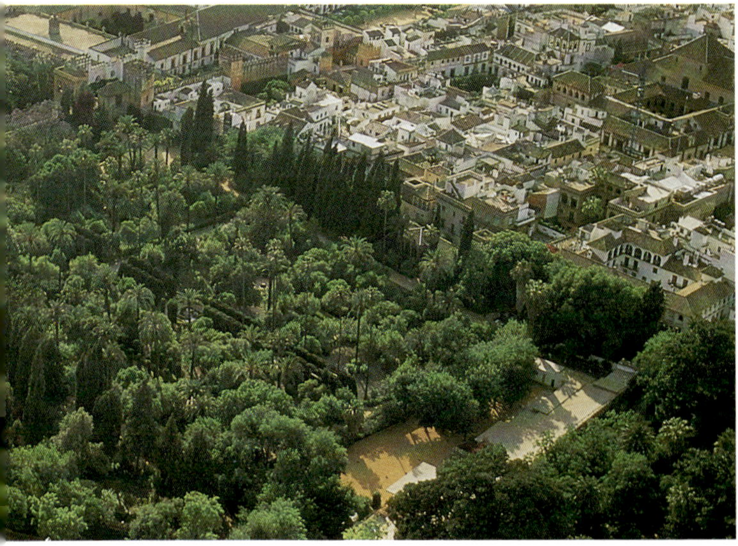

The visit to the Alcázar ends with a walk through the Gardens, each of which has a name: Garden of the Prince, Garden of the Ladies, Garden of the Dance, etc.

The Archivo de Indias

After leaving the Alcázar, we find on the same plaza del Triunfo the Archives of the Indies, before which there is a monument in the shape of a stone lantern called «The Earthquake Lantern», a beautiful monument in the Baroque style erected to commemorate the earthquake which destroyed Lisbon and other cities on November 1,1755, leaving Seville undamaged. Inside the lantern there is a small image of Our Lady, to whom this monument of popular thanksgiving is dedicated.

The Archives building overlooks the plaza del Triunfo, calle Santo Tomás, calle Fray Ceferino González and avenida de la Constitución. The main door was in older times the one on calle Fray Ceferino González . The building was constructed during the reign of Philip II as a market, so as to eliminate the trading of valuable wares on the Cathedral steps, which was quite often irreverent. The building was designed by Herrera, the same architect who built El Escorial, in his own personal style.

In the doorway opening onto Fray Ceferino street, under the steps, there is a great marble cross known as the Cross of Oaths, for upon it, the merchants buying and selling in good faith took an oath.

In the 18th century, with the disappearance of the monopoly of shipments to the Indies and the removal of the Exchange

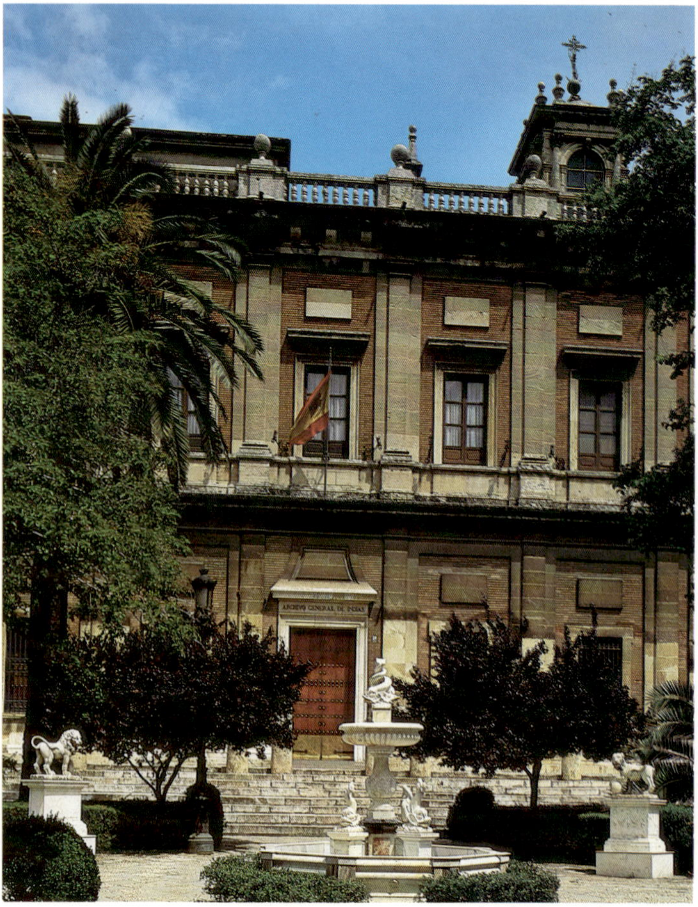

The Archives of the Indies.

(Casa de Contratación) to Cádiz, the merchant's guild decreased so much that the market was closed and the building became the headquarters of the General Archives of the Indies.

This Archive houses countless documents pertaining to the Spanish Colonial Empire, from the first discoveries to the loss of the colonies, so that it can be asserted that its shelves hold the greatest and best part of the history of Spain. The entrance is on avenida de la Constitución.

Torre de Abdelaziz

On the corner of calle Santo Tomás and avenida de la Constitución, there is a small hexagonal tower embedded in a building belonging to a travel agency. It is of Moslem origin, built around 1180, and known as the Tower of Abdelaziz. It is traditionally supposed that

King Saint Ferdinand hoisted his colors here, when his victorious Christian troops entered Seville in the year 1248.

Panoramic view of the city center.

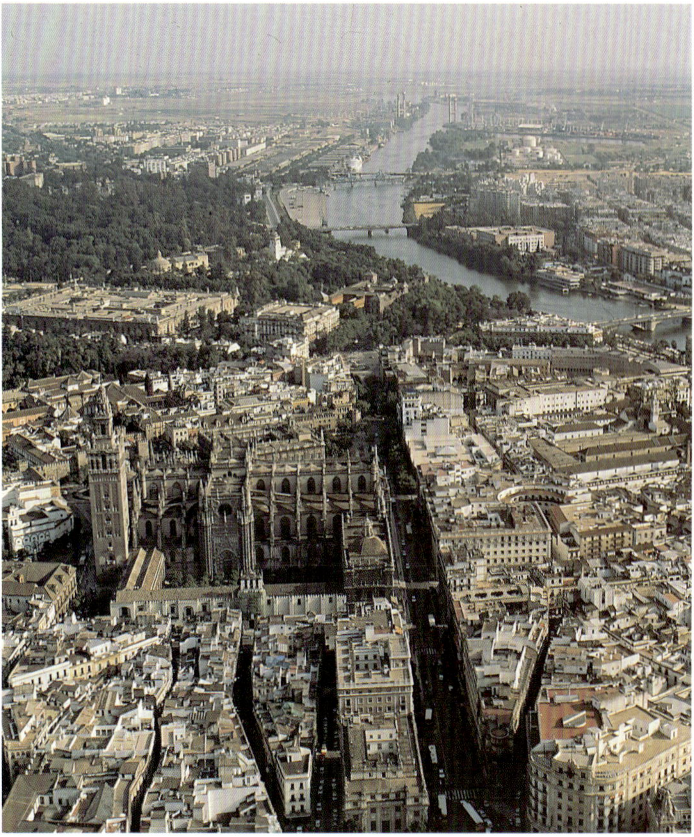

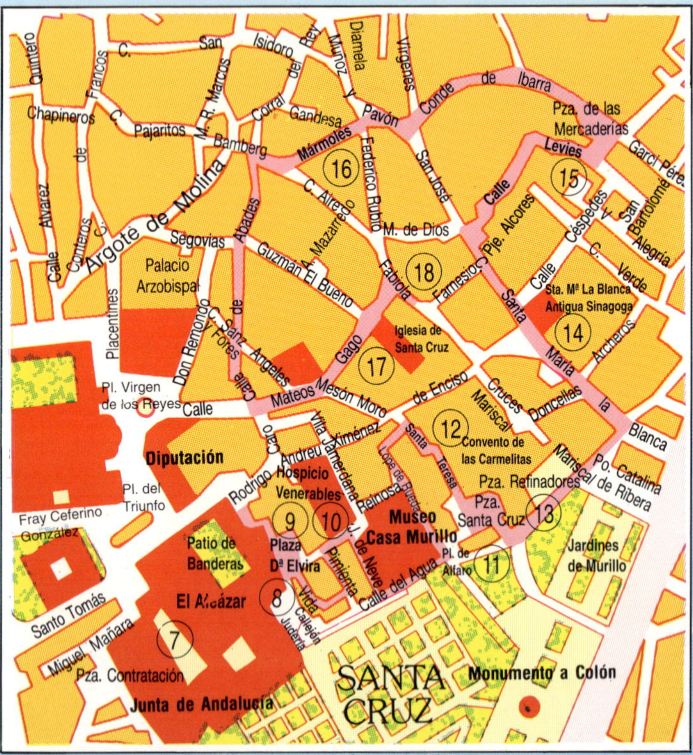

ROUTE 2
SANTA CRUZ QUARTER

PLACES OF INTEREST

⑦ **Court of the Banners**
Former Court of Arms of the Alcázar.

⑧ **Judería Alley**

⑨ **Doña Elvira Square**
Former open air theatre.

⑩ **Hospice of the Venerables**
Magnificent baroque palace and church of the late 17th century.

⑪ **Alfaro Square Rosina's**
Balcony, where «The Barber of Seville» took place.

⑫ **Santa Teresa Street**
Convent of Las Carmelitas.

⑬ **Santa Cruz Square**

⑭ **Santa María la Blanca Street**
Baroque church, former jewish synagogue.

⑮ **Levíes Street**

⑯ **Mármoles Street**
Remains of the temple of Hercules.

⑰ **Mateos Gago Street**
Church of Santa Cruz

⑱ **Fabiola Street**
House of birth of Cardinal Wisseman.

STARTING POINT	Plaza del Triunfo
EXIT TO NEXT ROUTE	By Mateos Gago street back to the Cathedral and Plaza del Triunfo. From there, along Avda. de la Constitución to reach route 3.

USEFUL ADDRESSES NEARBY

Chemists:	Santa María la Blanca, 2 and 11 Mateos Gago, 14
Photo Service:	Souvenirs shops on Calle del Agua and Mateos Gago, and around the Hospicio de los Venerables.
Restaurante La Barca de Don Raimundo:	Placentines, 25
Restaurante Los Alcázares:	Miguel de Mañara, 10
Restaurante Self-Service:	Santa María la Blanca, 34
Restaurante Modesto:	Cano y Cueto, 5
Restaurante La Judería:	Cano y Cueto, 13
Restaurante El Cordobés:	Santa María la Blanca, 18
La Hostería del Laurel:	Venerables, 4. Typical food and drink inn, called after the famous place in which Don Juan Tenorio encountered Don Luis Mejía. Decorated in the style of those times.
Tapas Bars	
Bar Juan Gracia Aguilar:	Mateos Gago, 20
Bar La Gitanilla:	Ximénez de Enciso, 9
Casa Ramón:	Plaza de los Venerables, 1
Casa Robles:	Alvarez Quintero, 58. Especiality: «pescaíto» (fried small fish).
Bodeguita Romero:	Harinas, 10. Especiality: «pringá» (fried assorted meat served with bread).
El Trasiego:	Harinas, 8
La Carbonería:	Levíes, 18

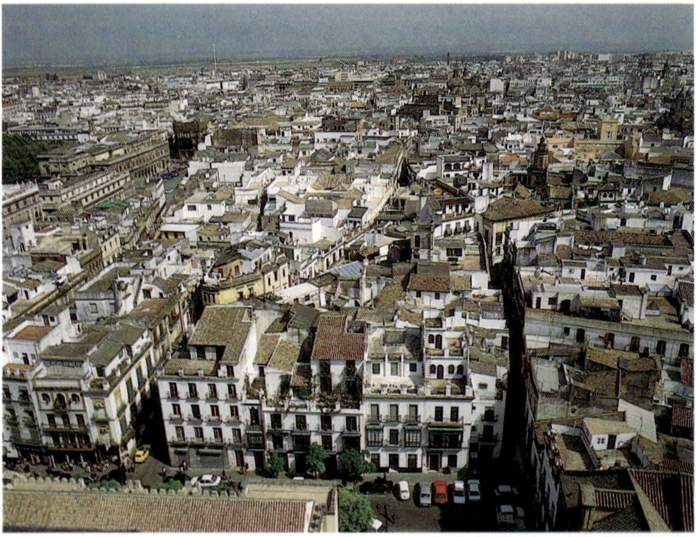

View of Santa Cruz Quarter from the Giralda.

Calle Mateos Gago in 1927.

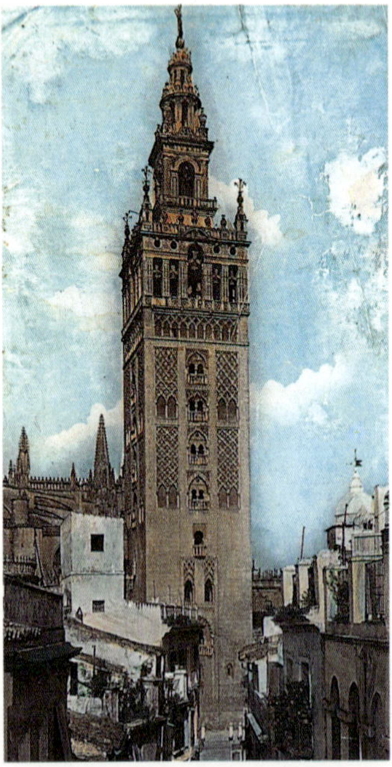

ROUTE 2: BARRIO DE SANTA CRUZ, PATIO DE BANDERAS AND LA JUDERIA

On the plaza del Triunfo, the walls of the Alcázar have a door opening onto the Patio de Banderas (Court of the Banners). It is called so because from the Reconquest of Seville by King Saint Ferdinand in 1248, until the Catholic Kings campaigned to reconquer Granada in 1492, Christian armies left from here to fight successive wars against the Moslems, and this was the gathering-place of the different militia, the military orders of Santiago, Alcántara, Calatrava and Saint John of Jerusalem, royal armies and militia from the different cities and towns.

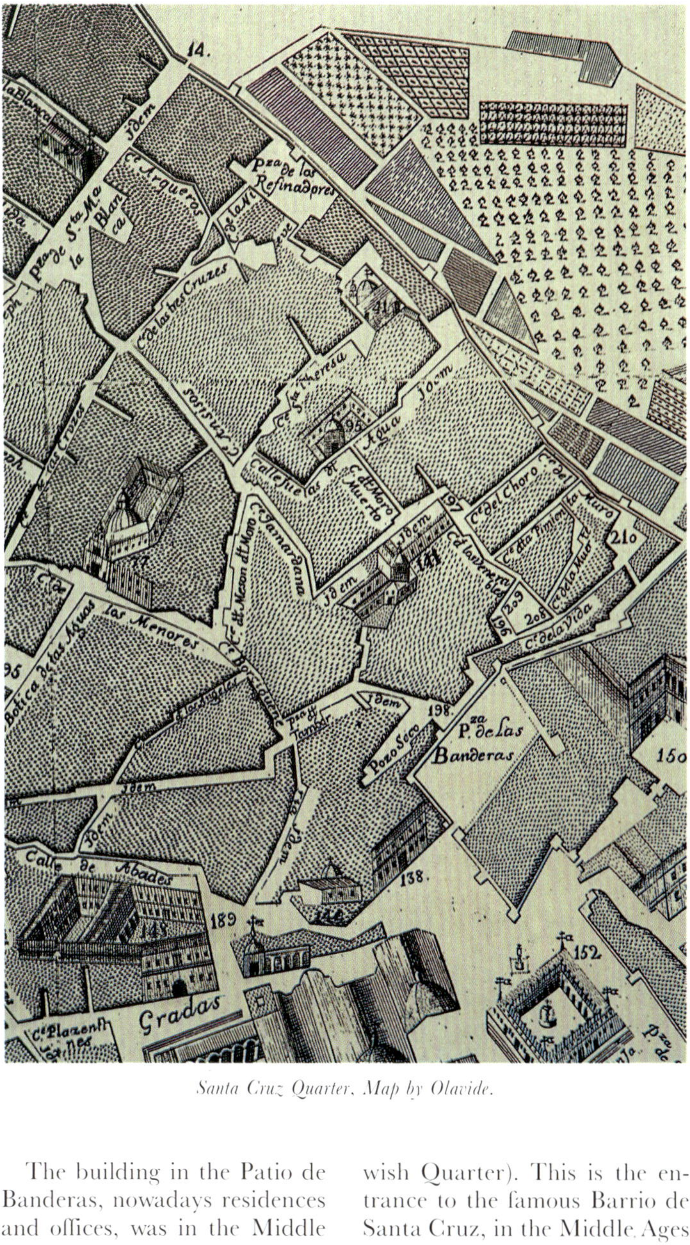

Santa Cruz Quarter. Map by Olavide.

The building in the Patio de Banderas, nowadays residences and offices, was in the Middle Ages the crossbowmen's barracks.

At the far end of the Patio de Banderas, on the left hand corner, there is a covered passage with a sign reading Judería (Jewish Quarter). This is the entrance to the famous Barrio de Santa Cruz, in the Middle Ages the Jewish Quarter of Seville, where over ten thousand Jewish families lived and prayed in three synagogues, later turned into the Christian churches of Santa Cruz, San Bartolomé and

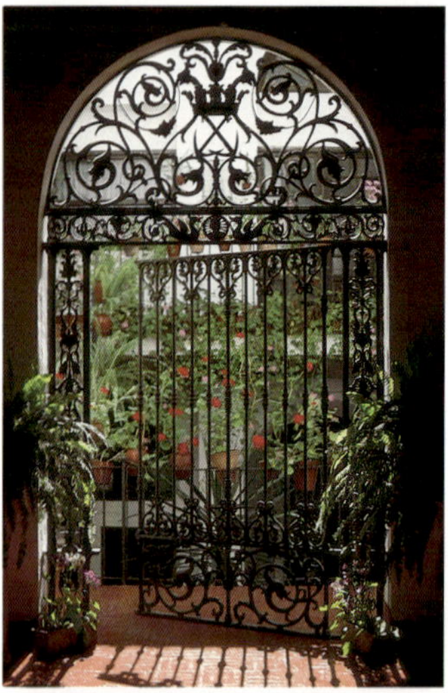
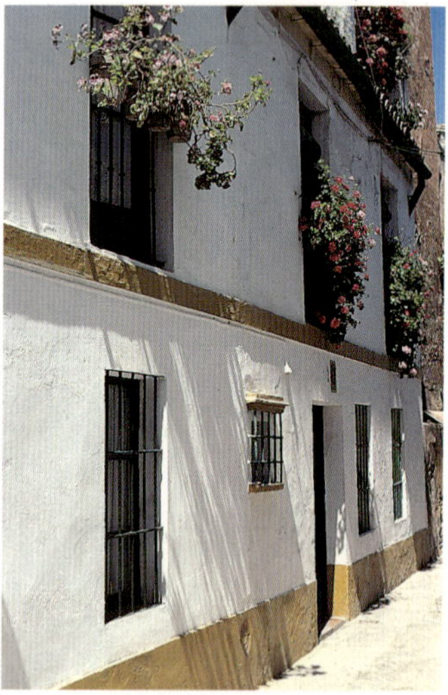

Different views of Santa Cruz Quarter.

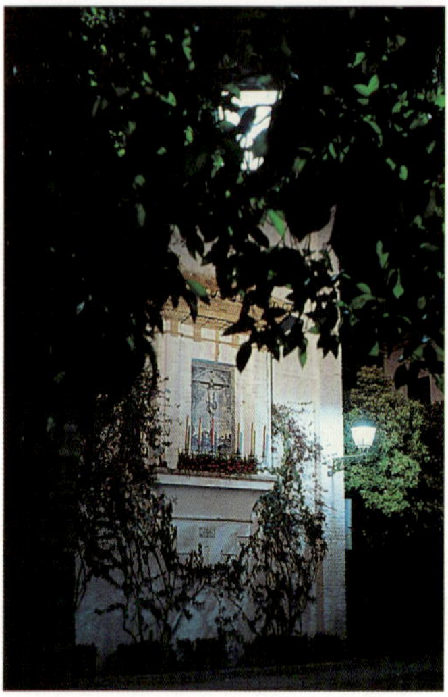
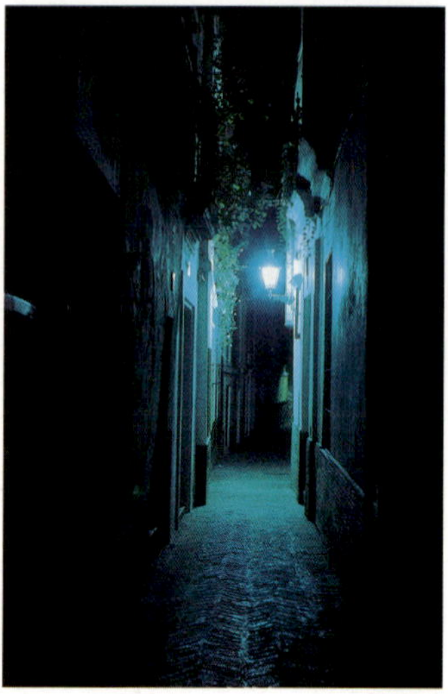

Santa María la Blanca.

The Barrio de Santa Cruz, even though five hundred years have elapsed since the Jews were expelled, still reveals the characteristic old «aljamas» in the layout of its streets, while at the same time it maintains the flowery and mysterious enchantment of the most typical area of Seville. Let us then enter the Callejón de la Judería which takes us to a small courtyard decorated with a marble fountain affixed to the wall, with a creeper vine overhanging it. It is said that this creeper was used a century ago by young King Alfonso XII to escape from the Alcázar each night to visit the Palace of San Telmo to see his beloved Merceditas Montpensier, whom he married and who died at age nineteen.

Through a wrought iron door we reach the Placita de las Cadenas ; to our left we follow calle Vida taking us to plaza de Doña Elvira.

Plaza de Doña Elvira

This beautiful plaza decorated with tiled benches and a profusion of flowers, is one of the most significant sites in the history of Spanish and universal literature. Together with the adjoining Hospicio de los Venerables, this square was a famous open air theater known as the corral de Doña Elvira , from the end of the 16th century through the 17th century.

Doña Elvira Square.

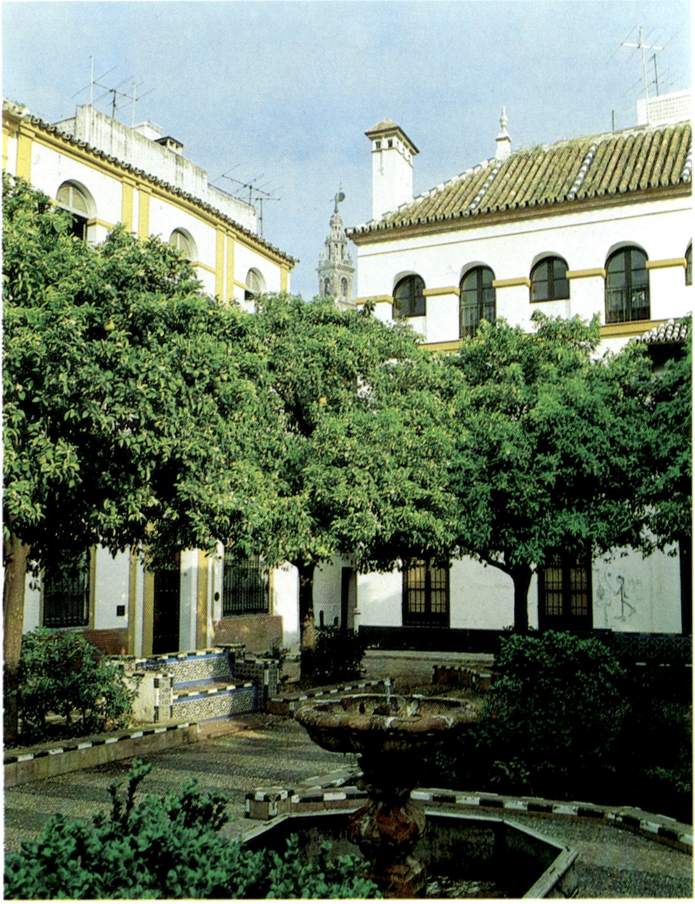

This theater was the stage where the most famous authors of the Golden Age premiered their plays, among them none less than Miguel de Cervantes Saavedra, who in 1582 signed a contract with the company of Rodrigo Ossorio to write six new plays for the price of fifty ducats each. This was also where the first advertising poster known to the world was made, an announcement notifying the public that Cosme de Oviedo's company would perform at three in the afternoon. The theater disappeared in 1631.

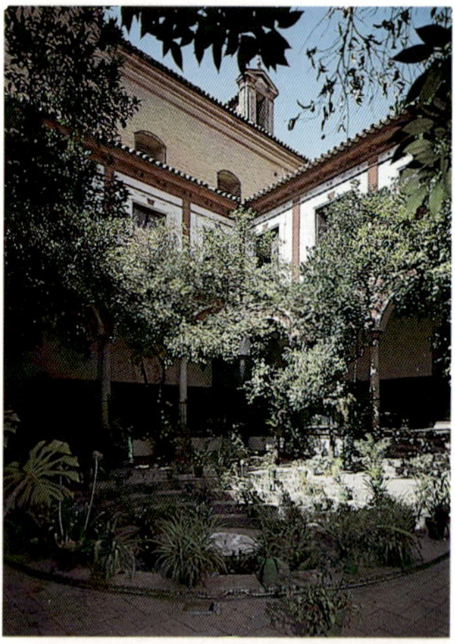

Courtyard of the Hospicio.

The Hospicio de Venerables

After the disappearance of the comedy theater the site was used by the priest Justino de Neve at the end of the 17th century to build the Hospicio de los Venerables Sacerdotes, a residence for old priests who had no family. The plans are attributed to Juan Domínguez, and the building was made in Baroque style with a residential wing surrounding a courtyard with arcades and a central fountain, and another wing for the church, with a single nave and a very beautiful façade.

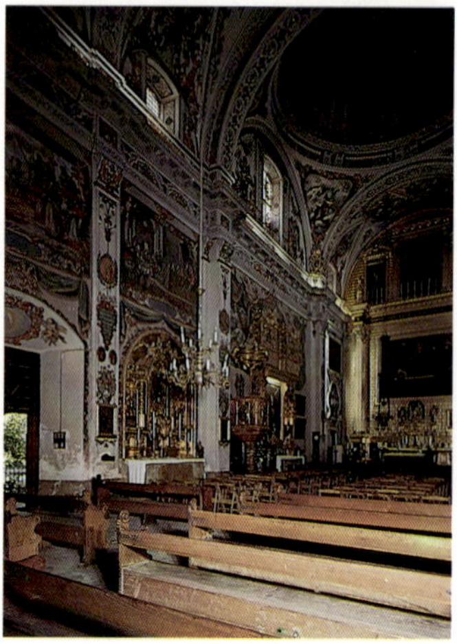

Church of the Hospicio.

The church contains magnificent paintings, murals and canvases, the best being the vault of the presbytery by Valdés Leal, and those by the same artist on the walls of the presbytery on the history of Seville.

Also worth admiring are the small paintings by Lucas Valdés depicting *The Baptism of Christ* and *The Healing of the Paralytic*, and in the sacristy, a scene of the *Presentation of the Child Jesus in the Temple* by the same artist.

There are also excellent sculptures by Martínez Montañés: a Saint Stephen, and by Pedro Roldán a Saint Peter and a Saint Ferdinand.

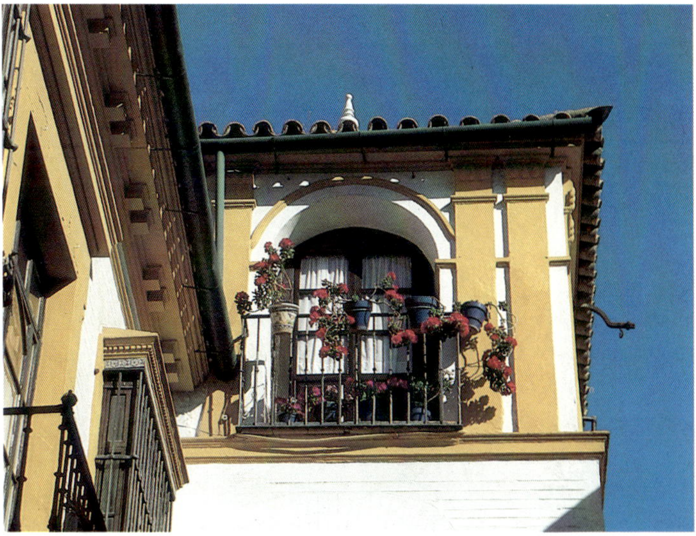

Doña Rosina's Balcony.

Walking through the Barrio de Santa Cruz

Coming out of the Hospicio de Venerables, through calle Justino de Neve, we go down the Callejón del Agua, so called because the wall that lines it, had a conduit on top to supply the Alcázar with water from the aqueduct of Carmona.

On the left sidewalk we see a house with a very beautiful patio, one of the most flowery in the Barrio de Santa Cruz , where several movies have been filmed, among them «Morena Clara» starring famous Spanish actress and singer Imperio Argentina.

The Callejón del Agua leads us to plaza de Alfaro. Here on the left, on the corner of calle Lope de Rueda is the house where, according to the legend, Rosina lived, with whom Count Almaviva fell in love. In Rossini's famous opera «The Barber of Seville» this is where Almaviva succeeded in entering Rosina's home in spite of her guardians's vigilance. The balcony is known as «Rosina's balcony».

Now we go up calle Lope de Rueda, which up to a century ago was known as calle de Barrabás, as shown in a tile set on a wall. The name Barrabás comes from a gentleman named Fernando Ortiz de Melgarejo, who was nicknamed «Gentleman Barrabás» due to his adventures and schemes, and died violently in 1630. This street has beautiful stone façades with noble coats of arms of the Clarebout family and others.

At the end we find calle Santa Teresa.

The convent of Las Teresas

On the street of the same name we find the convent of Las Teresas (although its real name is the convent of Saint Joseph). It is said to have been founded by Saint Teresa of Jesus, but this is not correct. When the saint was in Seville, she lived first in calle Zaragoza , in a house for this reason known as «casa de Santa Teresa». From

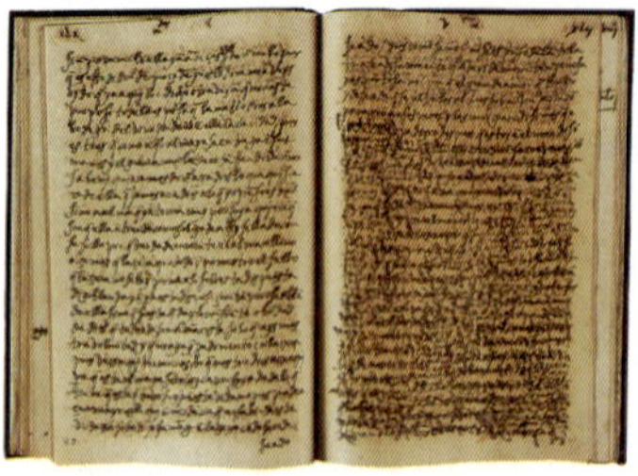

Manuscript of Las Moradas.

there, with a few nuns, she founded a convent on Armas street, today calle Alfonso XII, where the convent existed for several years. Later, when the Morga Bank went bankrupt, and had to quit this house, the convent moved into these premises in 1586. The church is the work of the architect Veremundo Resta and has a single nave. The main altar holds an image of the Immaculate Conception, made by the sculptor Juan de Mesa in 1620. On the left side of the presbytery there is an altarpiece depicting the well known scene of the Transfixion. The walls have several altars with noteworthy paintings and sculptures. The Sacristy has one of the most valuable documents in Spanish mystic literature: the original manuscript, written in the author's hand, of «Las Moradas» by Saint Teresa of Jesus.

Plaza de Santa Cruz

Going down calle Santa Teresa and its extension, calle Nicolás Antonio, we will find the plaza de Santa Cruz. This

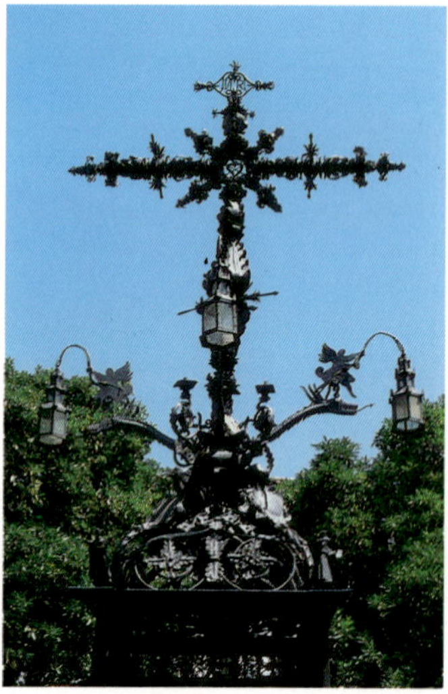

Santa Cruz Square.
The Ironwork Cross.

square has not been here very long as this site was occupied by the Church of the Holy Cross, an old Jewish synagogue which became a parish church in the 15th century, after the Jews were expelled in 1492. The church survived until the 19th century, when it was demolished to make the square. Because in past centuries there were no cemeteries, the dead were buried in their respective parishes. In this

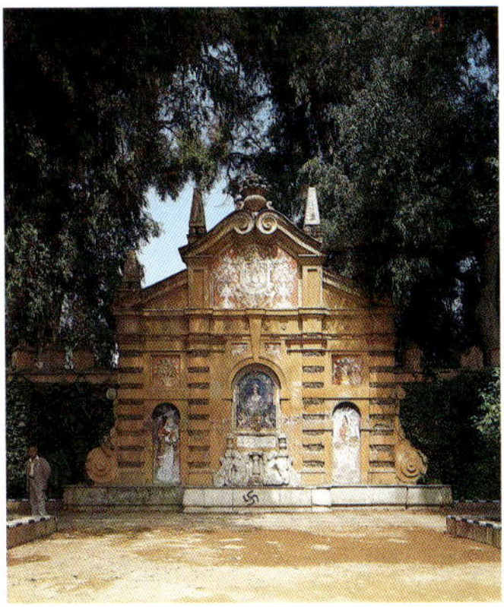

Fountain of Catalina de Ribera.

church the great painter Bartolomé Esteban Murillo was buried, but when the church was demolished, his remains were not rescued, and so we only know today that he is buried somewhere under this plaza.

In the center there is the exquisite Cruz de la Cerrajería (Ironwork Cross), made in 1692 by Sebastián Conde, an artist in iron, which offers the surprising quality of silver filigree, but worked in wrought iron.

Jardines de Murillo

From the same plaza de Santa Cruz we go down to the Jardines de Murillo (gardens) and Jardines de Catalina Ribera. These two gardens belonged to the Alcázar gardens but were separated from these by moving the wall back, in order to donate this public park to the people of Seville on behalf of Queen Isabella II and her grandson Alfonso XIII.

These gardens contain beautiful fountains, ponds, tiled benches and some old capitals as decoration.

To the north of the gardens we find calle Cano y Cueto , where the Saint-King Ferdinand is portrayed in tile at second floor level on one of the houses. The king slept in this house, according to tradition, the night before he victoriously entered Seville after the Moslems surrendered.

Santa María La Blanca

Calle Cano y Cueto takes us to calle Santa María La Blanca, and up this street we find to our right the Church of Santa María La Blanca, its true name being Santa María de las Nieves. This temple was a Jewish synagogue since it was built in the 13th century until 1309, when it became a Christian parish due to the decrease of the Jewish colony in Seville.

Synagogue of Santa María La Blanca.

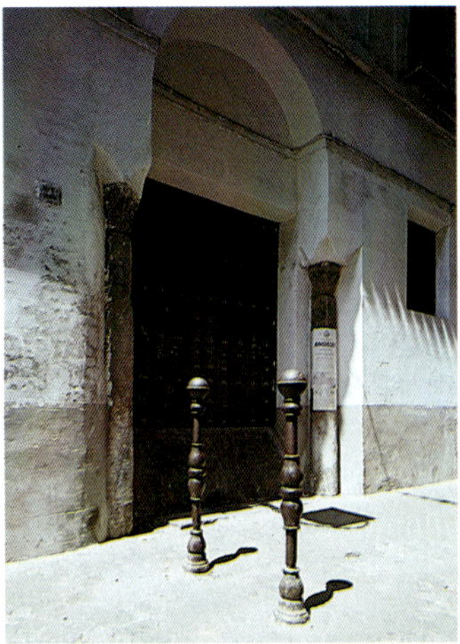

The synagogue was probably erected on the site of a previous Moslem mosque. After a partial reconstruction in the 14th century, and a complete one in the 17th century, all architectural remains, both Arab and Jewish, disappeared, and what we now see is a building in Baroque style, with three naves covered with small vaults and the high altar chapel with a cupola over a short crossing.

The ceiling is covered with Baroque plaster work by the Brothers Pedro and Miguel de Borja, the same as the arches resting upon red marble columns. This church housed a great number of paintings by Murillo, although some were stolen by Marshal Soult during the Napoleonic invasion, and others are today in the Prado Museum. However, there are still quite a few remains of its past wealth, and thus, in the Saint John Nepomuceno chapel we can admire a superb painting on wood depicting. *The Dead Christ* in the Arms of His Mother, signed by the great painter Luis de Vargas. In the communion chapel there is a picture representing the Virgin Mary and Saint John the Evangelist. Also by Murillo is the Last Supper, as recorded in the Records Book of the Brotherhood of Nuestra Señora del Pópulo, which owned the picture in its altar, later dedicated to Saint John Nepomuceno. This has been researched recently by historian José M. de Mena.

In this church, in the same altarpiece as the Virgin and Saint John, there is an Ecce Homo painted by Morales, known as «the Divine».

Plaza de Santa María la Blanca

The plaza in front of the church was during the Golden Age the meeting place of black and mulatto slaves, of whom there were many working as servants in Seville, in a state of semi-freedom. They were protected by the Hermandad de los Negritos and the church kept a watchful eye to avoid their being mistreated by their masters. Cervantes, in one of his comedies, Entremés de los Mirones, describes the colorful and festive air of this meeting place of colored servants. The building with a great façade next to the church is the palace of the Marquis of Astorga and Counts of Altamira, a family which was very prominent in society from 1500 to 1750.

Convent of Madre de Dios

Up the same street of Santa María La Blanca, on the left, we find the convent of Madre de Dios, founded in the 15th century. The Catholic Queen Isabella repeatedly stayed here, as she was a great patroness of the convent.

This monastery has a church which is truly a museum. In the high altar we can see Our Lady of the Rosary, a relief representing The Last Supper, and in the upper part, a Calvary. All the images are by the famous

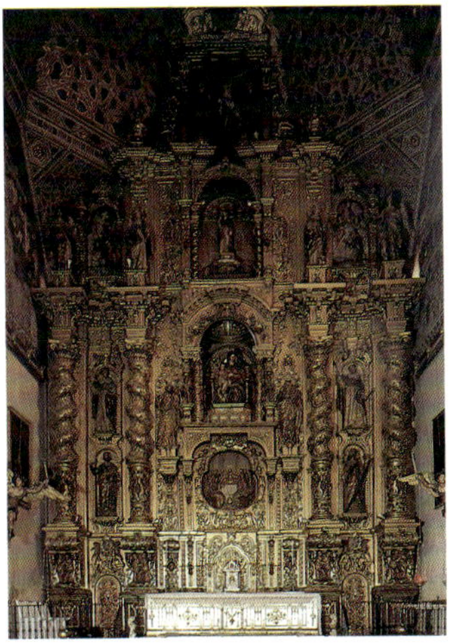

Altarpiece of the Convent of Mother of God.

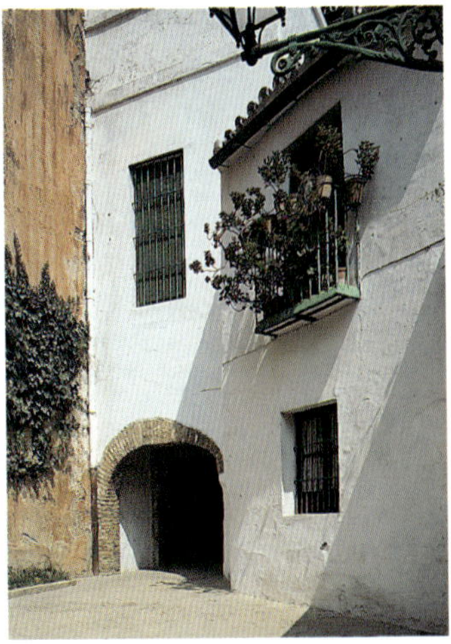

Street in the former Jewish Quarter.

sculptor Jerónimo Hernández. The rest of the altarpiece is by Francisco Barahona.

On the sides of the presbytery are two magnificent marble tombs with statues of the wife of Hernán Cortés, Juana de Zúñiga, and her daughter Catalina Cortés, statues made by Juan de Oviedo and Miguel Adam in the last third of the 16th century.

There are also sculptures by Jerónimo Hernández in the altarpiece on the left wall of the church and in the lower choir. As far as the paintings are concerned, the most noteworthy are those by Peter van Lint, a 17th century Flemish painter, a painting representing Saint Dominic by Juan del Castillo, and a Calvary attributed to Pedro Campaña. Another fine painting is The Burial of Christ, in which the holy women and other figures stand before the body of Jesus, while Joseph of Arimathea anoints His feet with perfumed balm. The artist is unknown, but belongs to the Flemish school of the 17th century.

Calle Levies

On the same street of Santa María La Blanca, on the opposite side and back a bit, we will find the calle de Levies, so named because in the Middle Ages Samuel Leví, treasurer to King Pedro I, lived here with his family. The house where they lived belonged later, in the 16th century, to the main courier Rodrigo de Xerez. In this street we find a marble slab placed on the façade of the most noble house, indicating that this was the birthplace of Miguel de Mañara y Vicentelo de Leca, a very powerful man, who was feared throughout the city for his wrath and arrogance. Later he repented and became a model of virtue. We will speak of this gentleman again when we reach the Hospital de la Santa Caridad.

The calle de Levíes opens onto the attractive and secluded plaza de las Mercedarias.

From here, and through calle Conde Ibarra we reach the crossing of San José, Vírgenes, Muñoz y Pabón and Mármoles streets.

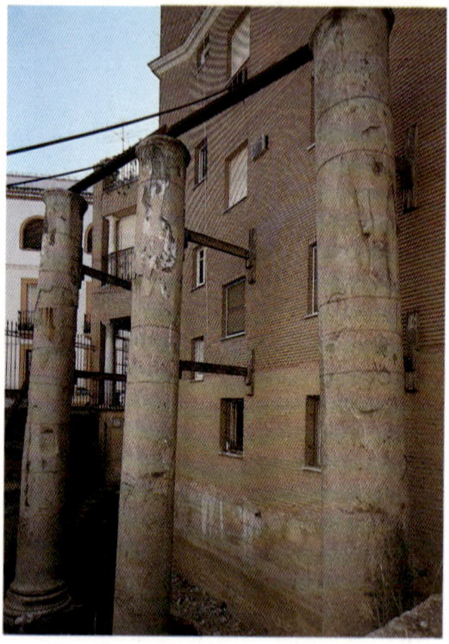

Roman pillars on Mármoles street.

Roman archeology

We take calle Mármoles, so called because it has several very tall pillars, the remains of a great Roman construction, possibly a temple, although some authors believe it was the Forum of the city.

In the Middle Ages, the existing pillars were more in number, but King Pedro tried to take two for the principal gate to his palace at the Alcázar and during transportation, one of them broke and was abandoned, being lost for all times. Another two were removed in the 16th century to the Alameda de Hércules, by the city official Francisco de Zapata y Cisneros, Count of Barajas.

In this area ruins and remains of Roman building have appeared on several occasions; the foundations of a Roman amphitheater were unearthed on the next street, Mateos Gago. And underneath all these streets, run impressive Roman sewers.

Calle Mármoles takes us to calle Abades, where we turn to the left. Here important personalities of the Moslem Era lived and inside some of the houses archeological remains of that era can still be found. A plaque tells us that in the house where Dr. Germán y Ribón lived, the Royal Sevillian Academy of Literature was founded in the 18th century.

The Church of Santa Cruz

We reach calle Mateos Gago and opposite is the parish church of Santa Cruz. It was originally the old convent of the Religiosas Menores which in the 19th century became a parish when the church on plaza de Santa Cruz was demolished.

Among the works of art it contains we will mention a painting of the Child Jesus in the tabernacle of the Saint Anne altar, by Valdés Leal. The altarpiece of Saint Anne is very interesting; it shows the saint teaching the Virgin Mary to read. This portrayal was quite common, and was used from the 16th through the18th centuries to encourage mothers to teach their daughters how to read. The theme is repeated quite frequently in different churches of Seville, such as Saint Laurence and others. This totally disproves the idea that women were illiterate at that time and that they were not taught culture so they would remain ignorant and dedicated solely to household chores. The work we are contemplating is by the famous sculptor Pedro Roldán.

Above the sacristy door there is a fine painting belonging to the Italian school, depicting the *Beheading of Saint John the Baptist*. The image of the Virgin with the Child presiding the church, set in a shrine in the presbytery, is the work of Jerónimo Hernández.

Cardinal Wisseman

To finish our tour of this sector, upon leaving the church of Santa Cruz we will walk a bit to the end of calle Mateos Gago, and to our right we will find calle Fabiola. The house in front of us has a large marble slab explaining that here the famous Cardinal Wisseman was born, glory of the Catholic Church and a great writer, author of the historical novel *Fabiola o la iglesia de las catacumbas*, novel whose title provided the name to the street.

Going back to calle Mateos Gago we reach the Cathedral and the avenida de la Constitución.

House where Cardinal Wisseman was born.

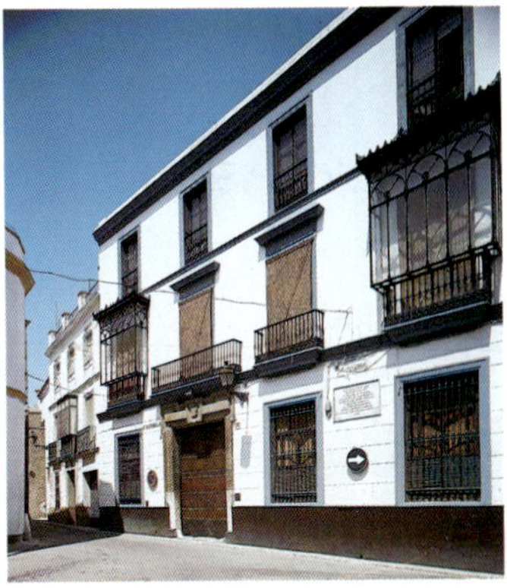

Church of Santa Cruz.

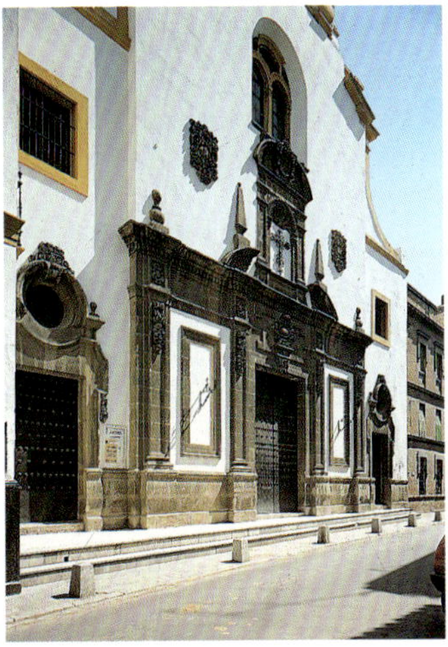

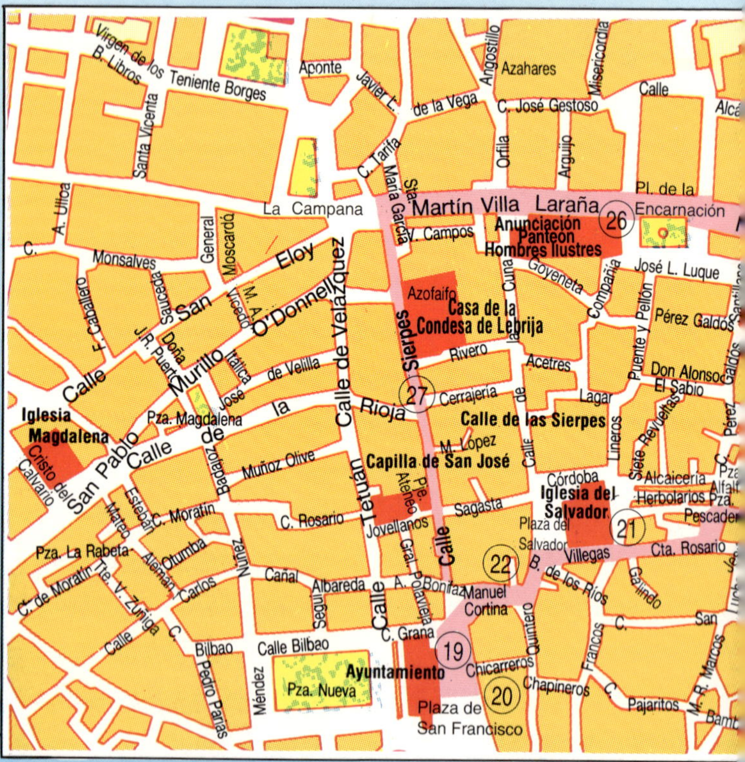

ROUTE 3: FROM CITY HALL TO PILATE'S HOUSE

PLACES OF INTEREST

⑲ **City Hall**
16th century renaissance style building.

⑳ **Court of Justice**
Today Caja de Ahorros de San Fernando (Savings bank).

㉑ **Collegiate Church of El Salvador**
Contains the Jesús de Pasión, by Martínez Montañés.

㉒ **Church of San Juan de Dios Hospital**
Contains sculptures by Juan de Mesa.

㉓ **Head of King Pedro**

㉔ **Pilate's House**
Palace of the Duke and Duchess of Medinaceli. Contains Roman sculptures and many other works of art. Plaza de Pilatos, 1. Tel: 422 50 55/52 98

㉕ **Churches of San Esteban, Santa Catalina and San Pedro**
Moorish and Christian medieval architecture.

㉖ **Church of La Anunciación and Panteón de Hombres Ilustres**
16th century building, once owned by the Jesuits. Contains paintings by Pacheco and sculptures by Martínez Montañés. Writers Reinoso, Alberto Lista and poet Gustavo Adolfo Bécquer among others are buried in the Panteón. Calle Laraña s/n. Tel: 421 61 47. Opening hours: 12.00 to 13.00 and 20.00 to 21.00.

㉗ **Sierpes Street**
The former royal prison, today Banco Hispanoamericano, is there.

STARTING POINT	Plaza de San Francisco

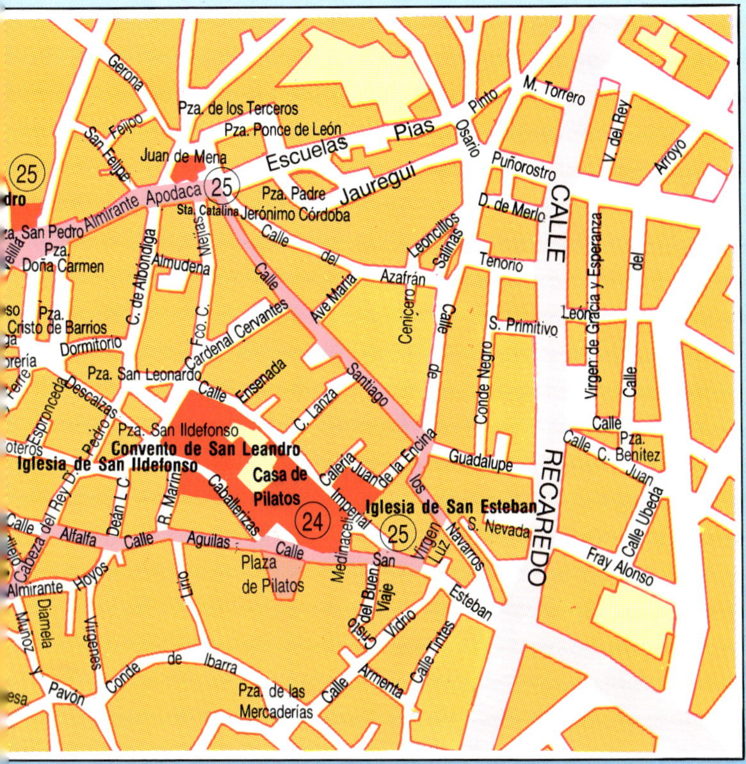

EXIT TO NEXT ROUTE	Plaza del Duque de la Victoria, starting point for route 4.

USEFUL ADDRESSES NEARBY

Chemists:	Alóndigas, 6
	Plaza del Cristo de Burgos, 3
Photo service:	Cuna 10 and 44
	Plaza de Jesús de Pasión, 4
Restaurante Abascal:	Plaza San Francisco, 10
Marisquería La Alicantina:	Plaza del Salvador
El Bacalao:	Ponce de León, 15. Especiality: «bacalao» (cod) and «cordero» (lamb).
Restaurante Victoria Eugenia:	Plaza de Villasís, at Cuna street.
Restaurante Almadraba:	Huelva, 8
Restaurante San Marcos:	Cuna, 6. Located on a 18th century palace. International cuisine.
Tapas Bars	
El Rinconcillo:	Gerona, 42. Established in 1600. Visited by artist and writers. There is a ceramic tile with the price of a glass of wine in the 1640.
La Antigua Bodeguita:	Plaza del Salvador 2. Especiality: iced manzanilla (wine).
Sopa de Ganso:	Pérez Galdós, 8.
Quitapesares:	Plaza Jerónimo de Córdoba, 3. Life «sevillanas» dance.

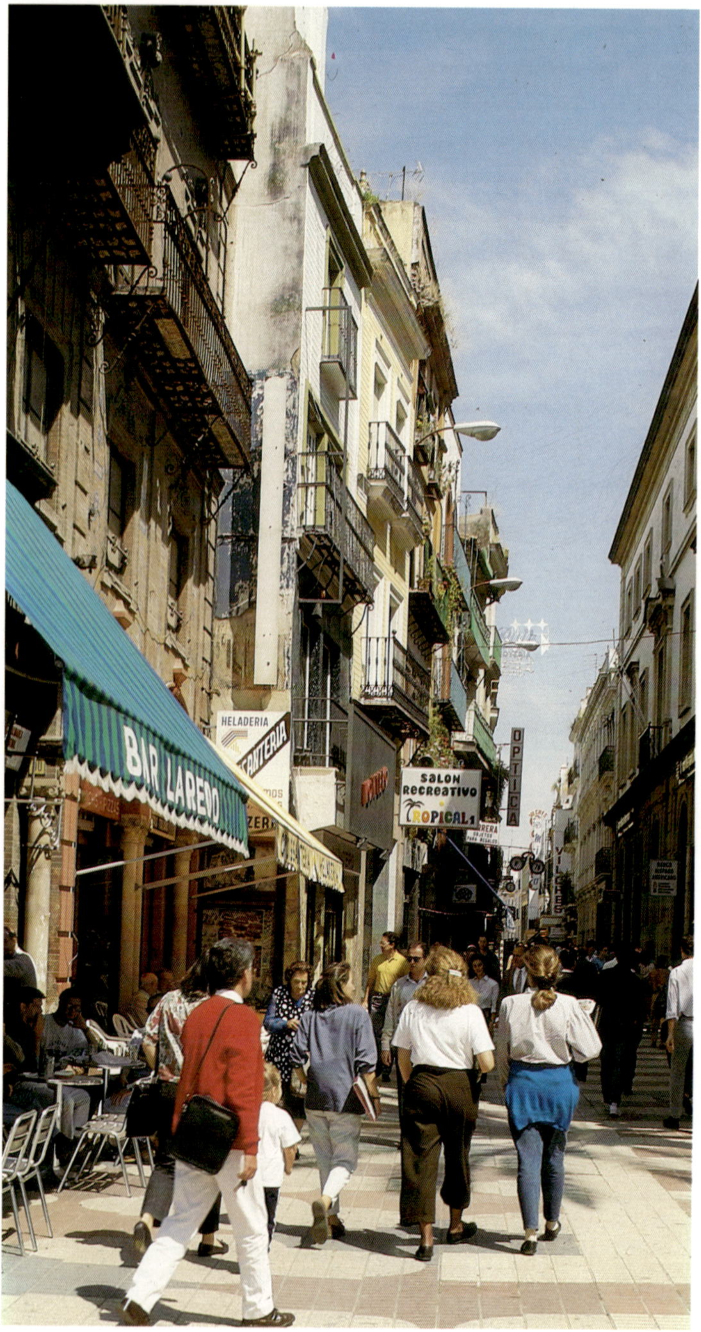

Sierpes Street.

ROUTE 3: FROM CITY HALL TO CASA DE PILATOS

Ayuntamiento (City Hall)

We will start our itinerary from plaza de San Francisco, where we find the City Hall. The square got its name from the monastery Casa Grande de San Francisco , which stood here and trained Franciscan priests as missionaries in the New World. At a time, up to three hundred missionaries lived here apart from the normal monastery community. Access to the Casa Grande was through what is today the Arquillo, or little arch of City Hall, an exquisite Renaissance arch we must stop and admire.

The Arquillo of City Hall has vaulted niches on both sides with statues of Julius Caesar and Hercules. Hercules (who was really a navigator before the Phoenician religion placed him on the altars) occupies this place of honor because he was, according to tradition, the founder of Seville and discoverer of these lands when he came with Phoenician ships to establish the first colonies in Celtiberian Spain. Precisely for the merits of such colonization, his countrymen made him a semi-god or saint of their religion.

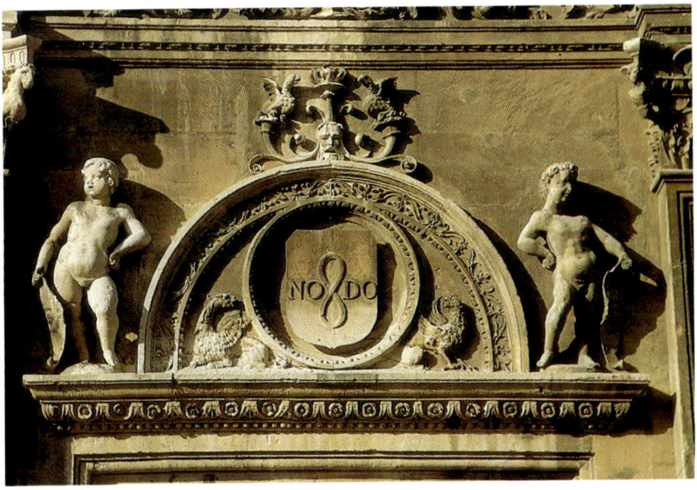

City Hall. Details of Hercules and Julius Caesar.

Julius Caesar occupies the other niche because Seville considers him a «Father of Seville», since he walled the city and turned it into a beautiful metropolis.

Over the Arquillo we can see two coats of arms with the five wounds of Saint Francis, as a sign that this was the entrance to the Convent.

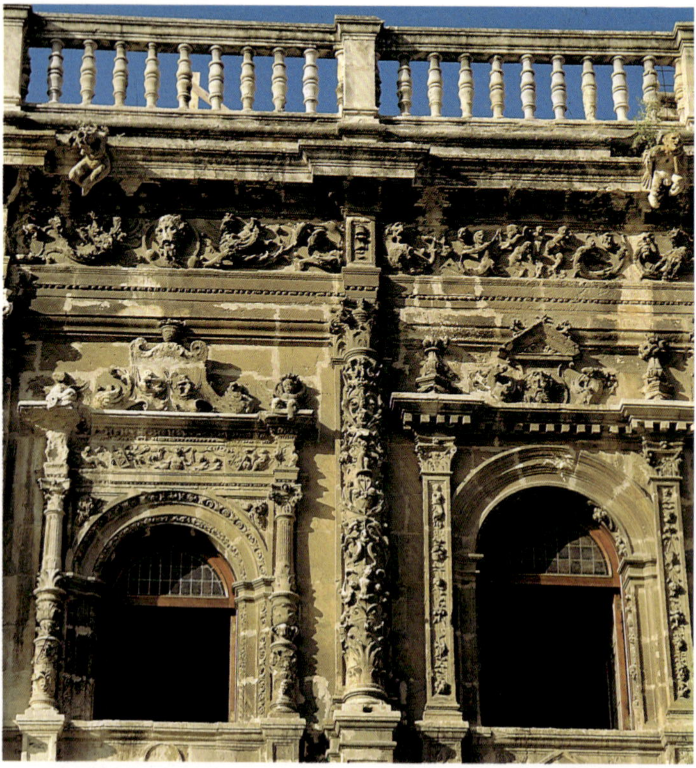

Two details of the façade of City Hall.

The City Hall building is magnificent and is considered by scholars to be one of the best Renaissance works in Spain. It is believed to have been built on initiative of Charles I, since the City Council lacked fixed headquarters and spread out its activity to corral de los Olmos for council meetings (next to the Cathedral), while the offices were in the corral de los Alcaldes Ordinarios in the barrio de San Pedro.

The place chosen to build City Hall was the site of the former Espartería Mayor or Espartería Vieja. The plans were probably by architect Diego de Riaño, since he commenced construction in 1527 and directed work for eight years, completing more than half the building.

More than half of the façade is carved in reliefs with figures and decorations framing and encircling doors and windows and filling stretches of walls. This has been carried out from the 16th century to the present time, uninterruptedly, little by little, employing the best sculptors of the city.

The interior of the City Hall building is partly Gothic and partly Renaissance. Next to the Arquillo is the room of the Fieles Ejecutores and the grand

Salón del Apeadero, with the start of the Gothic stairway which leads to the old archives.

The architectural masterpiece on the lower floor, is the Chapter Room or meeting room of the municipal council. This room has a flat stone vaulted ceiling, and each caisson holds a carved bust of one of the kings of Spain. The walls are covered with very intricate carvings in stone, resembling caves and grottoes, with inscriptions in Latin, allegories and coats of arms. The room is presided over by a monumental coat of arms of the city, made by the famous Renaissance sculptor Roque Balduque.

The Mayor's office is modern in decor, as well as the other offices and rooms. The main staircase is decorated in pink marble with a magnificent cupola, and leads to the upper floor where we find the Columbus Room, used for receptions and decorated with mirrors, tapestries and chandeliers.

The City Hall has a very valuable coin collection, and among the works of art it keeps are silver maces used by the mace-bearers in processions and civic activities. These date from the 16th century. An old the city banner is one of the prized objects, as well as a collection of paintings, including works by Juan Carreño de Miranda, Francisco Cabral, Gonzalo Bilbao, Joaquín Domínguez Bécquer, Alfonso Grosso, Zurbarán and other Sevillian masters.

The municipal archives are very rich in old documents and in extremely valuable incunabula. The most curious document is a letter from the Daté of Masamura (prince of a Japanese island) sending an envoy to the Council of Seville on October 26th, 1613. It is important in so much as it sheds light on the Japanese culture of that time.

The western wall of the City Hall, on Plaza Nueva, called the «Clock Wall» lacks interest as it was made in the 19th century when the Convent of Saint Francis was demolished and became a public square, which is why it is called Plaza Nueva (New Square).

The Real Audiencia (Court of Justice)

On the same plaza de San Francisco and facing the principal façade of the City Hall is the stately building of the Royal Audience Chamber of Seville, which at the beginning was called the «Casa Cuadra», and in the 16th century came to be known as the Audiencia. Of its original 16th century layout, the entrance hall still exists, which opens onto a magnificent courtyard through three arches with superb wrought iron gates.

The rest of the building has been reformed several times, adapting it to the bureaucratic needs of each period. The façade was reformed in 1824 by the architect Fernández Riosces, and again at the beginning of the 20th century, by Aníbal González, who gave it its present aspect and decorated it with the coats of arms of the provinces of Andalusia.

The building lost its judicial function some years ago, and

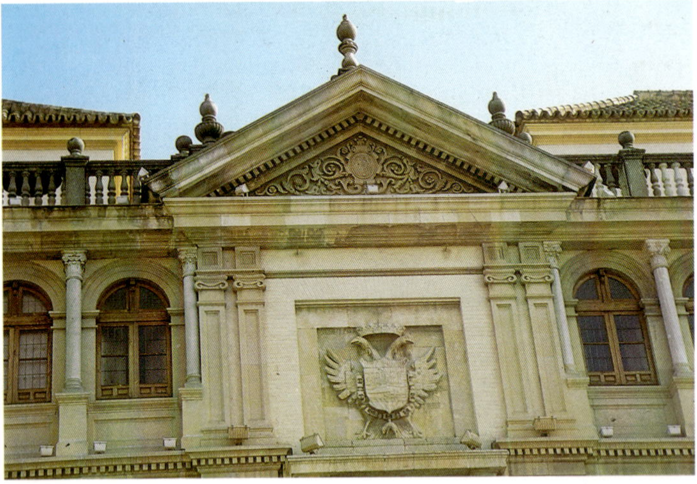

Royal Court.

now it is the headquarters and offices of the Caja de Ahorros Provincial de San Fernando which has transformed it into a bank without damaging in the least its architectural beauty.

Fuente de Mercurio

Also in plaza de San Francisco we can admire the Fuente de Mercurio (fountain), with a very beautiful basin and over it a statue of Mercury made by Juan de Bolonia and cast in bronze by Bartolomé Morel around 1570.

The fountain stands in front of a building that used to house the Consulate of Genoa, at a time when the Genoese were the bankers and brokers of the empire. It is now the Seville branch of the Bank of Spain. Mercury Fountain can be interpreted in many humoristic ways, and thus it was in the Golden Age, since Mercury was the god of trade as well as the god of thieves.

Mercury Fountain.

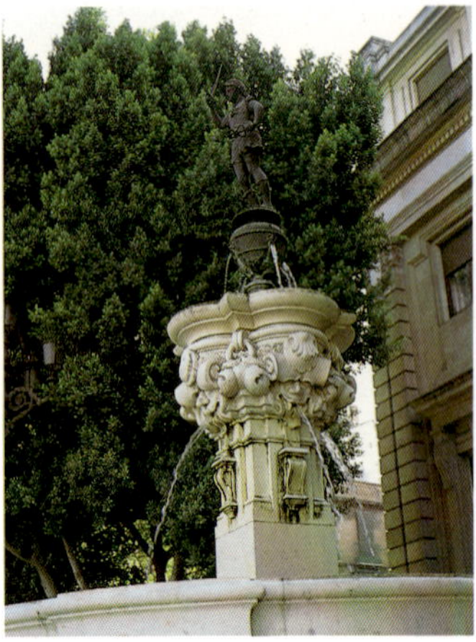

Plaza del Salvador

From plaza de San Francisco and through the small street bordering the northern wall of the former Audiencia, formerly called calle Entrecárceles and now calle Francisco Bruna, we come to another little street called Manuel Cortina, and reach the plaza del Salvador.

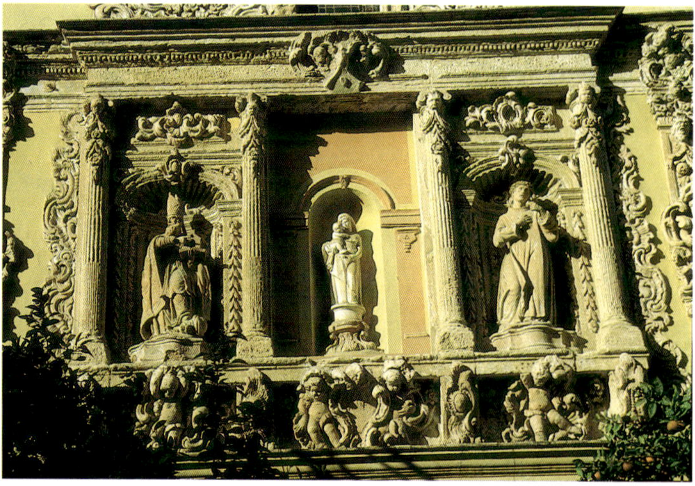

Façade of the Church of San Juan de Dios.

Church of San Juan de Dios

In this plaza we have two churches to see. In the first place we will visit the hospital church of San Juan de Dios, called Nuestra Señora de la Paz. This building has a curious history. It was owned by the Vega family. A gentleman of this family, Captain Vega, after fighting in Italy and against the Moriscos in Granada, in 1574, «not being able to adjust himself to a life of peace after nine years of war, decided to donate his palace as a hospital for the poor and left to continue warring in the New World». The hospital was established by the Order of San Juan de Dios for sick elderly people and the destitute. The entrance to the hospital is on calle Sagasta, but the church entrance is on this plaza del Salvador.

The church has its façade on this plaza, with two belfry towers. The frontispiece is transitional in style (Renaissance to Baroque) and is decorated with statues of Saint John of God, the Virgin and Saint Augustine. It has three aisles and the central nave has a noteworthy cupola over the transept. The main altar is by Francisco de

San Juan de Dios, Detail of a Tower.

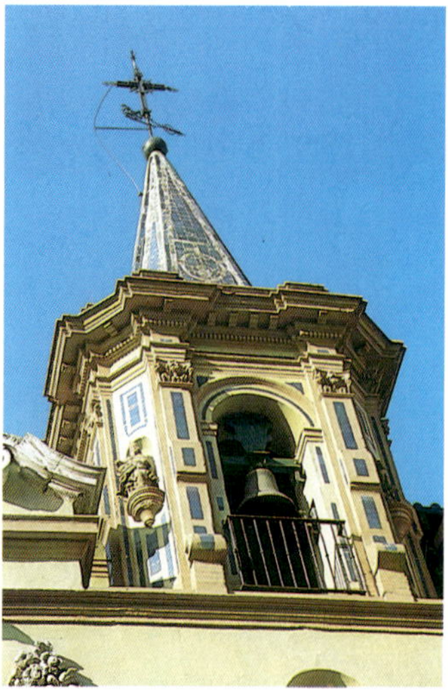

Ocampo and others, dating from the 17th century. The most valuable sculpture in the whole church is that of Saint Charles Borromeo sculpted by the great Juan de Mesa. The rest of the church and its statues date from the 18th century, all very fine and well kept by the Brothers of Saint John of God.

On the same street is the collegiate church of El Salvador. This church was in past centuries so rich and important that it competed with the Cathedral. It has the category of collegiate church and had a numerous chapter of religious canons and beneficiaries.

This church was formerly the Great Mosque of the Arabs until the 12th century (when the new Great Mosque was built, today the Cathedral).

Through an alley, we can reach the Patio de los Naranjos of the former mosque. Debris from demolitions made it necessary to raise the ground of the Court so much that the pillars hardly show more than their Abbasides style capitals. This was the Ad-Abbas Mosque, built in the 9th century and deteriorated by earthquakes and time, so that it had to be demolished in 1671 to build the present church. The only architectural remains of the Arab construction are the Patio de los Naranjos and the lower part of the tower or minaret. On the wall in the entrance to the church, on this court, there is a very beautiful inscription in Kufic characters from Arab times.

Inside the church we have a grand view, due to the width of its three aisles and the size of its pillars. The main altar has a Baroque altarpiece, the work of Cayetano Acosta in 1770, with a sculpted group of figures representing the Transfiguration of Our Lord. The cupola over the presbytery was painted by Espinal. The Tabernacle is a delicately carved guilded piece crowned by a 17th century image of the Immaculate Conception.

On the altarpiece to the left is the Cristo de los Afligidos, a splendid anonymous work dating from the same century.

Other valuable statues in this church include that of Jesús de la Pasión, a masterpiece by the sculptor Martínez Montañés. This image leads the Brotherhood of the Passion, one of the most famous during the Sevillian Holy Week, the Cristo de Amor, which is a magnificent figure of Christ crucified, by Juan de Mesa, whose altar is at the head of the right hand aisle. The Saint Christopher, also by Martínez Montañés, and Saint Anne teaching the Virgin to read, by the sculptor Montes de Oca, are other noteworthy pieces.

It is impossible to list one by one the sculptures and paintings kept in the Church of el Salvador, as well as the fine pieces in gold and silver and the liturgical silver objects it possesses.

Cuesta del Rosario

Going up this sloping street, we find a curious slab on the corner, under the Cruz de los Polaineros set there by the guild of leather craftsmen in the 16th century.

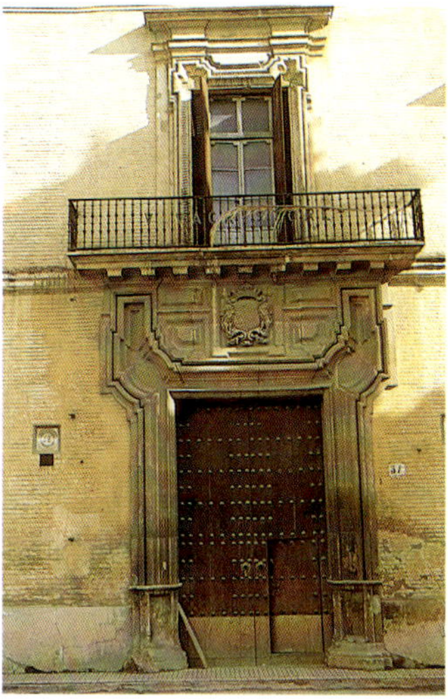

Palace of the Marquis of Villapanes.

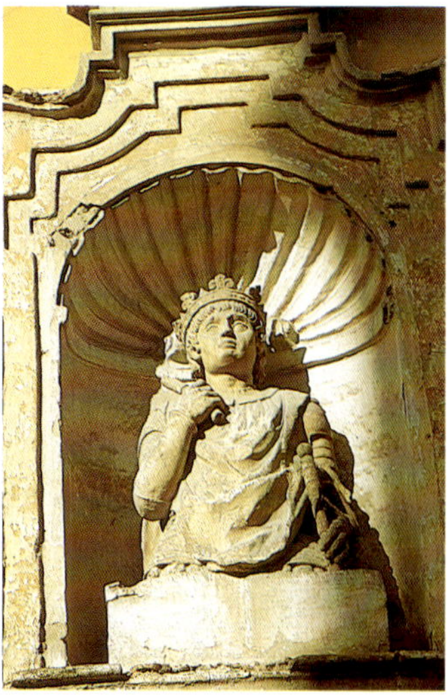

Head of King Pedro.

At the top of the slope we reach the old plaza de la Pescadería, «one of the three places that the King has not been able to conquer» (the other two were the plazuela de la Caza and the slaughterhouse of Puerta de la Carne, so reports Cervantes), since these three places were governed not by the Authorities, but by rogues and scoundrels.

After plaza de la Pescadería is calle Augusto Plasencia, and through it we come to calle Cabeza del Rey Don Pedro.

Cabeza del Rey Don Pedro

On one of the façade of the street of this name we can see a niche, just opposite the corner of calle Candilejo, which holds a marble bust of King Pedro I. According to legend, the king himself had it placed there as atonement, for in this place he killed a man he had challenged. However, historian Father Flórez asserts that after the Battle of Montiel, when Pedro was killed by his brother Enrique de Trastamara, the king was beheaded and his head brought to Seville, and was possibly exhibited in this place, where it was substituted later by this marble head so that the memory of the event might continue.

Casa de Pilatos

Following the same calle Cabeza del Rey don Pedro, a little further on to the right we find calle Aguilas, which we follow, past a beautiful palace with a magnificent balcony, the former house of the Count of Aguilas. The street leads to plaza de Pilatos.

The building on the left side of the plaza is the Palace of the Dukes of Medinaceli, known as

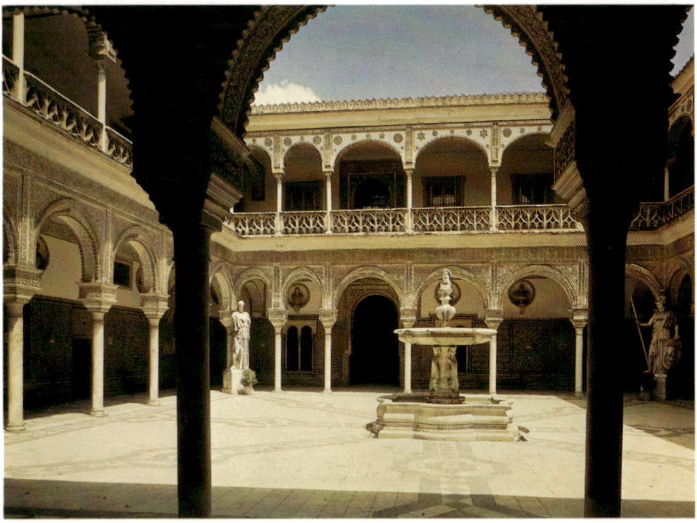

Pilates's house.

Pilate's House, because the same as Jesus Christ left Pilate's house to go to the Mount of Golgotha, from this palace the Via Crucis procession started out on Lent Fridays, leading outside the city walls to the Cruz del Campo.

The palace is Renaissance style combined with Mudejar.

Its construction was started by the Governor of Andalusia, Pedro Enríquez in 1492, and concluded by his son Fadrique Enríquez de Ribera, first Marquis of Tarifa, halfway through the 16th century.

The architecture of the building is noteworthy, beginning with the façade with the coats of arms of the Riberas and of the Holy Sepulcre in memory of Fadrique Enríquez's pilgrimage to Jerusalem in 1520. The main courtyard is impressive with its two large statues of the goddess Pallas Athena, one armed and the other unarmed, both brought from Italy, which seem to be copies after Phidias. The exterior of the palace and the pillars are by the Aprile, a famous Italian family of artists, and were made in Genoa in 1520. They were worked by Pedro de Aprile, Juan Antonio María Aprile, and Bernardino de Bisono, according to data that the historian Gestoso found in the Genoese archives.

The central fountain was also made by the Aprile, with a beautiful basin on an intricately worked pedestal and crowned by a classic bust.

Equally superb is the main staircase, decorated with tiles and with a guilded cupola in the ceiling.

Since the Ribera family had close connections with Italy and some members of the family held very important positions in Rome and Naples, they were

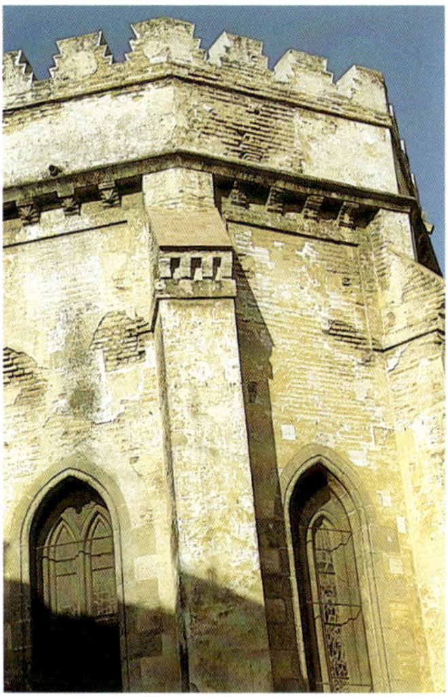

Saint Stephen.

cultured persons, loving antiques and sufficiently wealthy to enrich the palace throughout the 16th and 17th centuries with very valuable archeological pieces which today comprise a splendid collection of first class Roman statues and busts.

Thus, in the ground floor rooms and gardens, we find a series of statues of the twenty four Roman Emperors and the Latin authors Horace, Titus Livius and Cicero, as well as many other personalities, mythological gods and goddesses. On the ground floor there is also a collection of paintings from the Flemish and Italian schools, notable works by Sebastián del Pombo, A. Gaspar Crayer, Giuseppe Recco, Spanish masters such as Pantoja de la Cruz, Goya, Pacheco, Carreño de Miranda, and French painters such as Louis Michael Van Loo and Jean Thomas Thibault.

One of the jewels of the collection in Pilate's House is the tapestry El baile de bodas (The Wedding Dance) by the Flemish artist William Pannemaker, who weaved it in Antwerp in 1530. The large amount of tiles, reliefs, carvings and Mudejar decor make the interior of the palace a true architectural treasure.

San Esteban

We now go down calle San Esteban and to our left we find the church bearing this name. It is one of many which were restored after the earthquakes of the 14th century, in Gothic style, although they may previously have been mosques.

The interior has three aisles with a very valuable Mudejar ceiling in elaborately carved wood, made in the 15th century.

The main altarpiece has paintings by Zurbarán on the side panels, while those in the center are the work of the Polanco brothers.

Also important in this church is the image of the Cristo de la Salud y Buen Viaje, so called because travelers in past centuries left the city through this street, which leads to Puerta de Carmona Gate, and stopped to pray before this image to be free from accidents and attacking bandits.

On the wall of the sacramental chapel, there are tiles with medallions of warriors and animals from the 17th century, unique in their kind.

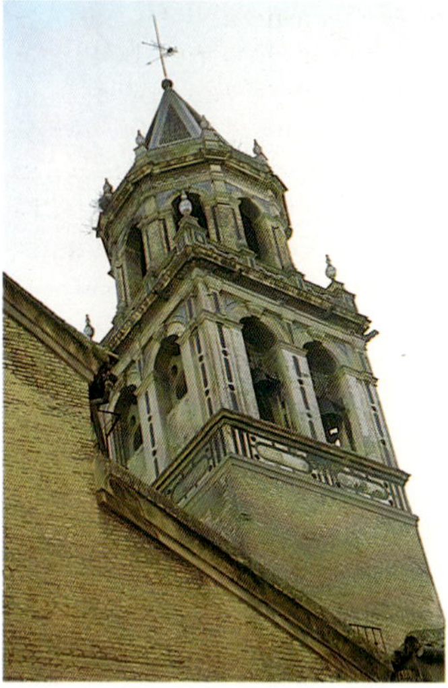

Church of Saint James.

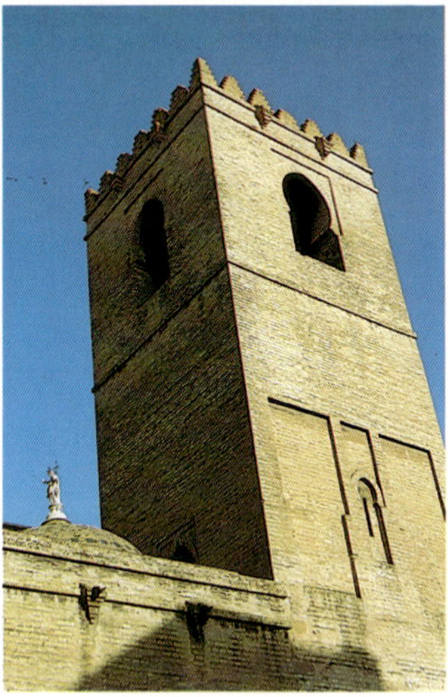

Church of Saint Catherine.

We leave the church of Saint Stephen and observe on the outside the remains of Arab art from the ancient mosque on the southern side and on the lower part of the tower, which was once a Moslem minaret.

Calle Santiago

From calle San Esteban where we are, we take calle Virgen de la Luz on the left, which leads us to calle Santiago.

Halfway down this street we will find López Pintado square, with the palace of the Marquis of Villapanés on one side. This palace has a spacious entrance showing, through its three wrought iron gates, a beautiful pillared courtyard. The façade of the building dates from the beginning of the 18th century. The building was the home of the López Pintado family, among whose members was Admiral López Pintado, one of the most renowned seamen of the 1700's.

On this square is the church of Santiago, one of the first parishes founded by King Saint Ferdinand in 1248. It was called the church of Santiago the Elder, not to be confused with the church of Santiago of the Sword or of the Knights, on calle San Vicente.

This church of Santiago is small and of scant architectural value, although it does have a beautiful painting on the main altar representing *Saint James at the Battle of Clavijo*, by Mateo Pérez de Alesio. To the right of the presbytery the historian Gonzalo Argote de Molina, author of *Nobleza de Andalucía*, is buried.

In the chapel on the Gospel side there are paintings by Pacheco representing several saints and the portraits of the protectors of the chapel, Captain García de Barrionuevo and his wife. There is also a sculpture.

The Church of Santa Catalina

At the top of calle Santiago we cross calle Almirante Apodaca, to find ourselves opposite the Church of Santa Catalina (Saint Catherine).

Its exterior is interesting, with a Mudejar tower, the lower part of which was used as minaret for the mosque which stood here in Arab times. If we go around the church to the back, there is a brick apse that some critics hold to be Arab from the Almohad Era, while others believe it is Mudejar from the 14th century, since the building underwent numerous restorations throughout its eight hundred years.

Standing in front of the main entrance to the church, we have before us a notable Gothic portal, but it does not belong to this church. It was brought at the beginning of the 20th century from the Church of Santa Lucía, which was closed to worship, as a plaque on the right hand side explains.

We enter the church through this Gothic portal and find the original door in beautiful Mudejar work. The church has three aisles with rich Mudejar coffered ceilings. The lovely main altarpiece has an image of Saint Catherine from the 17th century and paintings depicting the life of the saint by Diego López Bueno. The Sacramental Chapel, built by the architect Leonardo de Figueroa early in the 18th century, was decorated by the famous sculptor Pedro Duque Cornejo. The altarpiece in this chapel, extremely Baroque, was made by the Castillos, mostly by Benito Hita del Castillo, who also did the image of Saint Sebastian.

Christ of the Exaltation.

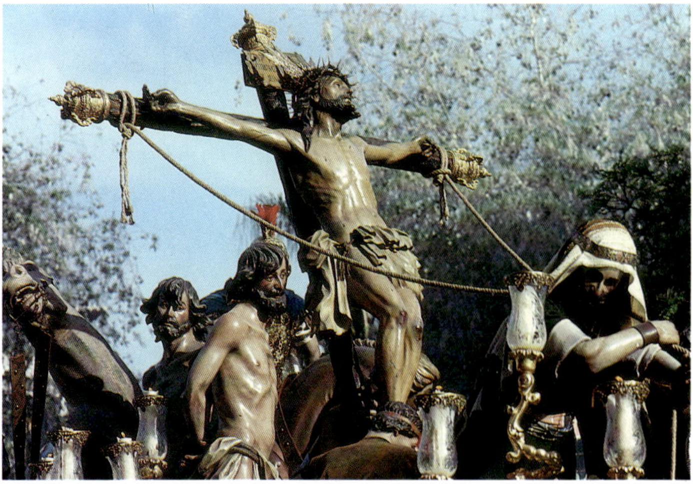

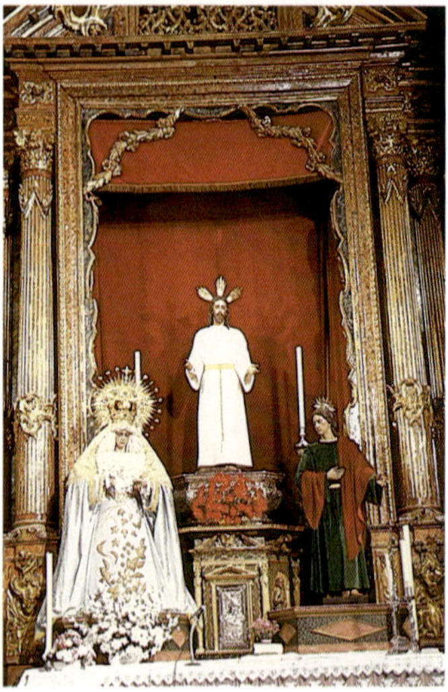

Belfry of the Church of St Peter.

The Cristo de la Exaltación (Christ of the Exaltation), belonging to the brotherhood of the same name, which comes out in procession during Holy Week, is the work of Pedro Roldán and the figures of the two thieves on the «paso» or float, were made by the sculptress Luisa Roldán de Mena, known as «La Roldana».

An interesting image of Saint Lucía presides over her altar at the foot of the church, this saint having received devotions in this church since the 16th century, according to Cervantes, although the present image could be from the 17th century.

This church of Santa Catalina is one of the best kept in Seville.

The Church of San Pedro

Going up calle Almirante Apodaca we find to our right the Church of San Pedro (Saint Peter). Its architecture is Mudejar from the 14th century, although it was possibly before that a Moslem mosque, one of the several damaged by earthquakes in the 14th century, and later reconstructed in the Christian Era in Mudejar style. This is the opinion of Gestoso, which we share.

The splendid frontispiece contains the figure of the saint and heraldic symbols of the pontificate.

The church has three aisles, the center one a bit longer, and the presbytery has a magnificent cupola with Gothic-style vaulting. The main altarpiece is by Pedro Delgado, with statues and bas-reliefs representing scenes from the life of Saint Peter.

Noteworthy is the Crucifix known as the Cristo de Burgos, and kept in the chapel of this Brotherhood. It is a masterpiece by the sculptor Juan Bautista

Burgos Crucifix.

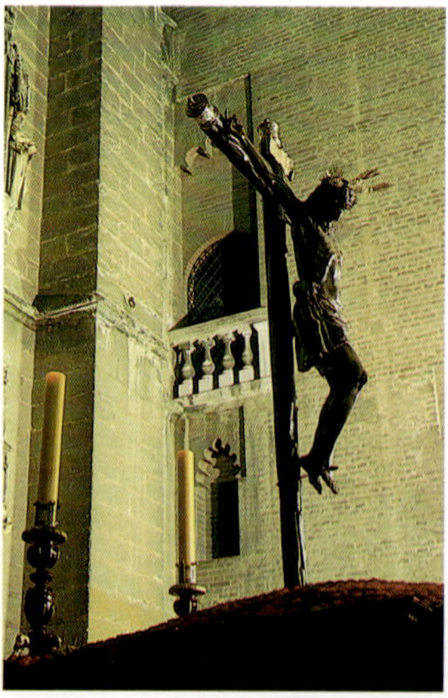

Vázquez the Elder, dated in 1573. This sculptor was one of the first image makers of Sevillian Baroque art, whose work is to be found not only in Seville, but also in Latin America, the most famous being the Christ of the chapel of the Manzipes in the Tunja Cathedral of Colombia, which is quite similar to this one.

Also worth seeing is the chapel at the foot of the church in the Gospel aisle. The altarpiece is composed of eight paintings of the Annunciation, several saints and the protector of the chapel and his family, all the work of the painter Pedro Campaña, as can be read on the pedestal of one of the statues painted on the Annunciation panel, which contains the signature of the artist: *«Petrus Kampania faciebat»*. The protector of the chapel was a wealthy citizen, Pedro de Santiago y Ferreol, who is buried in the same chapel, the tombstone informing us he died on January 23, 1600.

In the opposite aisle and facing this altar, there is another one with five very beautiful 16th century panels of the Italian school.

The Church of la Anunciación

From the church of San Pedro we go up calle Imagen, crossing plaza de la Encarnación, and on the corner of this square and calle de Laraña we will find the church of la Anunciación (the Annunciation), whose entrance opens onto Laraña street.

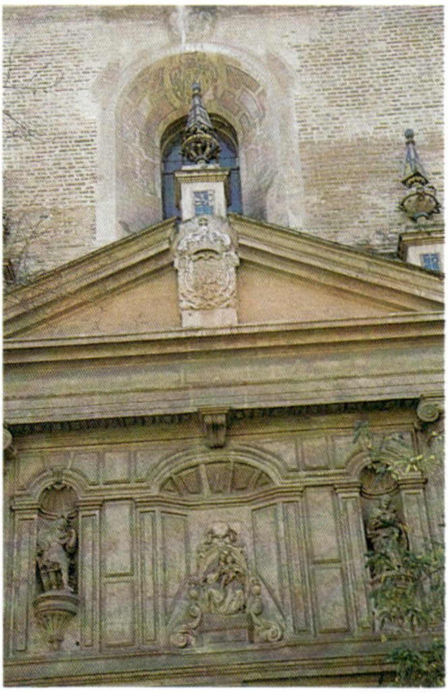

The Church of the Annunciation.

This church belongs to the no longer existing Casa Profesa de la Compañía de Jesús, built between 1565 and 1579. The Casa Profesa was, besides a Jesuit residence, the first school they had in Seville and where Miguel de Cervantes Saavedra

The Annunciation. Detail.

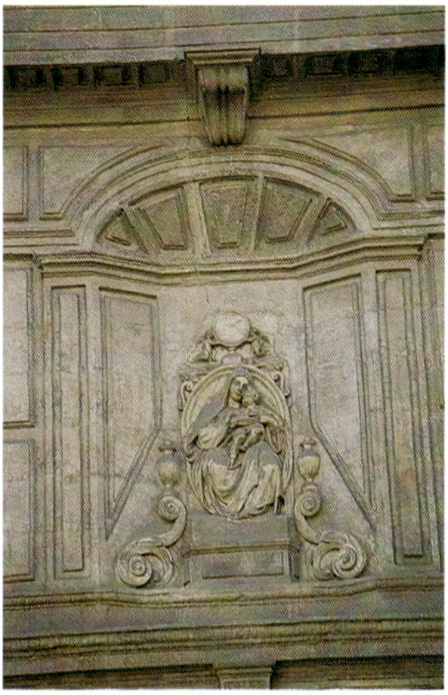

was a boarding student. The Casa Profesa became a university in the 18th century and was demolished several years ago to build the present School of Fine Arts of the University of Seville.

The church has been kept intact, and this is what we will visit.

Before entering, we must admire its Renaissance portal, and over the door, a large relief

We enter the church, whose layout is also controversial as it is attributed by some to Herrera, the architect who built the Monastery of El Escorial, while others assert that the drawings for this church were made by the Jesuit architect Bartolomé Bustamante.

The interior has a single spacious nave, with transept, whose arms contain beautiful altars.

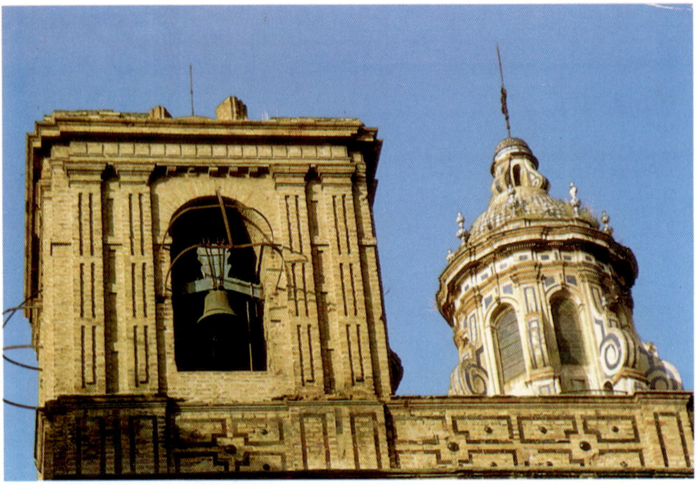

Belfry tower and dome of the Church of the Annunciation.

of the Virgin Mother by Torrigiano, the famous Italian sculptor who lived for a long time in Seville and died in this city jailed by the Inquisition. However, some modern authors believe this work is by the great image maker Juan Bautista Vázquez the Elder, who did the Burgos Crucifix we have already seen in the Church of San Pedro. Be that as it may, the medallion of the Virgin Mother is a Renaissance masterpiece.

The main altarpiece is Corinthian in style, made by the famous wood-carver Alonso Matías in the last third of the 16th century and divided into compartments containing magnificent paintings. Above, at the very top, is the Annunciation by Francisco Pacheco. In the center is The Sacred Family Accompanied by Saint Jerome and Saint Ignatius of Loyola, painted by Roelas, and on the sides The Nativity and The Adoration of the Magi., by his disciple Juan Varela.

In front there are two sculptures, Saint Ignatius and Saint Francis Borja, carved by of Martínez Montañés.

The other paintings are attributed to Alonso Cano and Mohedano.

The whole altarpiece was made between 1600 and 1606.

There are altars in the two arms of the transept. On the left, Our Lady of the Valley, work of Juan de Mesa in the 17th century, and the Coronation of Christ by Perea, made at the end of the same century.

In the right hand transept there is an altar with images of the Immaculate Conception, Saint Isabel, the Virgin and Child, and several saints, all by Juan Bautista Vázquez, the Younger.

On the left wall of the church is the superb tomb of Governor Pedro Enríquez de Ribera, finely worked in Carrara marble by the Italian sculptor Antonio María Aprile in Genoa at the beginning of the 16th century. This artist worked a lot for the Ribera family, as we have seen in connection with the Casa de Pilatos on previous pages. The right wall has another tomb of the same dimensions and style, work by Grazzini, but probably also designed by Antonio María Aprile.

These two tombs, which can be counted among the best funeral sculpture in Spain, were previously located in the Cartuja de las Cuevas, but were moved to this church when the monasteries were secularized in the 19th century.

In this church it is also worthwhile seeing the altar of The Virgin of the Milk, decorated with paintings attributed to Pacheco with scenes of the *Birth of the Virgin, The Presentation in the Temple, Martyrdom of a Saint Thrown to the Lions, The Betrothal, The Adoration of the Magi* and several saints.

There is also an interesting image of the Virgin in the presbytery, made by Torrigiano.

Panteón de Sevillanos Ilustres

Under this Church of la Anunciación, although the entrance is through the Facultad de Bellas Artes, the pantheon of famous Sevillians is located, where many personalities from the world of the military, literature, science, and art are buried. Among these are Gustavo Adolfo Bécquer, the poet, and his brother Valeriano Bécquer, the painter; Francisco Duarte, general purveyor to the Navy and his wife Catalina de Alcocer, who died in 1554; Lorenzo Suárez de Figueroa, master of the Order of Santiago, in 1409; Alberto Lista, a 19th century author and politician; Félix José Reinoso, also a 19th century author; Diego Gómez de Ribera, killed by the Moors after conquering Iznajas y Alora in spite of his offer to parley; and Pedro Ponce de León, first Count of Arcos; the famous philologist Benito Arias Montano, who died in 1598 and other Sevillians who have given glory and fame to Seville.

Calle Sierpes.

Leaving the Church of la Anunciación we go down Laraña and Martín Villa streets as far as a square known as La Campana, where we find the beginning of calle Sierpes.

The name of this street is universally known because it can claim to have been the center and hub of the world at the time of the Spanish Empire, in the 16th and 17th centuries.

All sorts of marvelous things have taken place in this street. Doctor Nicolás Monardes lived here and cultivated medicinal plants brought from the New World, which were unknown in Europe such as the castor oil plant, copal, guaiacol, the drumstick tree, plants which revolutionized Europe's knowledge of pharmacology, and others which were initially taken as medicine and later became generally used for other purposes, such as potatoes and tobacco. Here on calle Sierpes, a plaque recalls these facts.

But calle Sierpes was also important as a worldwide printing centre.

Books were printed here, which taught half the world to read in Spanish and to pray as Christians; for example, books printed in shops such as that of Alonso Díaz, who stamped his printer's mark as *In via Serpentina*, the latinized name of calle Sierpes.

Here there was also a famous shop that printed playing cards (known as «the book of the forty pages» among the rogues of those days), owned by a French hunchback, called Pierre Papin.

On this street there was also a Royal Prison, a «place where every discomfort is at home», as described by Cervantes, being its guest on two occasions. Precisely during his imprisonment he wrote the first part of Don Quijote. This is also commemorated by a plaque on the façade of today's Banco Hispanoamericano building.

Many newspapers were published here during the 19th century, and in cafés such as *La Cabeza del Turco*, political conspiracies were hatched.

But it was also, and still is, the place where cereal merchants, cattle traders and real estate brokers meet in bars and in the Círculo Unión Mercantil to discuss prices and close sale operations. Many of those who appear idle in these cafés are in reality active workers who in a few minutes can close trading operations worth several million pesetas.

Capillita de San José

Towards the end of calle Sierpes, two small streets meet it, one from each side. The first is calle Sagasta, where the Hospital de San Juan de Dios is located, which we visited before, and the other is calle Jovellanos. A short way up the latter, is the capillita de San José (little Chapel of Saint Joseph). It is a National Monument, for although small in size, it is one of the most important examples of

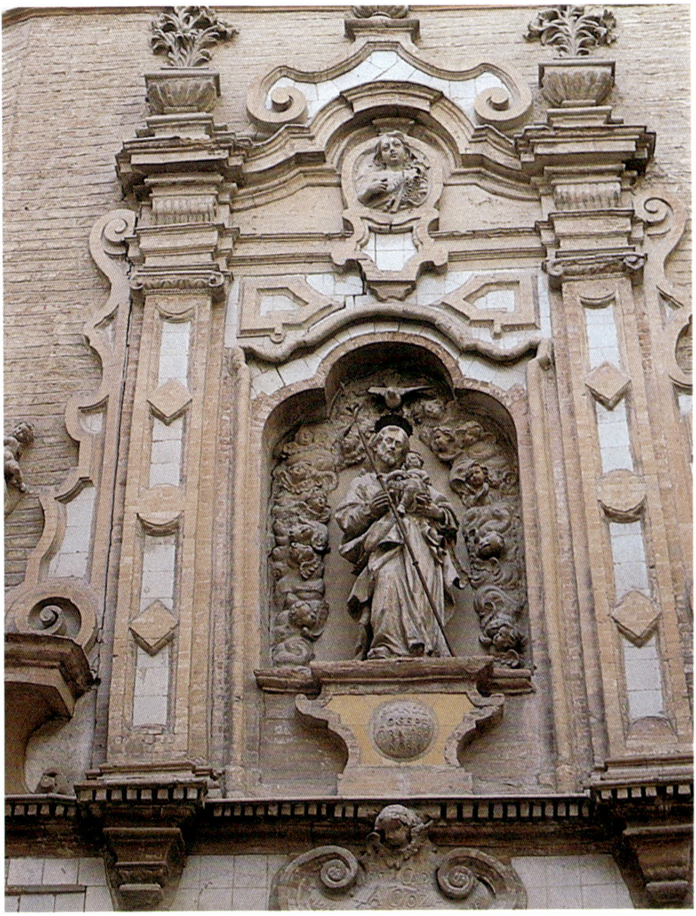

Capillita de San José. Detail of Saint Joseph and the Holy Child.

Spanish Baroque art. We will not stop at paintings such as the *Escape from Egypt, the Betrothal of the Virgin* and the sculptures of Saint Joachim and Saint Anne, since their merit is overshadowed by the richly decorated vault and walls, and the exceptional carpentry work of the reredos and altars. Baroque predilection for adornment reaches its climax in this small church, so much so that we can speak of «horror of emptiness», since even the smallest corner has its precise decor.

Leaving this chapel of San José we return to calle Sierpes, and continue to its end in San Francisco square, where we finish this route.

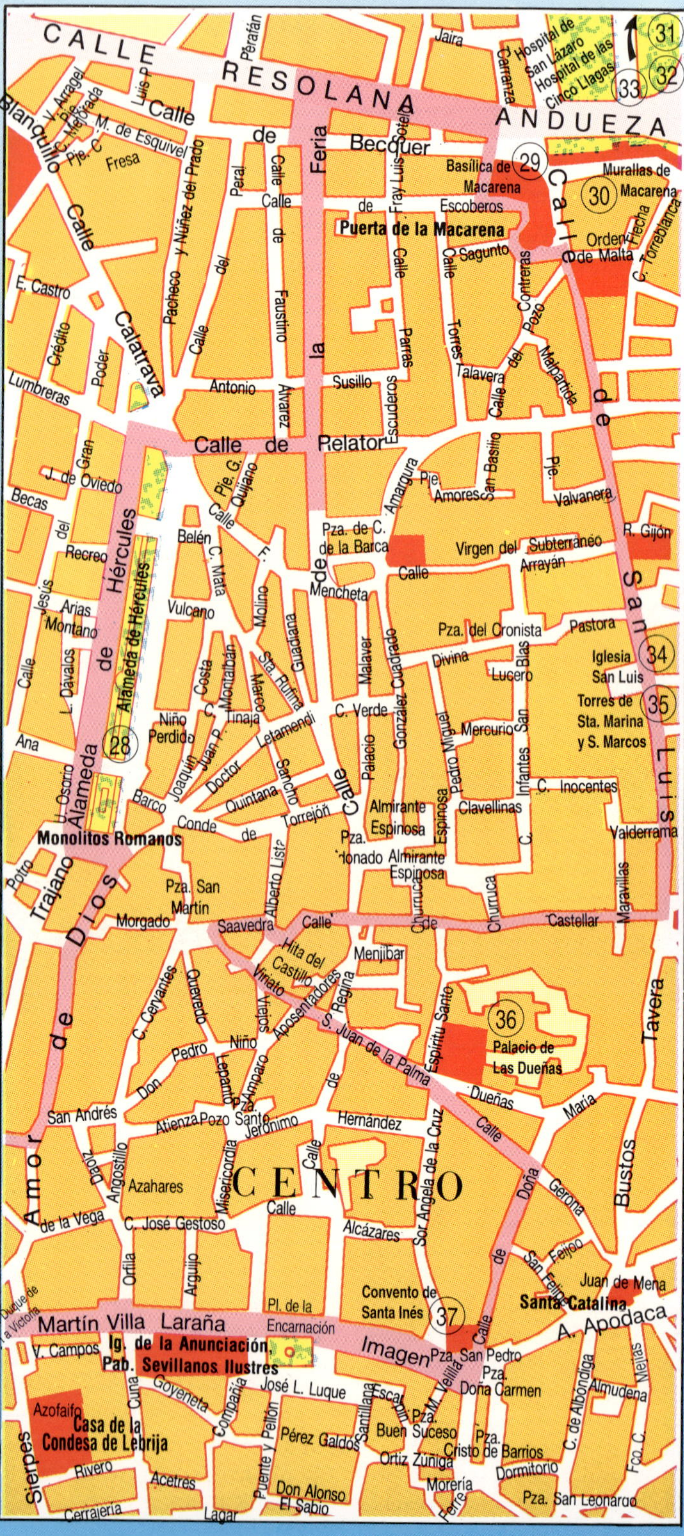

Calle Resolana
Andueza
Calle de Feria
Becquer
Basílica de Macarena
Puerta de la Macarena
Murallas de Macarena
Orden de Malta
Hospital de San Lázaro
Hospital de las Cinco Llagas
Calle de San Luis
Calle de Relator
Alameda de Hércules
Monolitos Romanos
Pza. San Martín
Trajano
Amor de Dios
Pza. de C. de la Barca
Pza. del Cronista
Iglesia San Luis
Torres de Sta. Marina y S. Marcos
Palacio de Las Dueñas
CENTRO
Convento de Santa Inés
Santa Catalina
Pl. de la Encarnación
Ig. de la Anunciación, Pab. Sevillanos Ilustres
Casa de la Condesa de Lebrija
Martín Villa
Laraña
Imagen
Sierpes
28
29
30
31
32
33
34
35
36
37

ROUTE 4: MACARENA QUARTER

PLACES OF INTEREST

(28) **Alameda de Hércules**
Main promenade of the city until the 19th century. Huge Roman columns with 16th century sculptures of Carlos I and Felipe II.

(29) **Church of Virgen Macarena**
Contains an image of the Virgen de la Esperanza Macarena, a museum of religious art and the tomb of Captain of Queipo de Llano.

(30) **Macarena Walls**
Magnificent Roman fortress rebuilt by the arabs.

(31) **Hospital of the five wounds**
The largest in Europe until the 19th century. It now holds the seat of the regional government.

(32) **Hospital of San Lázaro**
Hospital for lepers. It has a little arab tower from the Almohade era. The chapel with important artistic treasures.

(33) **Cemetery of San Fernando**

(34) **Church of San Luis**
Ornate baroque style with magnificent sculptures by Pedro Duque Cornejo. Appointment required: Dirección técnica del patrimonio de la Diputación Provincial de Sevilla. Tel: 421 40 24.

(35) **Towers of Santa Marina and San Marcos**
Moorish towers rebuilt in the 14th century; mudéjar style.

(36) **Palace of Las Dueñas**
Noble house belonging to the Alba House. Appointment required at the Alba House in Madrid.

(37) **Convent of Santa Inés**
Medieval 14th century building famous due to the legend of Maese Pérez the organist.

STARTING POINT	Leave Plaza del Duque by calle Trajano
EXIT TO NEXT ROUTE	From Plaza del Duque de la Victoria towards calle de la campana.

USEFUL ADDRESSES NEARBY

Chemists:	Amor de Dios, 2 and 36
	Trajano, 40
	Doctor Letamendi, 5
	Feria, 69, 126 and 160
	Macarena, 50
	Don Fadrique, 3
	San Luis, 87
	Duque Cornejo, 52
	San Marcos, 5
	San Juan de la Palma 15
	Plaza Cristo de Burgos, 3
	Laraña, 6
Photo Service:	Amor de Dios, 44
	Trajano, 12
	Feria, 97
	Bécquer, 2
	Don Pedro Niño, 17
Restaurante Las Columnas de Baco:	Santa María de Gracia, 2
Senra:	Pacheco y Núñez de Prado, 61

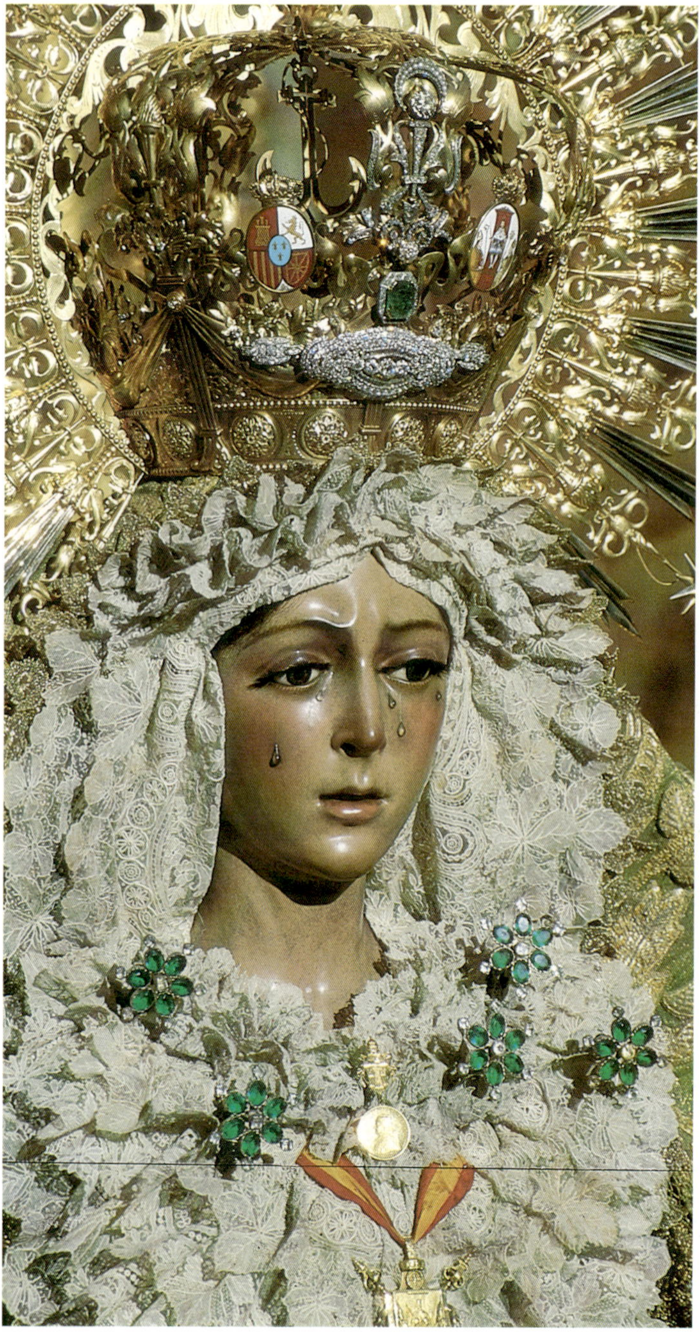

Virgin of the Esperanza Macarena.

ROUTE 4: BARRIO DE LA MACARENA

We start off from La Campana, where we entered calle Sierpes. Opposite this street, there is another one named Santa María de Gracia, after the convent of Santa María de Gracia, which stood here from the 16th century until the 19th century.

Further on it changes its name to Amor de Dios, after the Amor de Dios hospital, the most important one in medieval Seville. In the 19th century this street was famous for its cafés chantants or night clubs, such as *Salón Olimpia*, *Variedades*, *Salón Barrera* and others, where the present day form of Flamenco singing and dancing took shape.

Continuing Amor de Dios street we find, on the right, the San Isidoro Institute, the first high school opened in Seville and the second most important educational centre after the University. It was founded in 1846 by the famous author, poet and politician Alberto Lista. This institute taught students who later became relevant figures in Spanish literature, such as Francisco Rodríguez Zapata, Gustavo Adolfo Bécquer, Joaquin Guichot, Manuel Machado, and the brothers Joaquín and Serafín Alvarez Quintero.

The San Isidoro Institute, although the building has been renovated and modernized, has one of the best libraries in Seville, especially with regard to 19th century Spanish literature.

On the opposite sidewalk we can see the Cervantes movie theater, which was originally a theater, although it is nowadays used as a cinema. Built in 1873 by architect Juan Talavera de la Vega, it has exceptional acoustics. In this theater the first comedy plays by the Alvarez Quintero brothers had their premiers.

On the same side as the San Isidoro Institute a bit further on, we find the corner of calle Morgado. In the wall of the house on this corner, several feet high, there is a niche holding two small Roman style statues that tradition claims were the models used to make the statues of the Alameda de Hércules. If we look at them carefully and compare them with the figures we will see shortly, we will have to admit that there is not the slightest similitude between them, for which reason we can discard this popular belief which calls them the «Old Hercules». These are probably small Roman statues excavated nearby and placed here as a memento or decoration.

Following the same street we reach the spacious park of Alameda de Hércules.

Alameda de Hércules

This place was formerly an unhealthy lagoon which filled the whole city with stench and mosquitoes during the summer months. For this reason, a wise city official, Francisco de

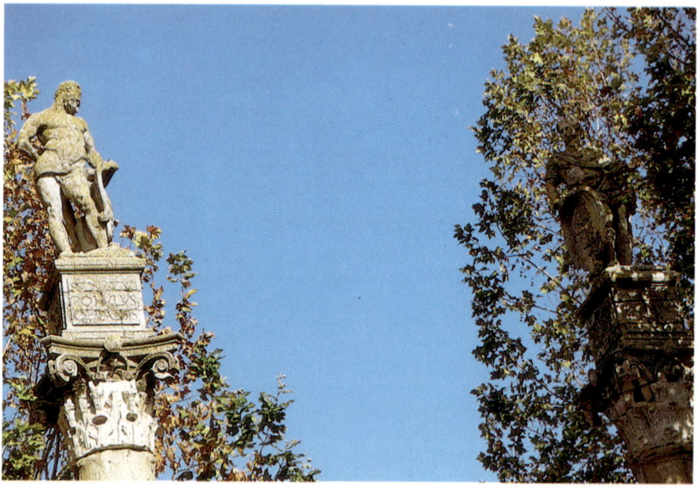

Alameda de Hércules.

Zapata y Cisneros, Count of Barajas, decided to fill it with earth and plant poplars to dry it up. Furthermore, he had two enormous Roman pillars brought from the ancient temple or forum on Mármoles street (which we have seen in the previous chapter). Due to the huge weight and size of the pillars, this task was compared in the chronicles of the time to «the labours of Hercules». The work of transporting the pillars was supervised by the 16th century architect and engineer Juan de Oviedo. On top of the two pillars we see the statues of Hercules and Julius Caesar, made by the sculptor Diego de Pesquera. In order to honor Emperor Charles I and his son King Philip II, he sculpted portraits of these two monarchs in the faces of Hercules and Caesar.

Alameda walk was during the 16th and 17th centuries one of the most beautiful, and undoubtedly, the most elegant in Europe. It was decorated with beautiful stone fountains and bronze statues, some of which still stand elsewhere, such as the famous Pila del Pato, today in plaza de San Leandro.

It was a popular promenading place where ladies in elegant carriages were to be seen with gallant young men on magnificent steeds trotting alongside courting them. When royalty visited Seville, grand «carousel» performances were held in the Alameda with hundreds of horsemen participating in quadrilles, dressed in Italian, German or Turkish fashion, with silk costumes embroided in gold and silver.

In the 18th century, the Alameda became the place where the «enlightened « and «progressive» intelectuals met to read the first newspapers, dis-

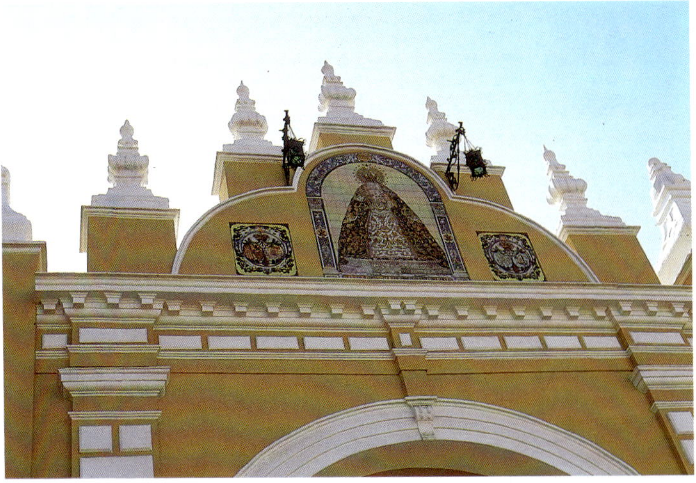

Entrance to the Macarena. Detail.

cuss politics, pass on war news, distribute leaflets against the Inquisition and comment on the events of the French Revolution.

In the 19th century it became a meeting place for rogues, dandies, bullfighters, flamenco singers and bronze craftsmen. At the turn of the century, small open air theaters, refreshment stands and the first movie theaters were set up here, where people could sit down if they paid or see the show standing up without paying. Later, the Alameda fell into disrepute becoming a marketplace of cheap love.

At the northern end of the Alameda we can see another two pillars with heraldic lions, placed here in the 18th century, shortening the park which previously extended to Calatrava street.

La Macarena

From the Alameda, taking the last street to the right, named calle Relator after a well-known clerk of the Audiencia who lived here in the 17th century, we reach calle Feria, famous in the past for its rufians and browbeaters, according to Cervantes. It is also known in the history of Seville for a great uprising, called the «motín de los ferianos o del perdón verde», which occurred here in 1521, coinciding with other rebellions in Castile and Valencia.

We turn right on this street to find at its end calle Resolana, which formerly bordered the city wall on the outside. Resolana street takes us to the Macarena Gate.

This is the only remaining gate. Next to it there is a long stretch where we can admire the solidity and height of the

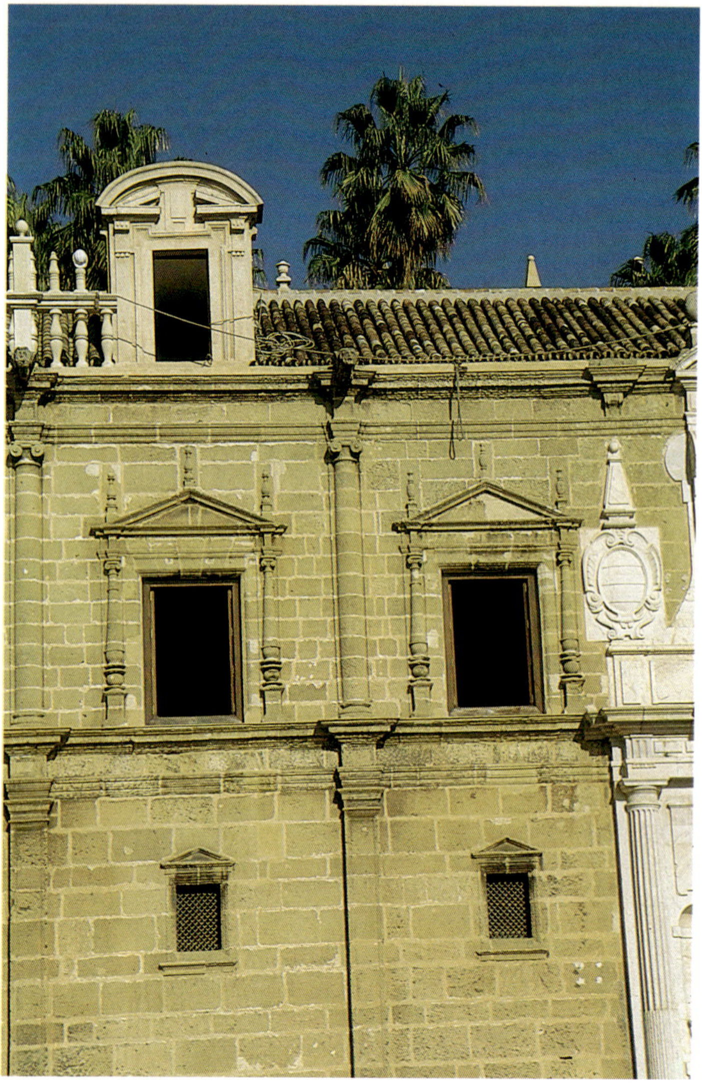

Detail of the Hospital of the Five Wounds.

wall and the barbican in front of it. King Alfonso X the Wise said in 1260 that the walls of Seville were so strong, that with only a barbican or front wall like this one any city could be considered well defended.

The wall was built in Roman times, when the danger of Goth invasions commenced, and was later reconstructed with battlements by the Arabs in the 12th century.

After seeing the walls, we can now turn our attention to the Hospital de las Cinco Llagas opposite, now the Parliament of Andalusia.

Hospital de las Cinco Llagas

This magnificent building was built in the 16th century by Doña Catalina Ribera, wife of the governor Pedro Enríquez de Ribera, who was immensely rich and dedicated a large part of her fortune to the construction of this hospital, the largest in Europe, for which Pope Alexander VI granted her a papal construction bull on May 13, 1500.

After being housed provisionally in another place, the hospital was created on this site, designed according to the medical needs proper to a hospital by architect Francisco Rodríguez Cumplido after visiting the best hospitals of France and Portugal. The plans were drawn by the famous Martín Gainza, who found a way to combine medical needs with the demands of art, constructing this monumental building with capacity for three thousand patients. In addition, when floods or other public disasters occurred, it provided up to 400 refugees with bed and board.

Frequently, when the fleet from the Indies arrived, over two hundred men had to be hospitalized, as they had fallen ill during the long voyage from Mexico or Peru. In the course of time, from 1559 to 1960 when it was closed, the hospital has successively been called Hospital de la Sangre (Hospital of the Blood), Hospital de las Cinco Llagas (Hospital of the Five Wounds), and Central Hospital.

The main front of the building is 167 meters long (548 feet) and the sides are 153 meters (502 feet), so that it totals 25,500 m2 (274,488 ft2), the largest building in Spain until the Real Fábrica de Tabacos was built, also in Seville.

We will not describe its galleries, inner courts and rooms, for the interior of the building has been modified in order to adapt it as the seat of the Regional Parliament of Andalusia. We shall only say that the chapel has a Latin cross layout with a vault in stone, and a chancel with an altarpiece made by Diego López in 1601, with paintings by Alonso Vázquez. In the remaining chapels there are numerous paintings and statues, the most important by Roelas and Zurbarán.

Hospital de San Lázaro

We have two options, either to visit the Hospital de San Lázaro (Saint Lazarus Hospital) and the cementerio de San Fernando (Saint Ferdinand cemetery), or leave them out and remain at the Gate of La Macarena. If we decide to visit these two monuments, which are about ten minute walk away, we will go up the street in front of the Macarena Gate, called calle Don Fadrique,

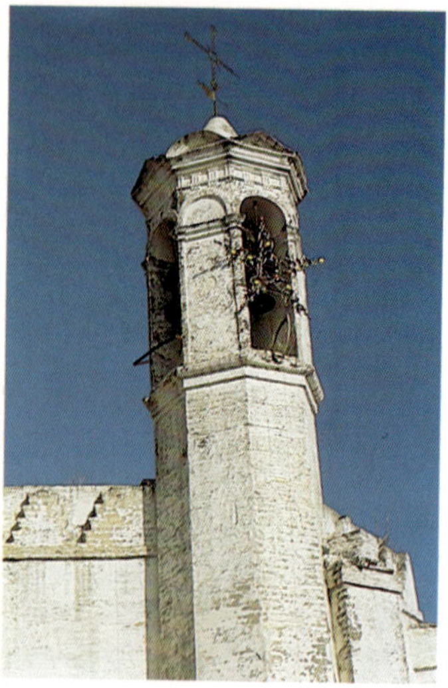

Hospital of Saint Lazarus.

reach the spot where it opens into avenida Doctor Pedriani. Crossing this, on the right hand side, we will find the Hospital de San Lázaro.

This building was the Wazir palace in Moslem times and there is still a small Arab-style turret on the outside, popularly known as «Gausín Tower».

In 1248 the palace was turned into a hospital for lepers by King Ferdinand the Saint, under the care of the Order of Saint Lazarus.

The façade was built during the reign of King Alfonso X the Wise and restored in the 16th century.

The façade has some curious little tiles dating from the 17th century. Inside, there is a medium-sized Renaissance court and a very attractive church, with a main altarpiece containing paintings *of Christ on the Road to Calvary, Christ with the Cyrenian, Raising of Lazarus, Mary Magdalene, The Apparition of Christ to Mary Magdalene, and The Martyrdom of Saint Lazarus,* by 16th century artist Villegas Marmolejo.

Cementerio de San Fernando

A few meters further on the same side of the street, is the cementerio de San Fernando (Saint Ferdinand cemetery), built in the middle of the 19th century. The façade and entrance courtyard is noble and severe, with wrought iron gates and pilasters topped by bronze statues and urns.

Inside the cemetery a beautiful garden covered in flowers makes for a pleasant surprise.

Near the entrance, on the main path, we come across the mausoleum of Joselito «el Gallo», his brother Rafael «el Gallo» and his brother-in-law Sánchez Mejías, all of them famous bullfighters. This large monument was made by the renowned sculptor Mariano Benlluire in the 1920's, representing the burial of Joselito «el Gallo». It is all in bronze, except for the head in white marble. The body is carried upon the shoulders of a group of bullfighters, cattlebreeders, flamenco singers and gypsies. Among them the figure of a distinguished elderly man with long sideburns: it is the portrait of a prestigious breeder, Eduardo Miura.

In front of the group carrying an image of the Virgin

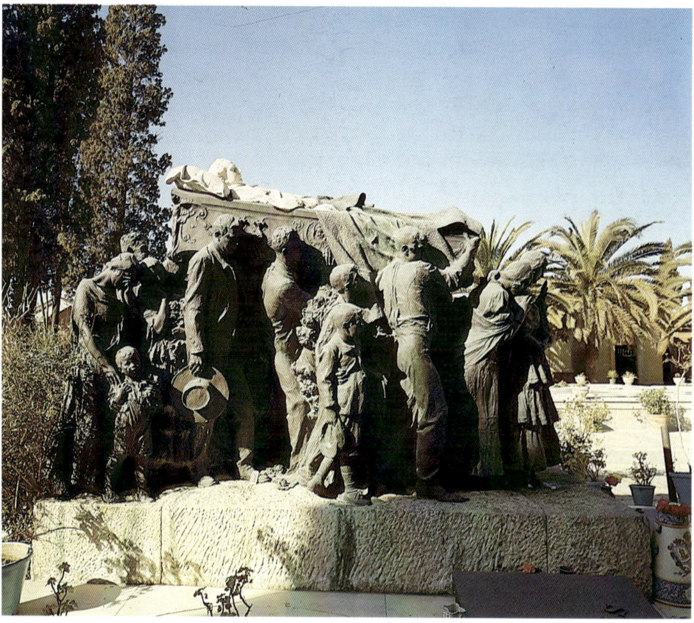

Tomb of Joselito el Gallo.

is María «the Gypsy», wife of the famous Flamenco singer Curro *el de la Jeroma*. This mausoleum is considered to be Benlluire's masterpiece.

Next to it, we see another tomb with a large statue of the bullfighter «Paquirri» cast in bronze, by the sculptor Victor Ochoa in 1989.

Tomb of Paquirri.

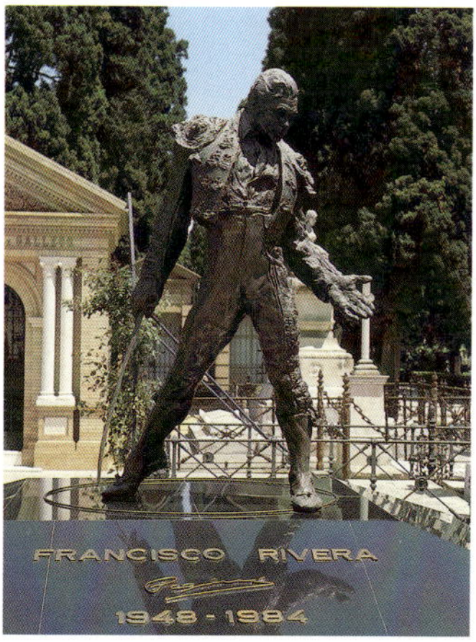

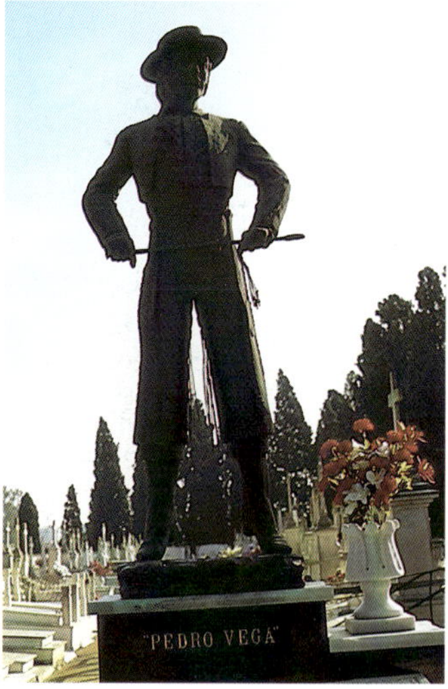

Tomb of the Flamenco dancer P. Vega.

About halfway along the same lane there is a mausoleum with two very simple tombs, which belong to the famous writer Gertrudis Gómez de Avellaneda and her husband.

On the opposite side is the tomb of the Flamenco dancer Pedro Vega with a statue in bronze, dressed in Andalusian costume.

At the entrance to the central square a beautiful reclining Christ in white marble, by Delgado Brackembury catches our eye, and in the center, the magnificent Cristo de las Mieles, by the sculptor Antonio Susillo, who committed suicide in 1896 and is buried at the feet of Christ.

On the path to the right of the square, in the second row on the left, several tombs with striking colored ceramic tiles from Triana can be seen.

If we walk slowly through the cemetery, which requires a whole morning, we will find mausoleums of other famous bullfighters (in the central square, to the right, Maera, and Gitanillos de Triana), and on the central path to the left, in the second row, guitar player Niño Ricardo, with an angel lifting up a guitar with broken strings.

The large number of beautiful tombs and sculptures by famous artists make this cemetery a true museum.

Back to La Macarena

We return to the Arch of La Macarena, and next to it we will find the Basilica de La Macarena where Our Lady of the Esperanza de la Macarena is venerated. The building dates from 1949, and was made by architect Gómez Millán in regional Andalusian style.

The high altar contains the image of Our Lady of La Macarena, a work attributed to Luisa Roldán de Mena «La Roldana», dating from the end of the 17th century.

Legend has it that this image was left by a navigator returning from the Indies who died in the neighboring hospital of las Cinco Llagas, and the hospital, to collect its fees, traded the image to the Brotherhood of La Macarena for a clock for the hospital tower.

The image is dressed in splendid velvet and silk robes, embroidered in Baroque style. She is set in a camarín or small chamber, almost as large as a medium-sized room, which can be reached by means of a staircase located to the left of the main altar. The walls of the camarín are covered with plates of engraved metal, the work of the contemporary goldsmith Fernando Marmolejo.

In the left hand aisle, near the entrance, is the tomb of General Gonzalo Queipo de Llano, one of those responsible for the uprising of General Franco in 1936, and who occupied Seville.

In this same aisle behind the chancel, a door on the left leads to the museum of the Brotherhood. It is a very fine museum, maybe one of the best in the world as regards embroideries and church plate. Near the entrance on the lower floor the «Paso», or float, of Jesús de la Sentencia is displayed which comes out in Holy Week with the Brotherhood of the Macarena. Life size figures represent the scene in which Pontius Pilate sentences Jesus Christ to death. It contains a figure of Jesus, by Felipe Morales, dating from the 17th century, and others of Pilate, Jews, Romans, and a black slave offering a washbasin and water jug for Pilate to symbolically wash his hands. All the figures are by Antonio Castillo Lastrucci, made this century.

On the top floor we find horns, command staffs, long poles canopy censers, navilula and other liturgical objects in engraved silver, splendid cloaks for Our Lady in velvet embroidered in gold and a small chamber with the gold crowns of the Virgin. Only seeing these cloaks embroidered in the Renaissance and Baroque style, can we understand the sublime artistic height of religious embroidery.

Calle de San Luis

The street leading to the Arch of La Macarena is calle de San Luis. It was also called the Land Gateway because Seville is a city embraced by two rivers, the Guadalquivir and in old times, the Tagarete, and the other gates opened onto the rivers, this being the only one through which one could reach land directly.

For this reason King Ferdinand and Queen Isabel passed through here on their visits to the city, also Isabel of Portugal when she arrived to marry the Emperor Charles V, and going further back in history, under Arab rule, the magnificent cortege with the venerable body of Saint Isidore to be deposited in the church of Saint Isidore in León.

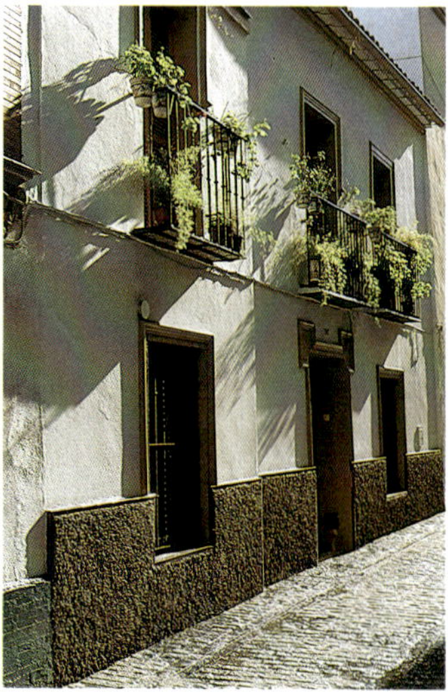

Saint Louis street.

At the beginning of this calle de San Luis, which was formerly called calle Real, we come past the church of San Gil, today of scant touristic interest, since its altarpieces disappeared when it was burned by the Republicans in 1936. The building is Mudejar in style dating from the 14th century.

A bit further on, there is another church on the opposite side. It is Santa Marina's, with an interesting Mudejar tower and the remains of a former mosque. This one was also burned in 1936, losing all of its

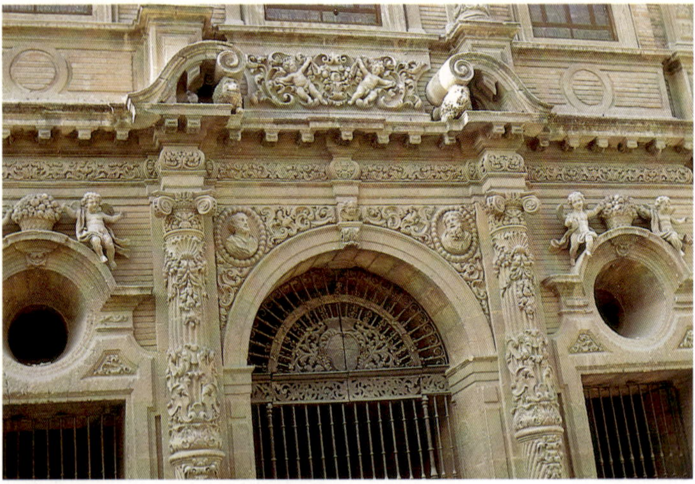

Façade and tower of the Church of Saint Louis.

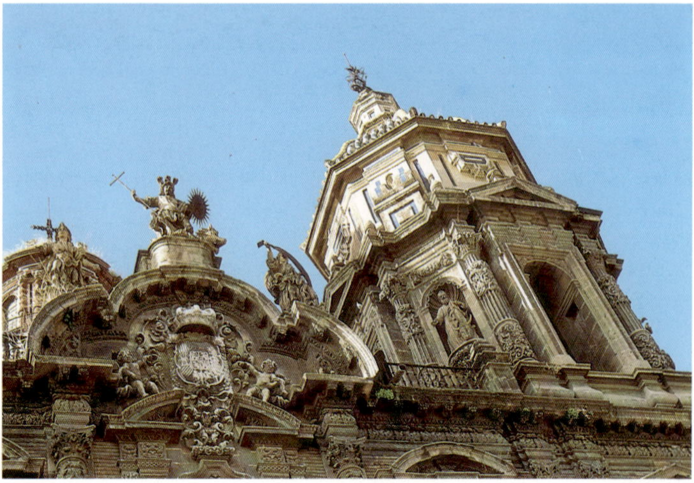

paintings, sculptures and altarpieces.

The Church of San Luis

On the right we find next the Church of San Luis, one of the marvels of late Baroque style. This church, with the adjoining building, belongs to the jesuit seminary of Saint Louis of the French. The façade is impressive, with an explosion of decorations which Gestoso called «insolent pomposity». Although the building was built according to some by architect Romero and according to others by Figueroa, in reality, the Jesuits wanted the building to be in line with the architectural trends of the times and ordered the builders to follow the style of José Churriguera, at the time the most prestigious Spanish architect.

The inside of the church is very rich and over the main altar there is a large painting of Saint Louis by Zurbarán. The sculptures are almost all by Pedro Duque Cornejo, one of the best Sevillian artist of the early 18th century, and the paintings depicting scenes from the lives of Jesuit saints: Ignatius of Loyola, Francis Xavier, Stanislaw of Kostka and others, are by Domingo Martínez, as well as the paintings in the vault. It is an authentic Baroque marvel, which although at the time could be called «excessively ornate», today can rank as one of the best examples of Spanish religious art.

The Church of San Marcos

We will not go into this church either, as it was burnt in 1936 and its images are not the original ones, whereas the church itself has been considerably altered by renovation work.

But we should stop to look at its magnificent tower from all angles. It is believed that the church was formerly a mosque in Arab times and that it was reconstructed in the 14th century in Mudejar style. The tower copies successfully the Almohad style, with the addition of a technical novelty in the mullioned windows which consists of increasing the size as they go higher, so that they look harmonious from below.

The tower is shaped like a Moslem minaret, topped with

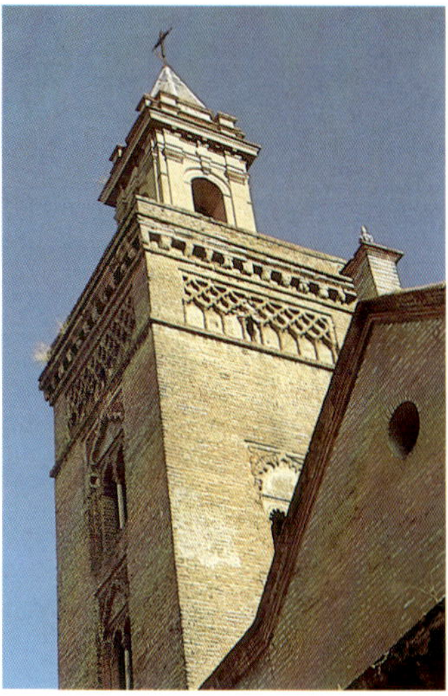

Tower of the Church of Saint Mark.

a Christian belfry, and finishing up in a pointed roof covered with tiles. However, the tower as a whole is Christian, dating from the 14th century.

Calle Castellar

From plaza de San Marcos we turn to the right into calle Castellar, named after the Count of Castellar who had his palace here.

The house which today bears number 40 is where the palace of the Guzmans stood, where Doña Leonor de Guzmán, the mistress of King Alfonso XI, lived and where the children of this love, Enrique II and Fadrique de Trastamara, were born. Doña Leonor has inspired numerous novels, dramas and operas, among them the opera with lyrics by Roger y Baez and music by Cayetano Donizetti: *La Favorita*.

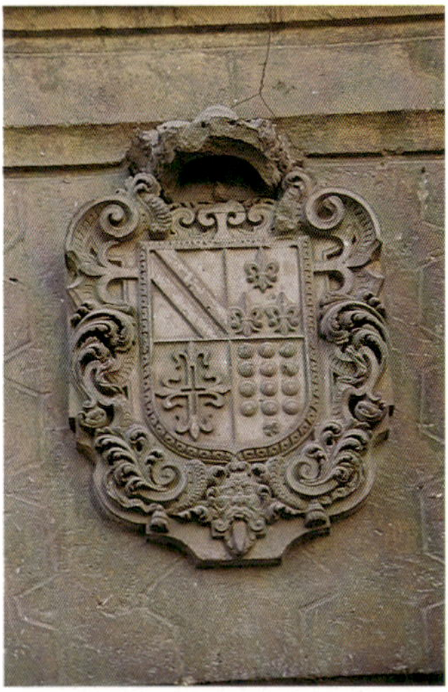

Coat of Arms on the House of Artists.

Casa de los Artistas

At the end of calle Castellar, on calle Feria and taking a left turn, we reach the church of San Juan de la Palma. Opposite it we see a great palace with a coat of arms over the stone portal. The palace belonged to the knights of Levantos and to the Marquis of Torrenueva, whose surname was Díaz-Lavandero, and his is the coat of arms. It is also known as the Casa de los Artistas (House of the Artists) because at the end of the 19th century and beginning of the present century, several studios and workshops were set up here for artists, sculptors, painters and the dance academy of the famous master Pericet.

The Church of San Juan de la Palma

The church of San Juan Bautista, popularly known as de la Palma, was rected over the remains of a mosque built by King Almotamid's mother in Moslem times.

It was reconstructed in the 17th century, and its interesting façade dates from that ti-

Palace of Las Dueñas. Coats of Arms.

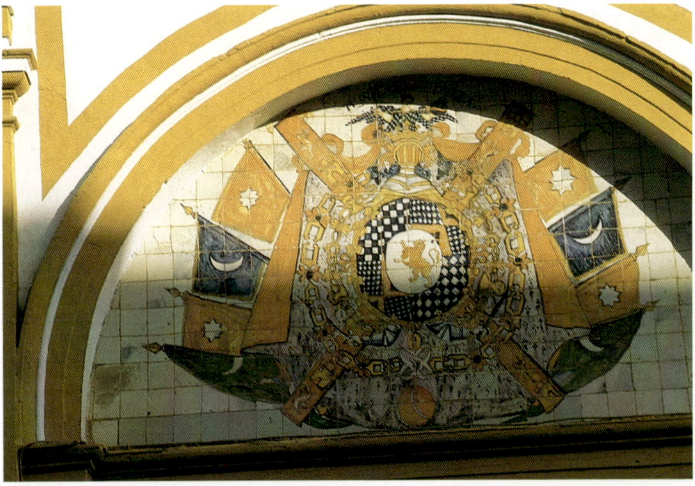

me. The illustrious Maldonado family were the patrons of the chancel and their coats of arms are carved in the pendentives there. As to works of art, there is a notable *Saint George* painted in the 16th century on the right hand wall, as well as figures belonging to the Brotherhood of La Amargura which are the *Virgen de la Amargura*, by the famous Luisa Roldán de Mena «La Roldana», Saint John, by Benito Hita del Castillo, and *Jesus en el Desprecio de Herodes*, by an unknown 17th-century artist.

Leaving the church we turn left and follow calle San Juan de la Palma.

The Palace of Las Dueñas

At the end of the street and to the left, is calle Las Dueñas, and on the left hand side is the Palace of Las Dueñas, the residence of the Dukes of Alba in Seville. Although not open to the public, as it is a private home, we can mention that the palace was built by the Pineda family in the 15th century, and later sold to the Riberas in order to pay the ransom demanded by the Moorish King of Granada for their eldest son, whom he held prisoner. The building, in Mudejar style, was embellished with Triana tiles in the Baroque style of the 17th century. Today the palace is much smaller in size, maintaining its great Mudejar courtyard with a handsome arcade.

The most interesting part of Palace of Las Dueñas is not its artistic value but its historic significance, including the fact that the famous poet Antonio Machado was born in this building as his father was the administrator. The poet's childhood was spent within these walls, which he mentioned in his poems:

Mi infancia son recuerdos
de un patio de Sevilla
(My childhood has memories of a
patio in Seville)

One last look at the noble coat of arms of the House of Alba, surrounded by banners won in battles against the Moors, as well as in Flanders and Italy; it is painted on Triana ceramic tiles dating from the end of the 17th century.

We will return by calle Dueñas and then fork off into calle Gerona, and then turn right into calle Doña María Coronel.

The Convent of Santa Inés

At the end of the street on the right is the convent of Santa Inés. Apparently, Doña María Coronel was married, in the 1360s, to don Juan de la Cerda, a knight who participated in the uprising against King Pedro I. The monarch had him killed, but smitten by the beauty of the young widow, pursued her in such a manner that she disfigured her face with boiling oil so as to destroy her beauty and force the king to leave her alone with her grief.

Later, Doña María obtained permission from the Archbishop of Seville, Fernando de Albornoz, to build a convent in her grand house, and this is the convent of Santa Inés, run

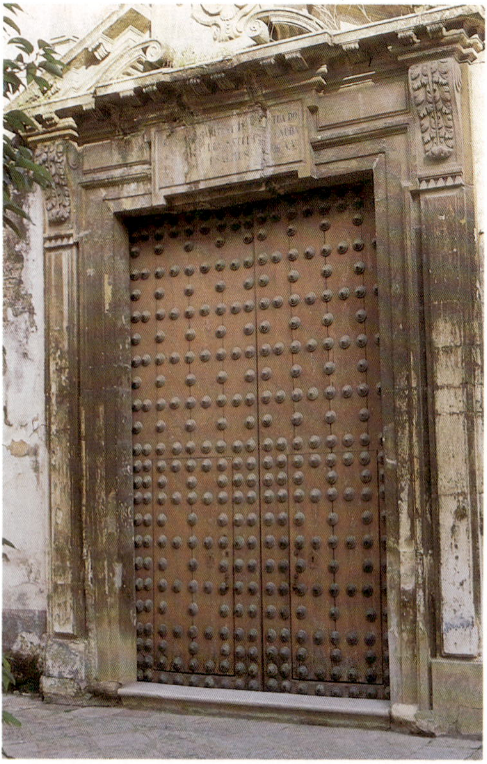

Convent of Santa Inés.

by nuns of the order of St. Clare.

The church is small but charming, as it combines Medieval and Baroque styles. The main altar dates from the beginning of the 18th century, made by the wood carvers José and Francisco de Medinilla, but the sculptures belong to a previous altarpiece dating from the 17th century. In the right hand aisle, at the top, there is an altar with beautiful paintings, which Gestoso attributes to the German school, but which Montoto believes are by the painter Andrés de Segura in the year 1505.

In the lower choir is the tomb of the founder, Doña María Coronel. Once a year, the urn containing her remains is opened so that the faithful may see the scars on her face, proof of her dramatic determination.

It was said that the organ in this church could only be heard on Christmas Eve, when it was played by the soul of the organist Maese Pérez, who died before being able to play for the first time the Christmas Eve Midnight Mass he had composed. Gustavo Adolfo Bécquer used the story to write one of his best legends.

With the visit to the convent, we conclude this route.

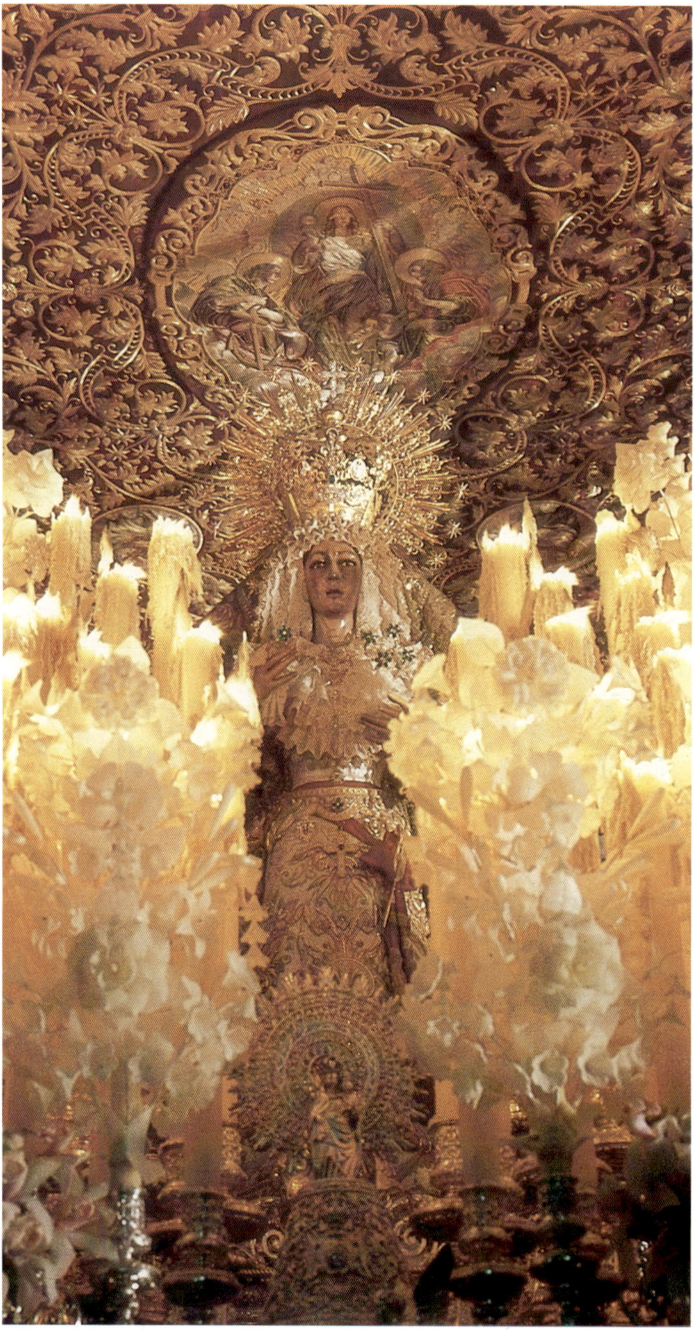

La Macarena on her covered float.

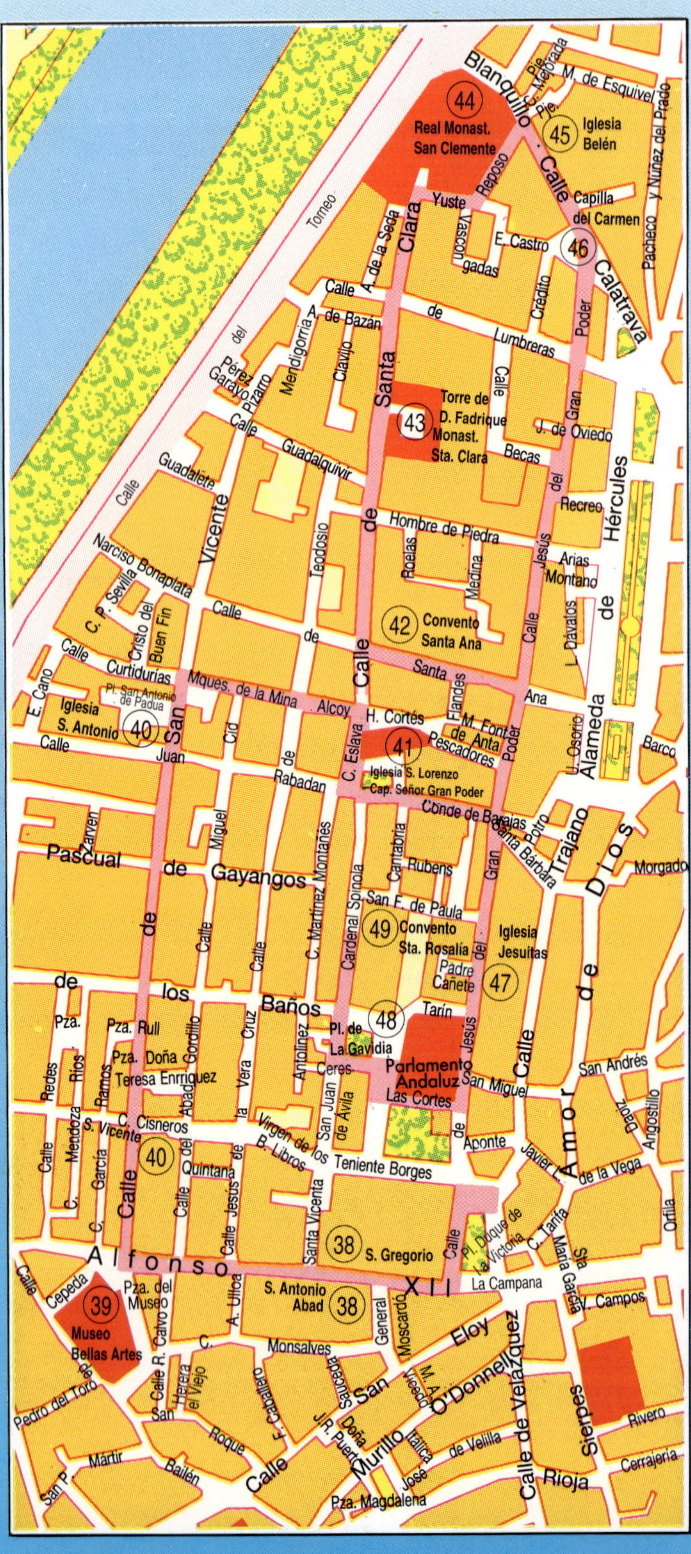

Real Monast. San Clemente
Iglesia Belén
Capilla del Carmen
Torre de D. Fadrique Monast. Sta. Clara
Convento Santa Ana
Iglesia S. Antonio
Iglesia S. Lorenzo Cap. Señor Gran Poder
Convento Sta. Rosalía
Iglesia Jesuitas
Pl. de La Gavidia
Parlamento Andaluz
Las Cortes
S. Gregorio
S. Antonio Abad
Museo Bellas Artes
Calle Santa Clara
Calle de San Vicente
Alameda de Hércules
Calle del Torneo
Calle Jesús del Gran Poder
Calle Alfonso XII
Trajano
Amor de Dios
Pascual de Gayangos
Calle de los Baños
Calle Calatrava
Calle Guadalquivir
Lumbreras
Calle de Santa Ana
Hombre de Piedra
Sierpes
Rioja
Calle de Velázquez
O'Donnell
Calle San Eloy
La Campana
Pza. del Museo

ROUTE 5: FROM THE MUSEO MURILLO TO THE MYTH OF DON JUAN TENORIO

PLACES OF INTEREST

(38) **Church of San Antonio Abad and San Gregorio**

(39) **Museum of Fine Arts**
Second art museum in importance in Spain. Contains paintings by, Murillo, Pacheco, Velázquez, El Greco and many other great masters. Plaza del museo, 9. Tel 422 07 90.
Opening hours: from 10 to 14 and 16 to 19 in winter; from 9 to 14.30 in summer.

(40) **Churches of San Vicente and San Antonio**

(41) **Church of San Lorenzo and Chapel of Señor del Gran Poder**
Contains a 13th century painting of the Virgen the Rocamador and an image of the Señor del Gran Poder.

(42) **Convent of Santa Ana and Monastery of Santa Clara**
Interesting altarpieces and tombs. They are only opened on Sunday mornings from 7.30 to 8.30.

(43) **Tower of Don Fadrique**
Unique sample of transitional style from Romanesque to Gothic.

(44) **Royal Monastery of San Clemente**
Contains the tomb of Queen Doña María and valuable paintings. It is now Sevilla Pavilion at Expo'92.

(45) **Church of Belén**
Former convent of the order of Calatrava.

(46) **Chapel of el Carmen**

(47) **Church of Los Jesuitas**

(48) **La Gavidia square**
Monument to Luis Daoiz.

(49) **Convent of Santa Rosalía**

STARTING POINT	Plaza del Duque
EXIT TO NEXT ROUTE	Along Avenida de la Constitución to Puerta de Jerez, starting point for Route 6.

USEFUL ADDRESSES NEARBY

Police Station:	Plaza de la Gavidia
Chemists:	Alfonso XII, 53 Jesús del Gran Poder 14 and 89
Photo service:	Trajano, 14 Amor de Dios, 44
El Corte Inglés (Department Store):	Plaza del Duque
Restaurante Camborio:	Baños, 3. Tourist menu.
Restaurante El Cantábrico:	Jesús del Gran Poder, 2
Restaurante América:	Jesús del Gran Poder.
Restaurante Bailén:	Bailén, 34
Restaurante A Babor:	Teodosio, 51
Restaurante Alvaro de Bazán:	Alvaro de Bazán, 2
Tapas Bars:	
Casa Ovidio:	Hernán Cortés. Typical bar. Fish and meat tapas. Music and videos about Holy Week.
Bar Doñana:	Plaza de la Gavidia. Decorated with pictures of famous bullfighters. Manzanilla wine and typical tapas.
Bar Los Cuarenta y ocho:	Cardenal Spinola, 31. Especiality: «pescaíto» (fried little fish)

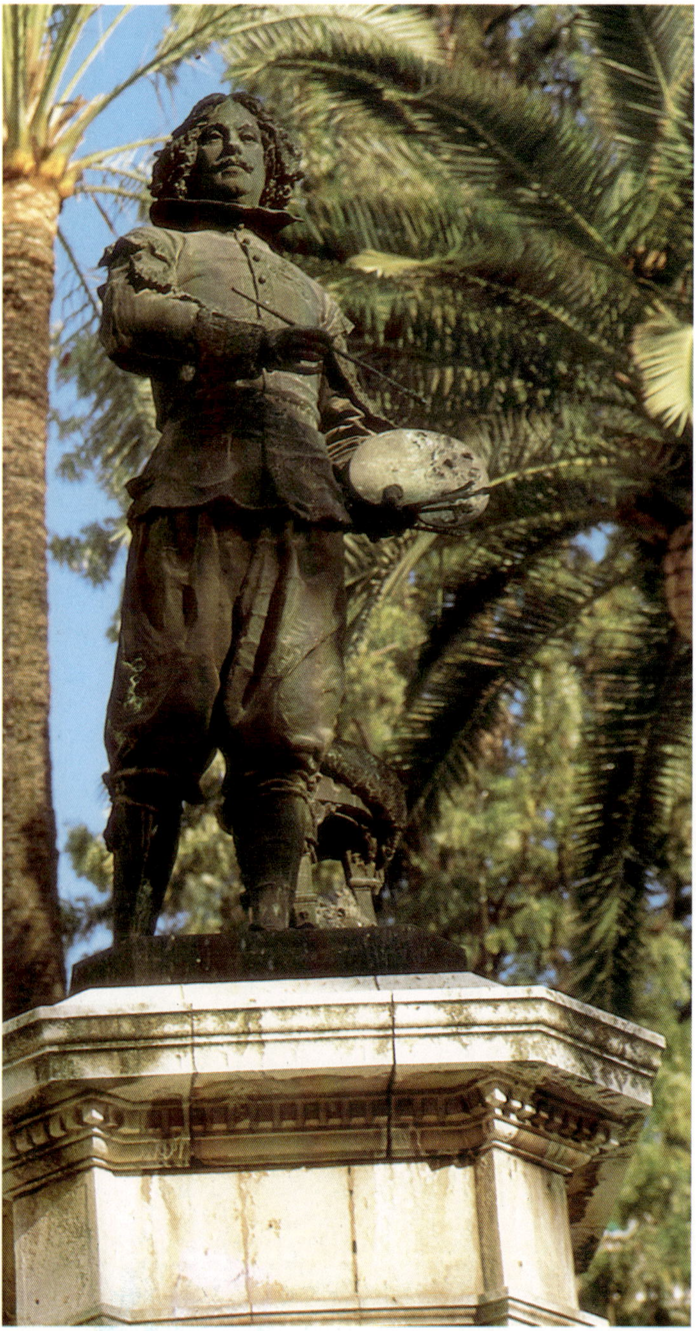

Monument to Velázquez.

ROUTE 5: FROM THE MUSEO MURILLO TO THE MYTH OF DON JUAN.

We will start off on our tour of this sector from the plaza del Duque, the main commercial center of Seville, where a bronze statue of the world famous Sevillian painter Diego Velázquez looks down from his pedestal over a small garden.

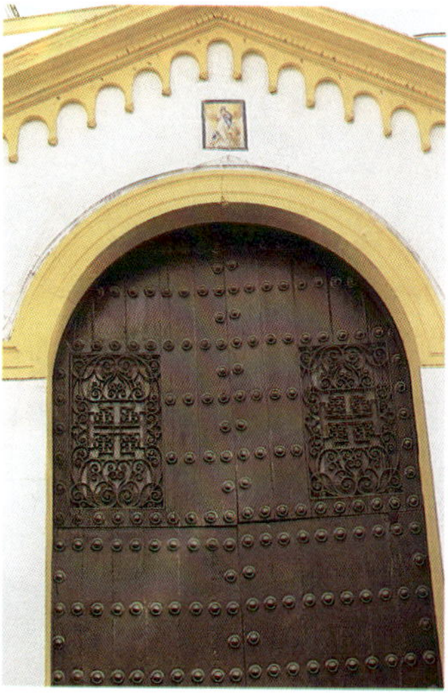

Church of Saint Anthony.

The Church of San Antonio Abad and the Hermandad del Silencio.

Walking up calle Alfonso XII on our left we come across the atrium of a church. This is the old hospital of San Antonio Abad and the Chapel of the Brotherhood of Jesus Nazarene, also known as the Hermandad del Silencio (Brotherhood of Silence).

In reality, this is not one church but two adjoined, which makes them look like a church with two aisles, as they intercommunicate. The first one is the chapel of this old hospital, founded in the 13th century for those suffering from scrofula or king's evil, also known as Saint Anthony's fire; while the second one dates from the 16th century and was built for the Brotherhood of Silence. Both churches were reformed later.

In the first one we find a Baroque main altar with an image of Jesus the Nazarene bearing the cross on His shoulders, known as Jesus of Silence, the work of Francisco de Ocampo in 1609. In this aisle there is also an image of Saint Anthony, by Francisco Ruiz Gijón, as well as a Virgin and a Saint Joseph by Martínez

A Penitent.

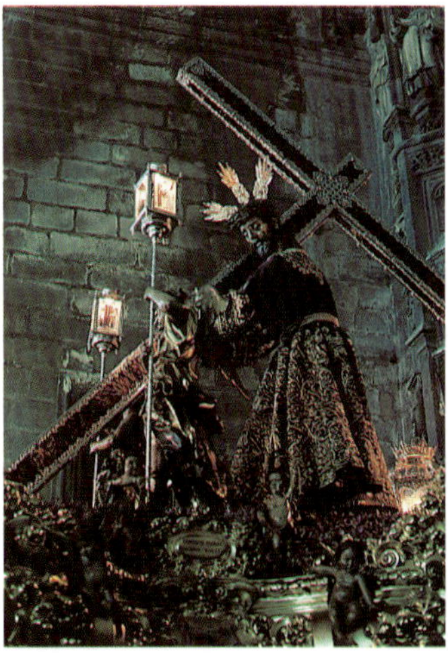

Montañés. The cross carried by Jesus is made of tortoise shell edged in silver, made in America and brought over by a pious worshiper.

In the second aisle, the main altar has an image of the Virgin, made by Sebastián Santos in this century, and an 18th century Saint John the Evangelist by Cristóbal Ramos.

We will now cross the street to enter another church opposite, the former chapel of the English Jesuit school.

Chapel of San Gregorio

This is the chapel of San Gregorio y del Santo Sepulcro (Saint Gregory and of the Holy Sepulchre), and is kept by the Mercedarian friars, who live in the adjoining residence.

Although not noteworthy for its architecture nor for its altarpiece, this chapel is important in relation to the Hermandad del Santo Entierro (Brotherhood of the Holy Burial), founded in the 13th century in the Humeros area, and that of Our Lady of Villaviciosa, founded in calle Colcheros in the 16th century, which merged and were raised to the status of Sacramental Brotherhood in 1759.

The images of this Brotherhood venerated here are the Reclining Christ, in a rich urn, sculpted by the famous Juan de Mesa about 1620. The figure of Our Lady of Villaviciosa is by Antonio Quirós, of about the same time, although restored by Astorga in the 19th century. Although not a religious

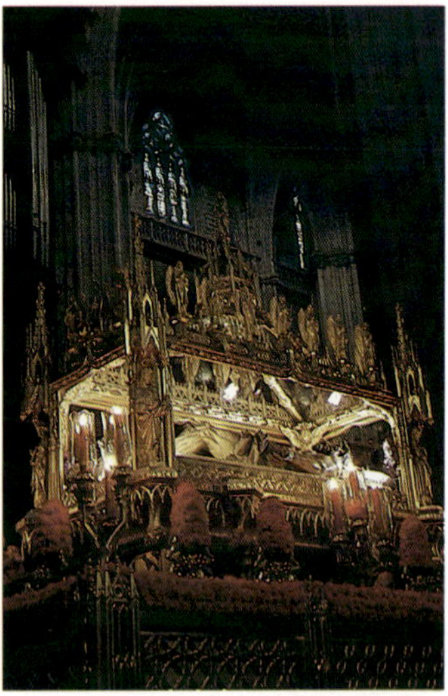

Reclining Christ.

image but rather a funeral sculpture, which is taken out in the procession of the Holy Burial during Holy Week, is the figure of Death, popularly known as »la Canina». It represents a human skeleton seated on the Globe, with its head

Triumph of the Cross over Death.

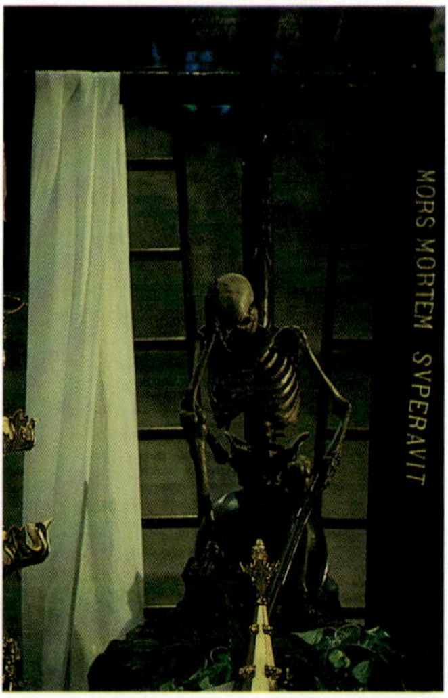

resting on its right hand in meditation, and the scythe in its left hand. In the procession, it is carried at the foot of a cross hung with a white shroud and a black cloth with a Latin inscription in gold lettering: *Mors mortem supera*.

The School of Spanish-American Studies.

Leaving the church and turning right, the following building with a splendid façade, is the headquarters of the Escuela de Estudios Hispanoamericanos (School of Spanish-American studies). It has been restored several times and was formerly the famous Anglo School of the Company of Jesus, where young Englishmen were educated when they could not study in their own country due to religious persecution. After the Jesuits were expelled in the 17th century, it was put to different uses, among them, headquarters of the Academy of Medicine, and now, as we have pointed out, the School of Spanish-American Studies. It has one of the best libraries in the world on American subjects, being frequently used by scholars from all the Latin American countries.

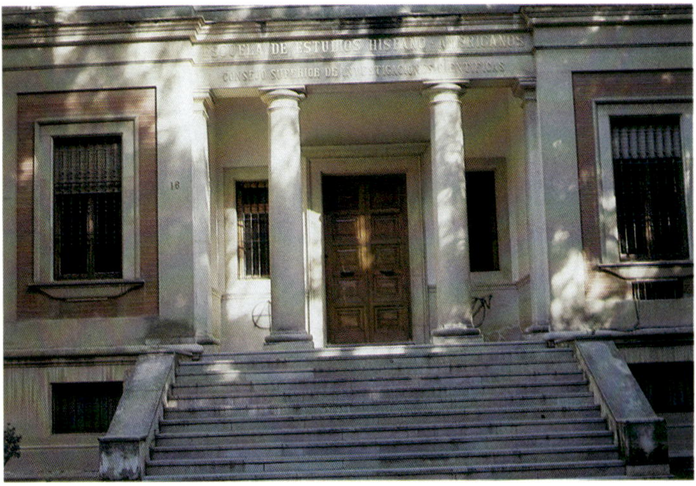

School of Spanish-American Studies.

The Museo de Bellas Artes

We continue on calle Alfonso XII and reach plaza del Museo so called for here is located the Museo Provincial de Bellas Artes (Provincial Museum of Fine Arts), considered the second most important picture gallery in Spain, after the Prado in Madrid.

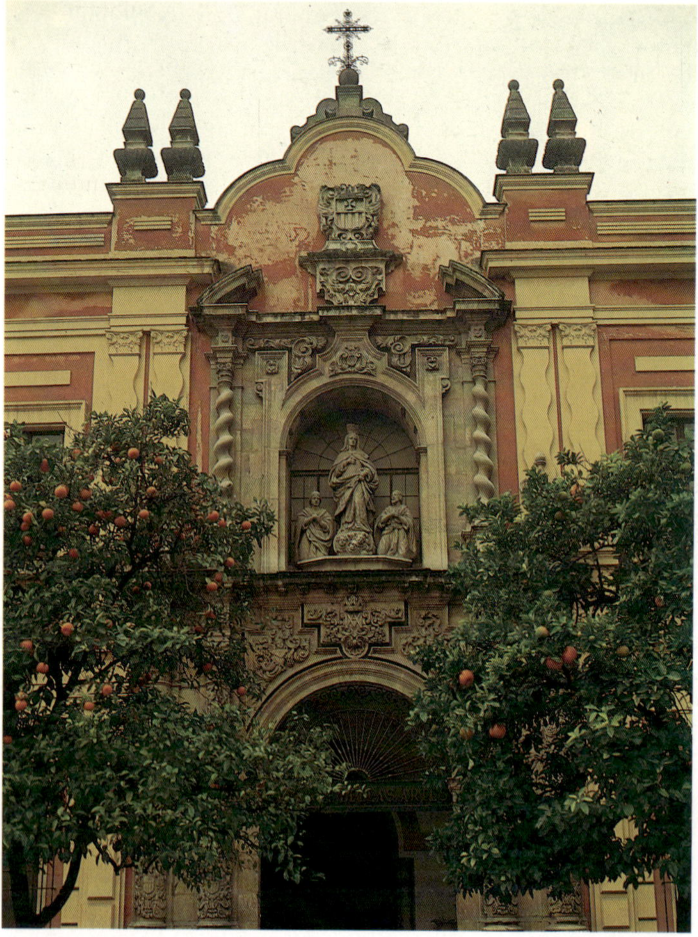

Museum of Fine Arts. Façade.

The building has a beautiful portal with two Solomonic pillars flanking an image of Our Lady of Mercy. It was in past centuries a monastery of the Mercedary Order, dedicated to saving Christian prisoners held captive by the Moors and Turks.

Their grateful families were generous in their donations to the Order for centuries, so that monasteries as grand as this one were built, with beautiful cloistered courts, marble staircases, great galleries and estately reception rooms.

After the secularization in the 19th century, it became a museum and houses an authentic treasure in paintings. We shall mention, among others, twenty two pictures signed by Zurbarán, some as colossal as *The Apotheosis of Saint Thomas*, or as delicate as *The Child Jesus Weaving a Crown of Thorns*. *The Miracle of the Holy Vow*, also known as *The Friar's Meal*, is impressive in its beauty and realism. Our *Lady of the Caves*, from the high altar of the Cartuja de las Cuevas, is a severe yet simple composition. The Virgin protects under her cloak, held up by two angels, the community of Carthusian monks.

There are twenty five Murillos here, among them three versions of the Immaculate Conception known as *La Grande (The Large One)*, *La del Padre Eterno (Of the Eternal Father)*, *and La Niña (The Child)*. Others include *Saint Thomas of Villanueva Distributing Alms to the Poor*, *Christ Embracing Saint Francis of Assisi Removing the Nail from the Cross*, etc.

Twenty three paintings by Valdés Leal include *The Betrothal of Saint Catherine*, *Saint Jerome Praying in the Desert*, *Saint Ignatius of Loyola Praying in the Manresa Cave*, and *The Assumption of the Virgin*.

By Francisco de Herrera the Elder there are twelve paintings, among them the splendid and detailed *Apotheosis of Saint Hermenegild*.

There are nineteen pictures by Francisco Pacheco, including two important ones of *Saint Peter Nolasco*. In one of them, the saint is accompanied by two servants loaded with bundles of gold coins, boarding a vessel sailing to Algiers to ransom captives, and in the other one, he is discussing with the Moorish Sultan in Algiers the ransom price while a friar counts the coins and through a barred window the captives can be seen in prison.

There is an interesting collection of Romantic paintings, by Joaquín Domínguez Bécquer, Antonio María Esquivel and other artists.

There is a collection of early 20th century works by the painter Andrés Parladé, Count of Aguiar, on bullfighting subjects, beautiful dogs and Andalusian scenes; there are also large size paintings by Virgilio Mattoni on historical themes, such as *The Last Communion of King Saint Ferdinand*, in splendid surroundings and with a complicated play of light and shade.

From the later 20th century there are works by Alfonso Grosso, Santiago Martínez and the late Romero Ressendi.

Among the visitors' favorite paintings are the *Portrait of Jorge Manuel Theotocopuli* painted by his father El Greco, *The Imposition of the Chasuble on Saint Ildephonse*, by Velázquez, and *The Calvary* painted by Lucas Cranach.

The museum also has a fine collection of sculptures, among which we should mention Saint Jerome by Torrigiano; Saint Dominic de Guzmán in Penitence by Martínez Montañés, an exquisitely delicate group slightly larger than life-size called The First Quarrel, where twins fight to be nursed by their mother, a work by Antonio Susillo, and Saint John the Baptist as a Child, by Pedro de Mena.

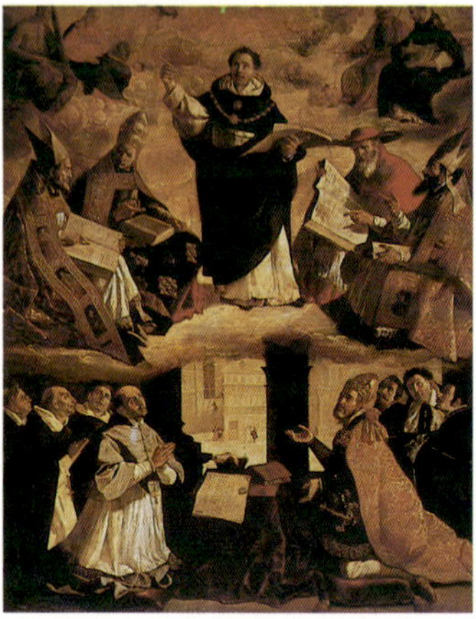

Apotheosis of Saint Thomas. Zurbarán 17h century.

The Child Jesus weaving a Crown of Thorns. ▷ Zurbarán, 17th century.

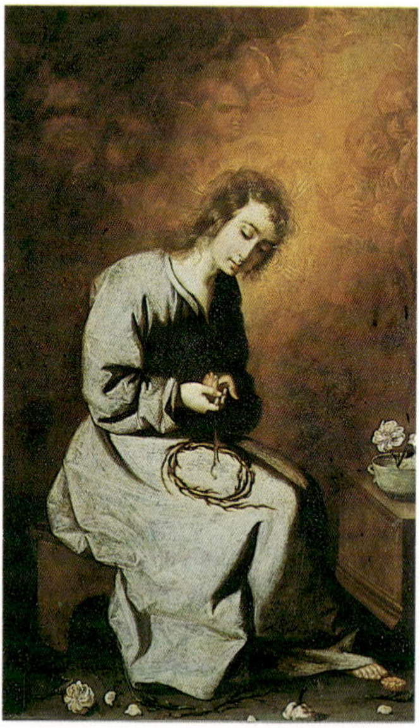

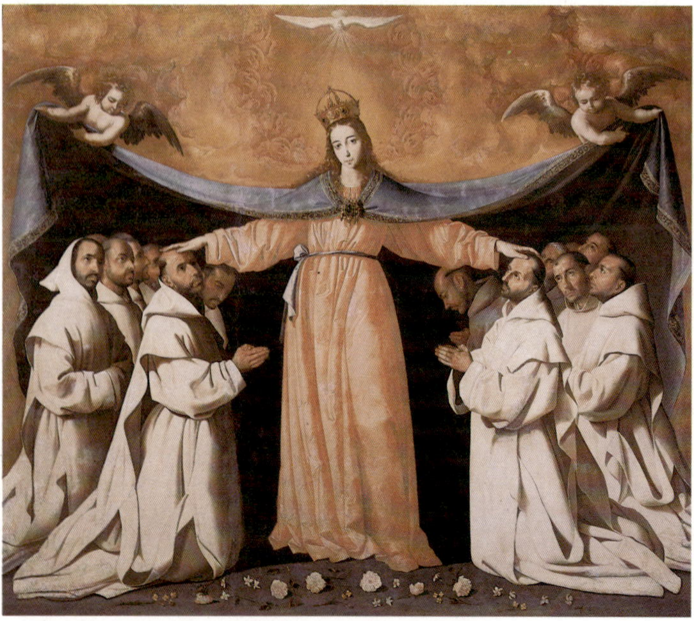

Our Lady of the Caves Zurbarán, 17th century.

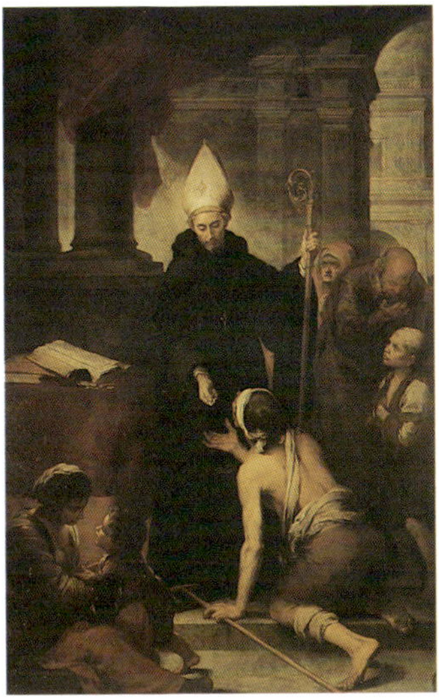

Saint Thomas distributing alms.
Murillo, 17th century.

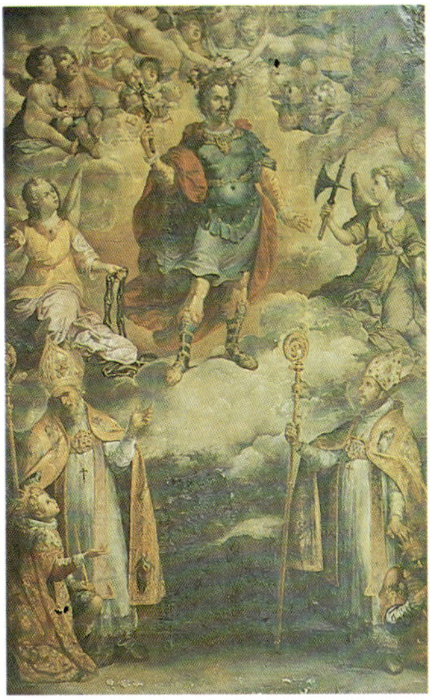

Apotheosis of Saint Hermenegild.
Francisco de Herrera, 17th century.

Saint Jerome praying in the desert. Valdés Leal, 17th century.

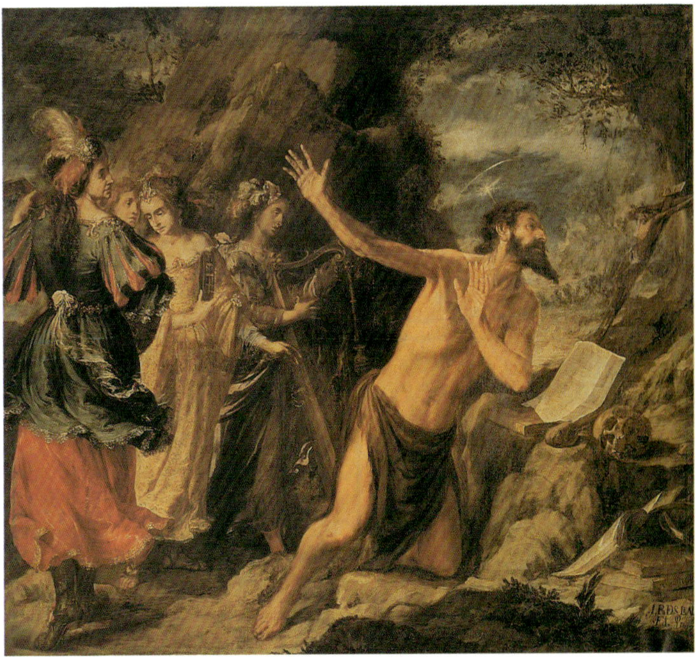

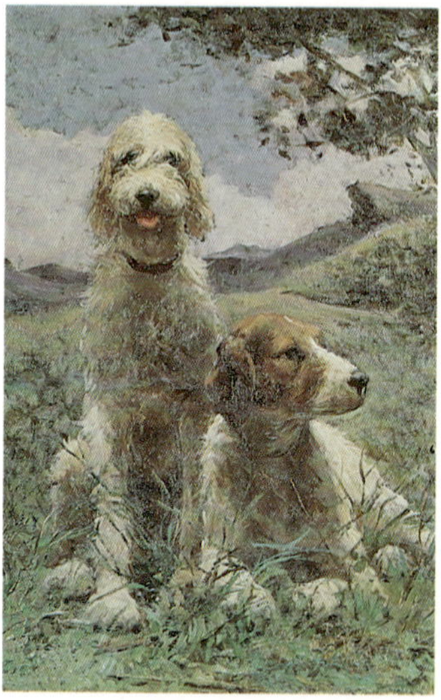

Dogs. Andrés Parladé. 19th century.

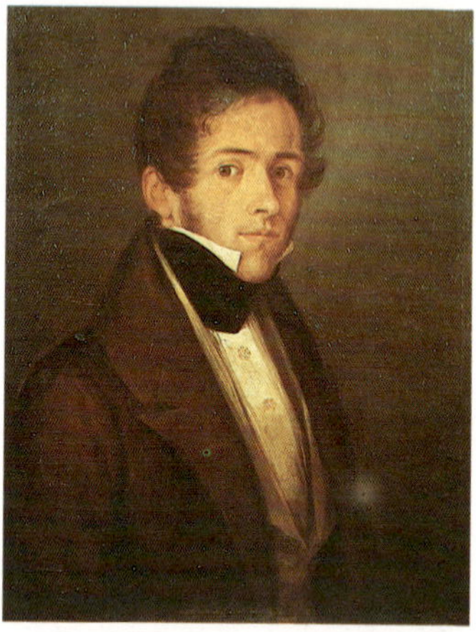

Portrait of José D. Bécquer 19th century.

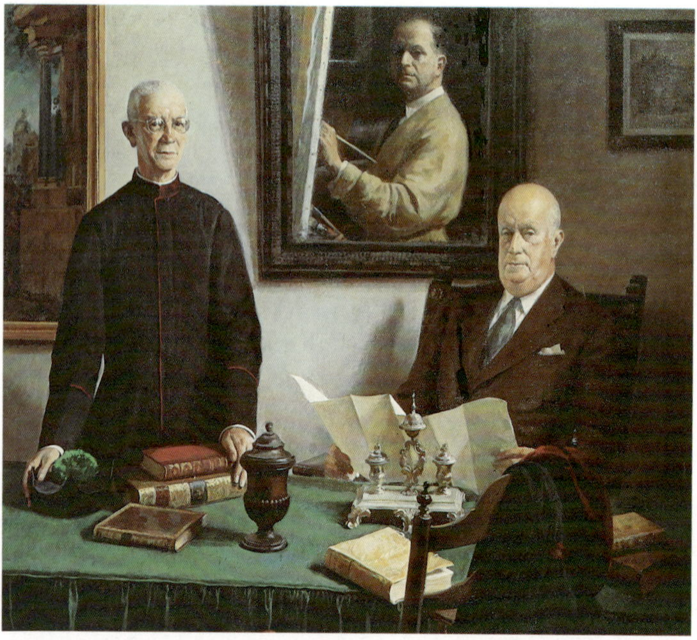

Patrons of the Museum Alonso Grosso. 20th century.

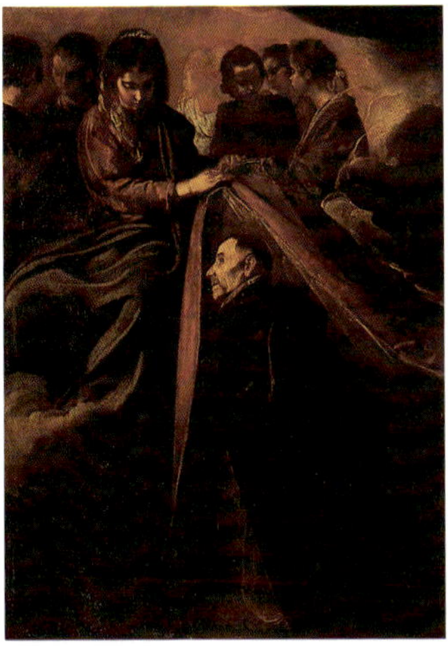

The Imposition of the Chasuble on Saint Ildephonse. Velázquez, 17th century.

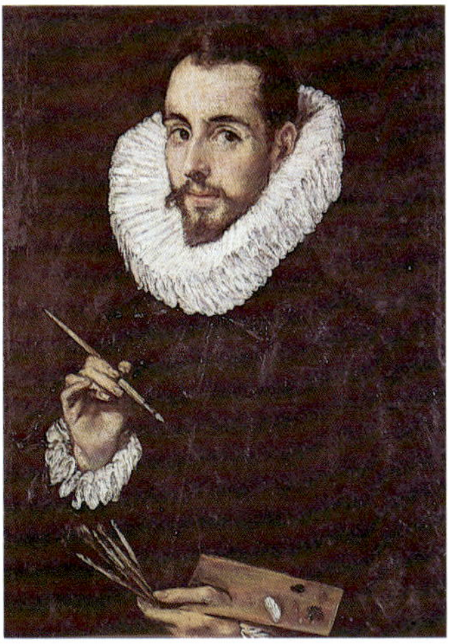

Portrait of El Greco's Son. El Greco, 17th century.

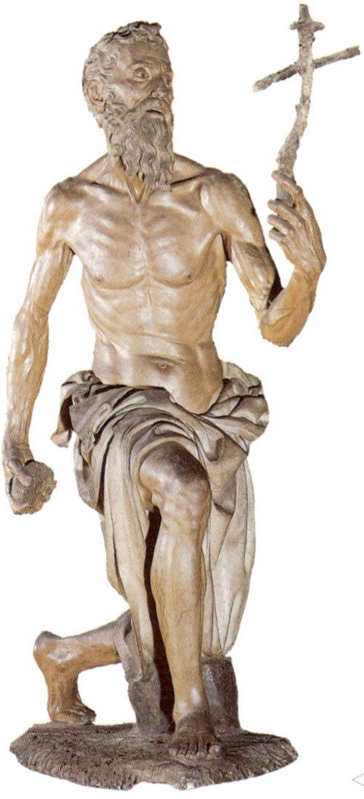

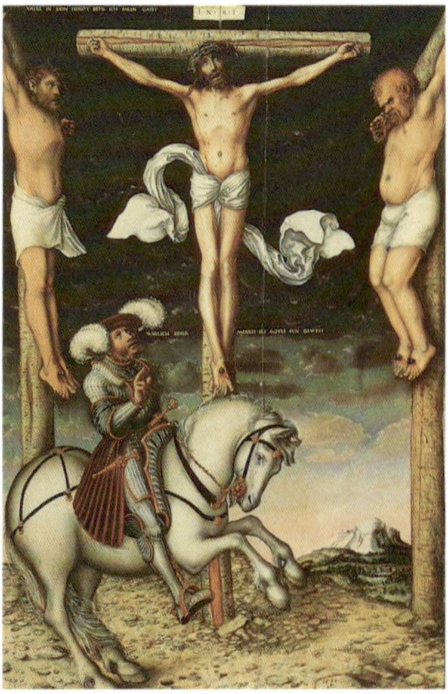

The Calvary. Lucas Cranach, 16th century.

◁ *Saint Jerome. Torrigiano, 16th century.*

Monument to Murillo in Plaza del Museo

Upon leaving the Museum, we will see in the center of the square a large monument with a statue in bronze of the painter Bartolomé Esteban Murillo, as a tribute that Seville pays to its most distinguished artist. The monument has three parts. The first is the base, the second one is decorative, with moldings and arches on Renaissance-style ledges and pearl-string ornamentation, all in marble. Over this, symbols of the principal Fine Arts are sculpted in bronze: Poetry, Painting, Sculpture, Architecture and Music. The third section bears the name of Murillo in bronze letters, decorated with acanthus leaves and a laurel crown with olive leaves and roses.

Finally comes the statue of Murillo with a brush in his hand, standing next to a pilaster with the palette and a sketch of his painting *The Large Immaculate Conception*.

The pedestal was designed by Demetrio de los Ríos and made in Italy by the best marble workers in the Carrara quarries, Guiseppe Vanelli, Antonio Caniparoli and Federico Giemignani. The whole of the pedestal comprises 86 pieces.

The statue of Murillo was modeled by the sculptor Sabino Medina and cast in bronze in Paris by Eck and Durand.

The monument was inaugurated on January 1, 1864.

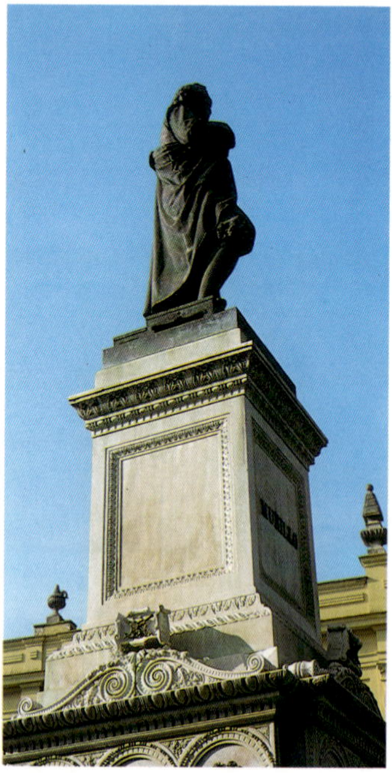

Monument to Murillo.

The Church of San Vicente

The statue looks towards calle San Vicente, which is the direction we are going to take. On our right we find the church of San Vicente. It contains a mixture of styles, since on the site of the former mosque of the Moslem era, a parish church was built, which was in turn reconstructed in the 14th century with a Gothic portal, now sealed, but of which we can still see a pointed arch on San Vicente street. Later, Baroque and Neoclassical style decorations were added, with still more additions in the 19th century.

The history of this church, according to Medieval tradition, dates back to the Visigoth era, when Bishop Saint Isidore established a school for training priests here, where he died. On the southern wall on Cardinal

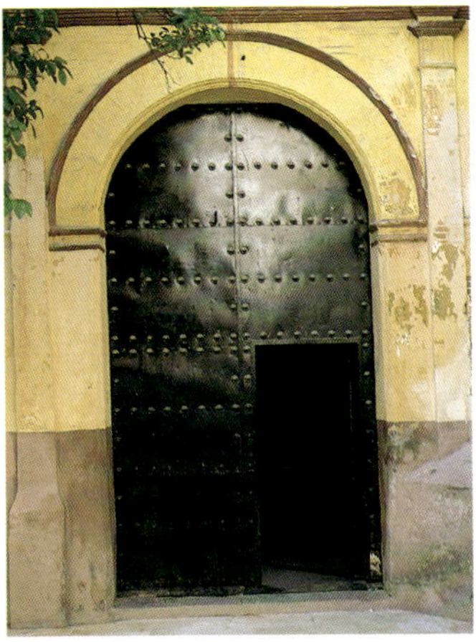

The Church of San Vicente.

Cisneros street, there is a plaque explaining in ancient script that the King of the Goths, Genseric, tried to desecrate and plunder this church but was killed by lightning when he passed the portico on horseback. Legends, maybe myths, but which may nevertheless hold a bit of truth in them.

The high altar dates from 1705, and has a noteworthy sculpture attributed to Martínez Montañés. The altar of the Descent has a handsome group in polychromed high-relief, considered by critics as the best of its kind in Spain. It is the work of Andrés de Ocampo.

Equally good are the images of Jesús de las Penas, by followers of Roldán in the 17th century, and the Virgen de los Dolores, by Blas Molner, from the same century.

In this church, the historical prevails over the artistic: the painter Antonio María Esquivel was baptized here, Juan Martínez Montañés was married here, as well as Luisa Roldán de Mena,«La Roldana».

But above all, this church was where the Sevillian Eucharistic devotion was established, mainly through Doña Teresa Enríquez, known as »the Madwoman of the Sacrament», who contributed to the creation of the Sacramental Brotherhoods at the end of the 15th century, under the protection of King Ferdinand and Queen Isabel. For this reason, the street behind the church was named after Teresa Enríquez.

Calle San Vicente

We follow calle San Vicente, which was considered the most fashionable in Seville in the 18th and 19th centuries. Some of the private palaces still exist, such as that of the Marquis of Tablantes, today the headquarters of the Spanish Socialist Party, which moved its offices here in 1980. On the façade there is a magnificent coat of arms of the Jácome family, who came from Flanders. The house opposite also bears noble crests, and others on this street are obviously ancestral homes.

Continuing along this street, we come to a religious building on the left, and a plaza on the right. The religious building is the Franciscan monastery of

San Antonio de Padua, of scant artistic interest.

Turning right on the square, we go down Marqués de la Mina y Alcoy street, until we join Eslava street, opposite Hernán Cortés street, so called because the last house on the left was the Conqueror of Mexico's mansion. To our right we find the Church of San Lorenzo.

The Church of San Lorenzo

This beautiful church captures our attention from the outside with its graceful Mudejar tower dating from the 14th century. Its architecture is very Sevillian, with two doors, one on Hernán Cortés street, and the other on the plaza de San Lorenzo. There used to be a third door, the oldest of all, Gothic, on Eslava street, but it has been blocked up.

Both doors have good stone portals, one with reliefs representing the grid-iron on which Saint Lawrence was martyred, and the other with his statue and a beautiful Latin inscription dating from 1625.

The reredos behind the main altar was designed by Juan Martínez Montañés, with reliefs of Saint Lawrence made by Felipe Ribas in 1645. The altarpiece is crowned by a Crucifix, and in the center there is a figure of Saint Lawrence, also the work of Felipe Ribas and Dionisio Francisco Ribas. Next to the presbytery there is a noteworthy chapel of the Immaculate Conception, with an altarpiece by Francisco Pacheco made in 1623, which is specially interesting because at the feet of The Virgin there is a panoramic view of the city of Seville as it was at the time.

The choir has fine choir stalls and over them one of the best Baroque organs in Seville.

Next to the choir there is a superb wall painting of Our Lady of Rocamador. Authors and critics have not come to agree-

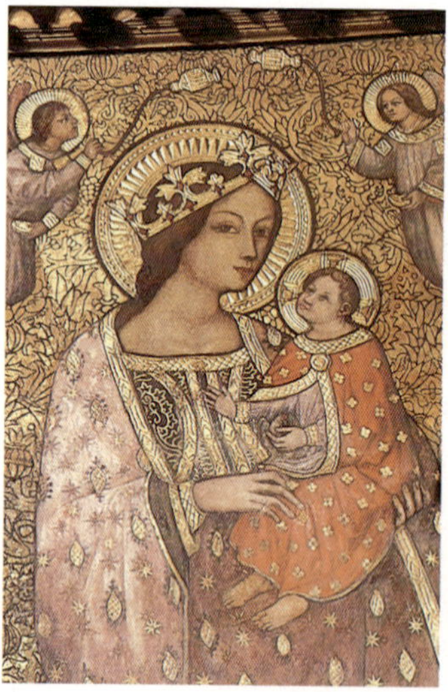

Virgin of Rocamador.

ment regarding its age, since some consider it Visigoth with Byzantine influence from the time of Bishop Saint Isidore, i.e. prior to Moslem rule, while others believe it to be Mozarabic, painted by the Christians who remained during Arab occupation. Finally, others believe it to have been painted in the 13th century, after the Reconquest by Saint Ferdinand, as devotion to this Virgin was French in origin and widespread among Castilian knights at that time.

Whatever its origins, it is a

splendid picture of Our Lady with the Child in Her arms, all polychromed and richly gilded. It is over three meters (10 feet) high. At the foot of the altar members of the Bucarelli family are buried, some of them generals of the fleet of the Indies and one of them Viceroy of Mexico.

The small altar opposite is interesting. The great painter

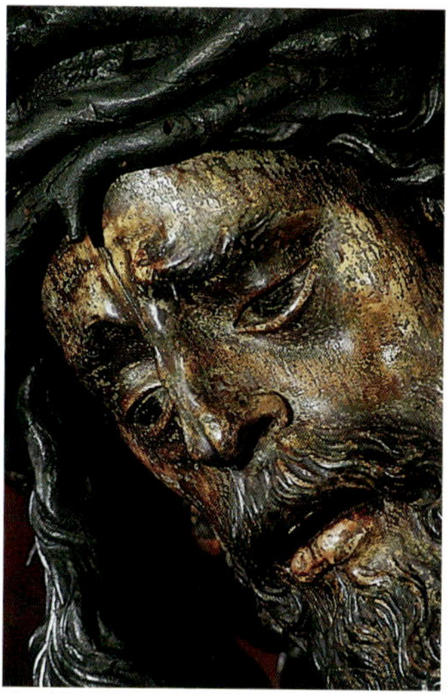

Jesús del Gran Poder.

Villegas Marmolejo is buried here.

At the foot of the left hand aisle we find the chapel of Saint Anne, which has a magnificent 17th century sculpture of the saint teaching her daughter the Virgin Mary as a child to read.

This aisle closes with the chapel of the Brotherhood of Solitude, with a beautiful anonymous figure of the Virgen de la Soledad from the 17th century.

In the right hand aisle, there is an altar with an image of Virgen del Carmen, and by the manner it is shaped following the curve of an elephant's tusk, we can deduce that this is a copy of a small one made of ivory, possibly a Virgin from the 12th or 13th century.

Also in this aisle is the chapel where the Brotherhood of Jesus before Anás and Holy Mary of the Sweet Name hold their services. This Brotherhood is popularly known as «La Bofetada» (The Slap), referring to the episode of the Passion in which He is slapped in the face by his executioners. On the main altar of the chapel is the image of Our Lady and on the left wall the Cristo del Mayor Dolor crucified, both made by Antonio Castillo Lastrucci at the beginning of this century.

The church has five aisles: the central nave, two wider aisles and two narrower ones.

The Church of Gran Poder

On the same plaza de San Lorenzo, and as à continuation of its façade, we find another church which is the Chapel of the Hermandad del Gran Poder, built in 1964. It is a beautiful church with a circular layout and a magnificent cupola. The floor is a huge mosaic in marble of different colors, with the coat of arms of the Brotherhood.

In a compartment over the altar the image of Jesús del Gran Poder is kept, one of the best Baroque sculptures in the world, the work of Juan de Mesa in the 17th century. All the physical signs of the Passion are visible with unique realism: weariness, resignation and pain. The figure is fully modeled, with a vigorous anatomy, although it is shown dressed with a beautiful tunic. One can go up to see it from close by.

On the right of the altar, is the other image, María Santísima del Mayor Dolor y Traspaso, an anonymous 18th century sculpture.

Bécquer's house

From the plaza de San Lorenzo we go down Conde de Barajas street and at number 18, on the left, an inscription informs us that this is the house where the poet Gustavo Adolfo Bécquer was born, a glory of Sevillian literature and forerunner of Romantic poetry.

Upon reaching Jesús del Gran Poder street, we turn left to find the building housing the Conservatory of Music, formerly the palace of the Count of Bagaes, and opposite a movie theater and shopping arcade «Alameda Multicines» built on the site of the former Irish Jesuit College of Saint Patrick, populary known as the «Colegio de los Chiquitos».

Following this street, the third on the left is Santa Ana street, where we find, to the right, the Convent of Santa Ana.

The Convent of Santa Ana

This convent of Carmelite nuns was established in 1606. They were later joined by the community of the Convent of Las Dueñas when their convent was closed. In the main altarpiece there is a fine image of Saint Anne, made by Martínez Montañés, who also sculpted the image of Saint John the Baptist on the altar on the left.

Saint John the Evangelist and Our Lady of the Star, both dating from the 17th century, are valuable but anonymous.

Calle Santa Clara

We leave the church and turn into calle Santa Clara, a bit further on. Number 12 is the palace of the Dukes of Torres de la Pressa, with a beautiful noble coat of arms over the entrance. Nowadays it is a religious residence and hostel.

On the other side is the palace of the Counts of Santa Coloma, a very large building built in the 17th century by the noble Bucarelli family, of Italian origin, who for over a cen-

Balcony on Santa Clara Street.

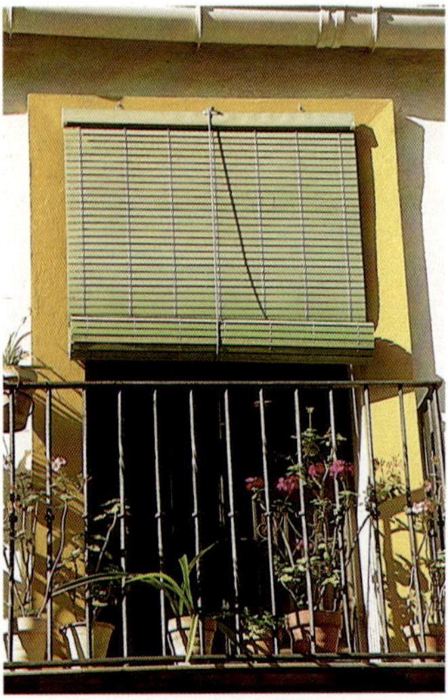

tury held positions as admirals, generals and viceroys of Spain in the Indies, so much so that this section of the street was known as the street of the Generals.

In the 18th century, when the Bucarelli lineage died out, the palace passed on to the Queralt family, Counts of Santa Coloma, who are still the owners, although most of the building today is a high school.

On this street of Santa Clara we can admire the typical Sevillian architecture of the 19th century, with abundant flower-lined balconies.

Torre de Don Fadrique

A bit further on the right hand side, there is a religious portal with an altarpiece in tiles representing Santa Clara of Assisi, dressed as a Franciscan nun and carrying in her hand a monstrance with which, according to tradition, she held back certain troops that were going to invade Assisi.

On entering we find a very pretty open courtyard, with a stone fountain in the center and full of flower pots, orange and lemon trees. Around the sides there are living quarters occupied by craftsmen making religious sculptures and silverwork.

At the end, there is a splendid church façade with a porch in front. Before entering the church, on the left a Gothic portal is visible with a wrought iron gate, providing access to a garden surrounded by stones, tombstones and archeological remains. This is a municipal archeological deposit, not a museum. In the center there is a pond, and opposite, the tower of Don Fadrique. It is very interesting from the point of view of its architecture since it shows exactly the transition from the Romanesque to the Gothic style around 1254.

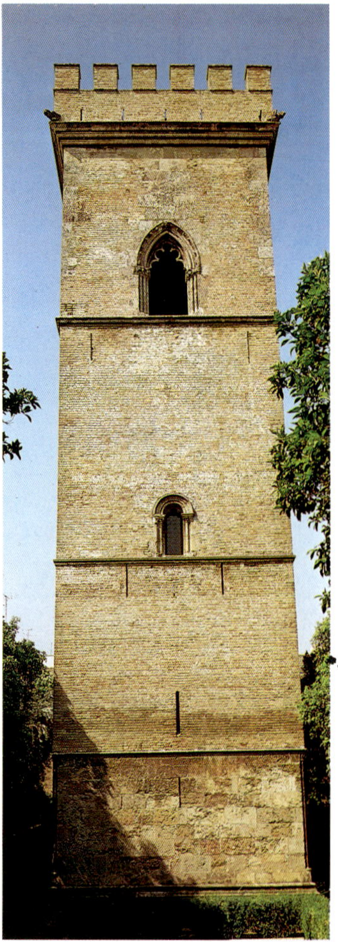

Tower of Don Fadrique.

The lower section is Romanesque, with arow-slits framed by Romanesque arches, while the upper section has Gothic windows and, a flat roof with crenellated battlements. Due to the proximity of the city wall, it is clear that this was a defensive tower, from which both the walls and the river bank could be defended with crossbows.

It was built by the Infante Don Fadrique, son of King Ferdinand and brother of Alfonso X the Wise. According to legend, this Infante fell in love with his father's widow, Queen Joan of Ponthieu, which caused a scandal at Court and led to his banishment. But he rebelled against his brother, who condemned him to death and had him executed, while Joan of Ponthieu was forced to return to France.

More than a fortress to defend the city, the tower of Don Fadrique, was the hidden love nest of a romance that ended tragically.

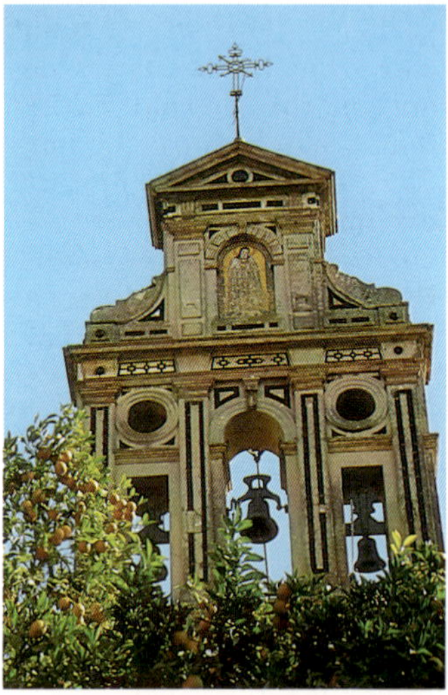

Belfry and façade of Santa Clara.

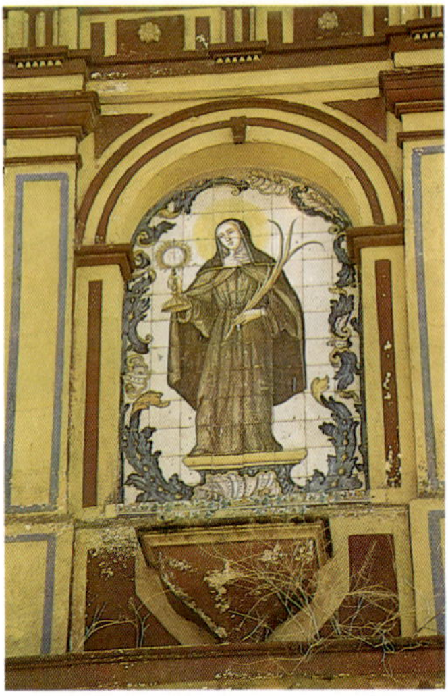

Convent of Santa Clara

Now we can visit the Convent of Santa Clara, founded on a property which belonged to Don Fadrique, expropriated upon his death and handed over to Franciscan nuns to build a convent, as a donation from King Sancho the Brave on November 15th, 1289. The convent was therefore originally Mudejar in style, but due to the weather and earthquakes, it had to be rebuilt in the 16th century, for which reason its style is Gothic. The church has socles over two meters high, covered with tiles made in 1575. The ceiling is coffered in Mudejar style and the lower choir is covered with a beautifully coffered and carved ceiling.

The main altarpiece was designed by Martínez Montanés in the 17th century and has excellent sculptures of Saint Claire, the Immaculate Conception, the Eternal Father and Christ Crucified, by unknown authors. Other altars have images of St. Francis, by a follower of Montañés, and by Hernando de Sturmio.

Near the entrance under the porch, there is a unique sculpture of Doña Ana Salgado, and a slab on the floor tells us that this lady was buried here because her six daughters were nuns in the convent, and since she could not be buried inside, she was content to lie near the door.

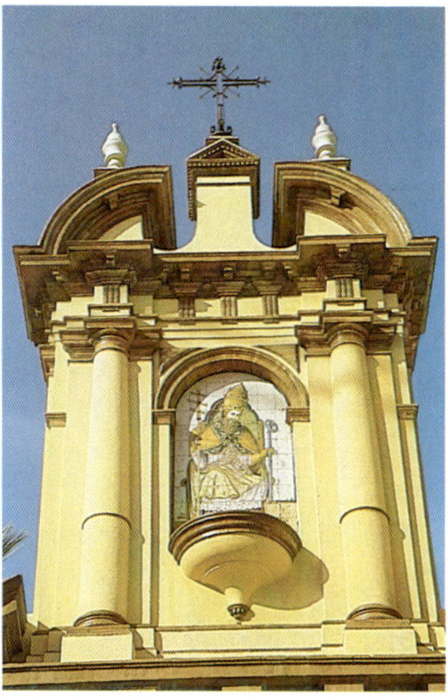

Convent of San Clemente.

The Convent of San Clemente

We go out through the courtyard into the street and follow on to the right until the end of the street, where we find the convent of San Clemente, where a tiled mural on one side tells the story of the convent, founded by King Ferdinand the Saint in 1250.

There is an open space with trees and then the church, which houses among other artistic and historical treasures the tomb of Queen María, the wife of Alfonso XI and mother of Pedro I, called the Cruel by his enemies, and the Just by his advocates. This lady's alliance with the sons of her husband's mistress Doña Leonor de Guzmán is one of the most surprising events in Spanish history, even more so, because this alliance was against her own son Pedro, and the cause of his losing both his crown and his life. Maybe her behavior has influenced the fact that there has never been any attempt to transfer her body to the pantheon of Kings in the Royal Chapel of the Cathedral, as would seem logical.

The main altarpiece was made by Felipe Ribas in 1640, with images of Saint Clement, Saint Benedict, the Immaculate Conception, Saint Hermenegild and Saint Ferdinand. The paintings in the presbytery are by Lucas Valdés, and at the foot of the church there is a very interesting one representing King Ferdinand entering Seville after conquering the city from the Arabs, a late 17th century work by Valdés Leal.

In this church, there is an image of Our Lady of the Kings, that is, a seated Virgin with the Child in her arms, which can be dressed in different costumes, similar to the image of Our Lady of the Kings of the Cathedral. This is one of the so-called «Ferdinand series», all from the 13th century and possibly from the same workshop, which are to be found in several churches of Seville, donated by King Ferdinand to start Christian worship after the reconquest of the Islamized city.

In the altar of Saint John the Baptist there are reliefs by Gaspar Núñez Delgado and paintings by Pacheco.

This convent lent part of its building to the Commissary of the Seville Pavilion in Expo '92, and after it has been renovated, it will once more become part of the community of Cistercian nuns, founded by a daughter of King Ferdinand the Saint.

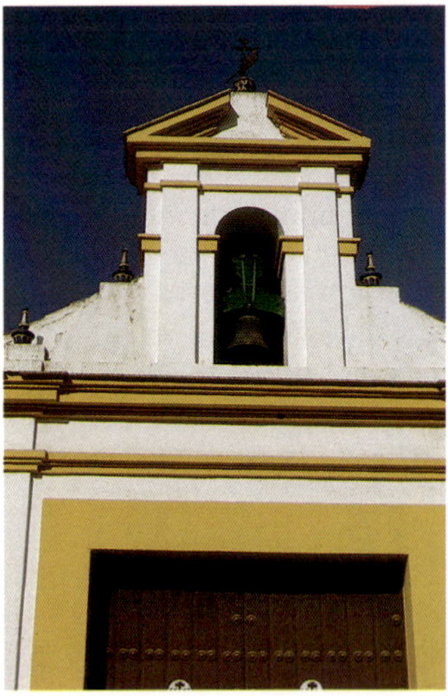

Chapel of Our Lady of Mount Carmel

The streets of Don Juan

We leave the monastery of San Clemente, and bordering it on Yuste and Reposo streets, we come to Calatrava street, of the knights of the Order of Calatrava. We turn into this street and then off to the right. A bit further down we will find opposite us, on the left hand side, a building which bears the sign of Parish of Our Lady of Bethlehem.

If we visit it, we will find a single nave of solid architecture dating from the 14th century and very high up on the main altar and at the foot of the church, coats of arms of the Order of Calatrava carved in stone.

We continue along this street and on the right we will find a small chapel, more like a shrine, with the coat of arms of Mount Carmel on the door. This is the chapel of the Virgen del Carmen built by the Ribera family, the Marquis of Tarifa, in 1639, in memory of their eldest son, Pedrito Ribera «el Mozo», who met his death on this spot. This character completes the legend of Don Juan Tenorio, which commenced with the true episode of a gentleman who challenged the nobleman Ulloa in his tomb in the convent of San Francisco.

If the chief theme of El Convidado de Piedra, written by Tirso de Molina around 1620, is that of an unbeliever daring to profane the repose of the dead, the event of don Pedrito Ribera «el Mozo» robbing a woman on Calatrava street will complete the plot of this literary myth, based, we insist, on real events. Don Pedrito had shortly before tricked the old bishop who lived in the Alameda out of his house at midnight to administer the sacraments to a dying man, only to duck him in the fountain in the Alameda. He then went still further in his defiance of the rules of social behavior by stealing from a woman on Calatrava street.

However, her relatives, armed with knives and tapestry weaving needles, cornered Don Pedrito, who fought back sword in hand, leaning against the pillar of a stone cross known as the «Cruz del Rodeo». However, he was outnumbered and died. The powerful Ribera family, which included the Dukes of Alcalá and Medinaceli, raised this chapel in his memory. Later, the dramatist José Zorilla included the episode in his «Don Juan Tenorio», although he made a nun out of the woman who had only been a resident of Calatrava street. Important operas have been written on the life of Don Juan, based on historical facts combined by writers, for example Don Giovanni by Mozart, Don Juan by Gluck and others by Carnicer and Alfano.

Calle Jesús del Gran Poder

In the same square as this small chapel we will find the street of Jesús del Gran Poder, which we enter. A bit further up we see on the right side that the street widens and that there is a small alley called Becas, which indicates that here stood the school of Becas (Scholarships) founded by the Jesuits in the 17th century. We do not enter this alley.

On the same street of Jesús del Gran Poder, there is a palace on our left, the so-called casa de las Sirenas (Mermaids' house), which was in total ruin until recently. It is not worthwhile visiting this because the architecture is mediocre, from the 19th century, and not original but a copy of a German mansion. We go ahead, passing the Conservatory of Music and beyond it to our left, stands the present church of the Sagrado Corazón, which was formerly the church of Saint Francis of Paola, with a beautiful brick façade and a belfry covered with fine tiles. Also on the church façade we can see very beautiful tiles.

Further on we turn to our right into a narrow street, called calle de Las Cortes.

College of San Hermenegildo

The 17th century building on our left houses the chapel of the former Colegio de San Hermenegildo (College). Until recently, it has been used as the headquarters of the Regional Parliament of Andalusia. The chapel is in the Baroque style, very beautiful though not original due to successive reforms. Here the Cortes or Parliament met in the early 19th century, and resolved to declare the monarch Ferdinand VII incapable of ruling.

On the same calle de Las Cortes, along what is now the

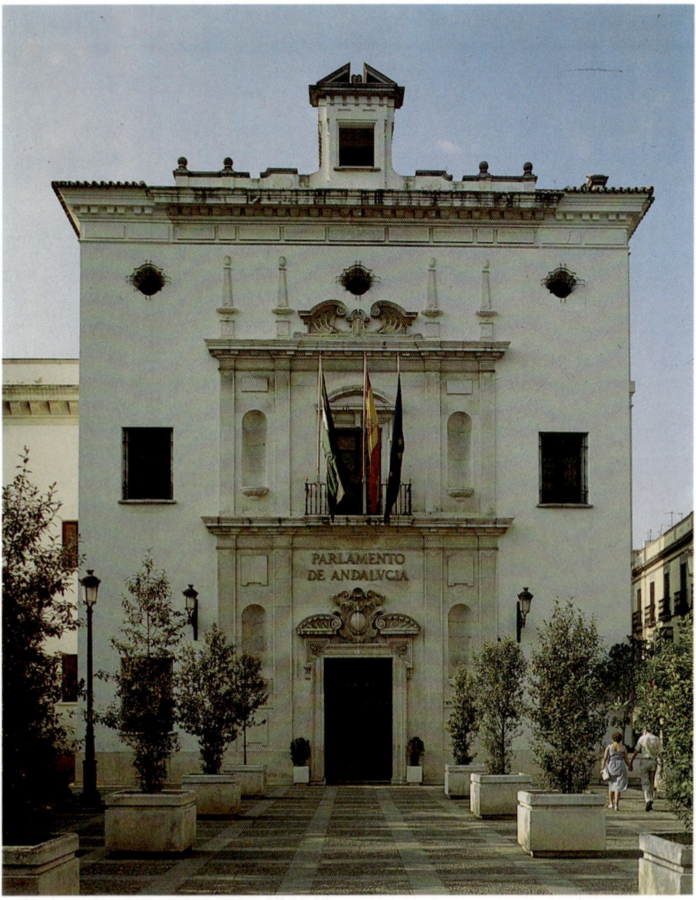

College of Saint Hermenegild

right hand sidewalk the Hospicio de Indias was situated, where Jesuit missionaries, aged and often in bad health, retired after preaching the Gospel in the New World.

And so we reach the plaza de la Gavidia.

The monument of Daoiz

At the center of plaza de la Gavidia, there is a monument to Luis Daoiz, as artillery captain and hero of the Spanish War of Independence (Peninsular War), who headed the rebellion against the Napoleonic troops in Madrid on May 2, 1808.

Luis Daoiz was born in the house which the statue is facing, on this same square. The magnificent monument was made by the sculptor Antonio

Susillo (the one buried in the Saint Ferdinand Cemetery, outside the Macarena walls), and is one of the best public monuments in Seville.

The Convent of Santa Rosalía

From Gavidia square we set off along calle Cardenal Spínola, and, almost at the beginning to the right is the convent of Santa Rosalía, with a Baroque portal including a figure of this saint.

It is a convent of cloistered Capuchin nuns founded in1700 and built in the Baroque style. However, it was destroyed by a terrible fire in 1761, as we can read in a slab on the convent wall. Rebuilding was paid by Cardinal Solís, but it no longer has the previous architectural quality. The church has a Latin cross ground-plan, with groined vaulted ceiling and octagonal pillars. The presbytery ceiling was painted by Espinal and represents the Eternal Father, Saint Lawrence and Saint Vincent, as this convent is located on the border between these two saints' parishes.

The main altar contains images of the Immaculate Conception, Saint Francis, Saint Clare, and Saint Rosalie. On other altars we see the sculptures of Saint Felix of Cantalicio, and other Capuchin saints. Although it is not known who executed them, as the documents were destroyed by fire, it is obvious that they were made by excellent artists, including Cristóbal Ramos.

The church is one of the tidiest and best kept in Seville.

And leaving this church we complete our itinerary by taking a left turn to plaza de Gavidia and crossing it, to return to the plaza del Duque.

Monument to Daoíz.

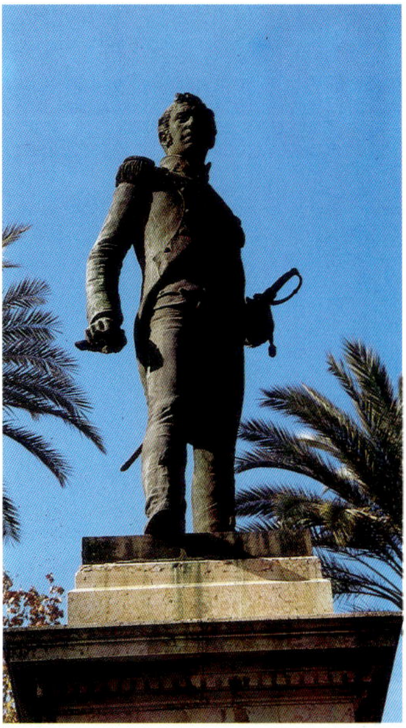

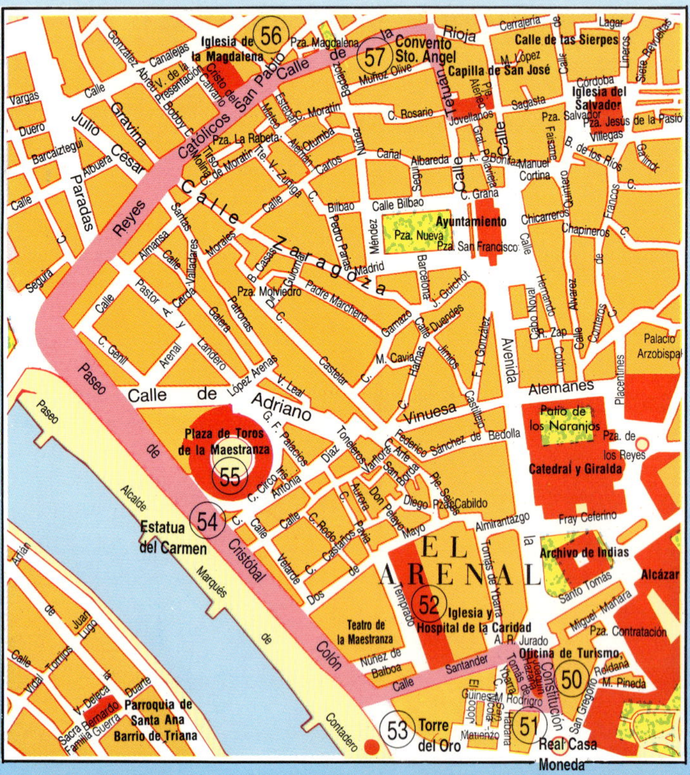

ROUTE 6: FROM THE HOSPITAL DE LA CARIDAD TO THE REAL MAESTRANZA BULLRING

PLACES OF INTEREST

(50) Chapel at Puerta de Jerez
Is the only remain of the ancient University built in brick in 1502 in Gothic style. Extremely valuable altarpiece by Alejo Fernández.

(51) The Royal Mint
Splendid building with interior alleys which houses the furnaces in which the gold and silver form America were melted.

(52) Hospital of Santa Caridad
Late 17th century Baroque building. The adjoining church of San Jorge, holds the best paintings by Valdés Leal and Murillo. Opposite there is the monument to Miguel de Mañara. Calle Temprado, 3. Tel: 421 77 38. Opening hours: 10 to 13 and 16 to 19

(53) The Golden Tower
13th century arab fortress; houses the Navy Museum. Paseo de Colón. Tel: 422 24 19. Opening hours: 10 to 14. Closed on Mondays.

(54) Statue of Carmen

(55) Real Maestranza Bullring
Houses the Bullfighting Museum. Paseo de Colón. Tel: 421 23 56

(56) Church of La Magdalena
Fray Bartolomé de las Casas was consecrated there. Great collection of paintings and sculptures.

(57) Convent of the Santo Angel
Sculptures by Pedro Roldán and Martínez Montañés.

STARTING POINT	Plaza Puerta de Jerez
EXIT TO NEXT ROUTE	From Plaza Puerta de Jerez along calle San Fernando towards the University, starting point for Route 7.

USEFUL ADDRESSES NEARBY

Chemists:	Gamazo, 1 García de Vinuesa, 38 Zaragoza, 17 San Pablo, 5 González Abreu, 7 Tetuán, 4
Photo service:	Antonia Díaz, 31 Galera, 25 Reyes Católicos Plaza de la Magdalena
Restaurante Torre del Oro:	Santander, 15
Restaurante El Postigo:	Tomás de Ibarra, 2
Restaurante Enrique Becerra:	Gamazo, 2. Local cuisine.
Restaurante La Isla:	Arfe, 25
Restaurante El Barranco:	Arjona, 12
Restaurante Llorens:	Pastor y Landero, 19
Restaurante El Burladero:	Canalejas, 1. Luxury restaurant.
Restaurante Las Piletas:	Marqués de Paradas, 28
Restaurante La Mandrágora:	Albufera, 11
Tapas Bars	
Bar Los Tres Reyes:	Reyes Católicos. Meeting point for bullfighters and bullbreeders. Excellent tapas.

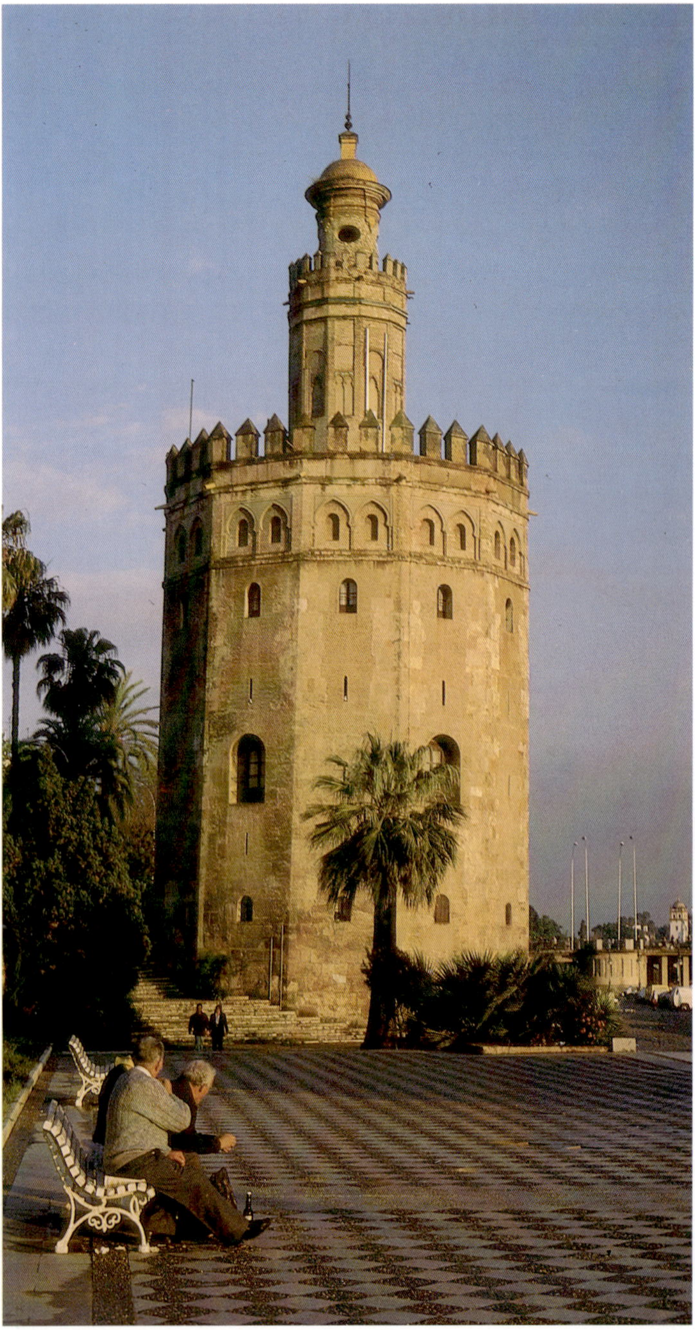

The Golden Tower.

ROUTE 6: FROM THE HOSPITAL DE LA CARIDAD TO THE REAL MAESTRANZA BULLRING

At the end of Constitución Avenue, beyond the Cathedral and the Archives of the Indies, we reach a spacious square with gardens on the far side, called Puerta de Jerez because on this site the old city walls had a gate leading out towards Jerez de la Frontera.

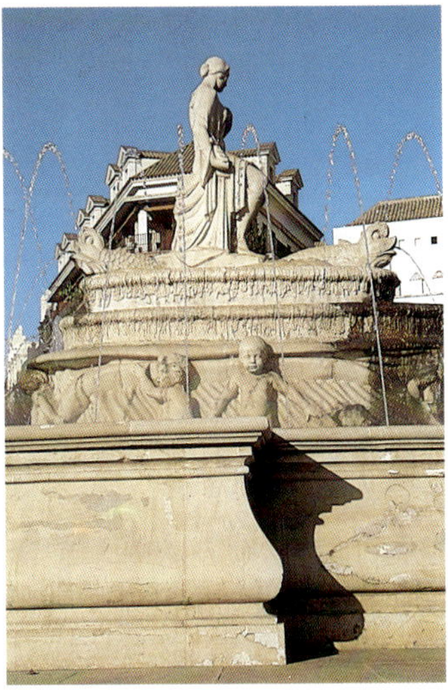

Puerta de Jerez. Square.

Chapel at Puerta de Jerez

On the same corner of the left hand sidewalk of Constitución Avenue and Puerta de Jerez square, there is a tiny religious brick building with a small portial and wrought iron gates. Its style is Gothic but in brick, and the belfry is also in brick.

This chapel has several names – Chapel of Maese Rodrigo, Chapel of Saint Mary of Jesus, Chapel of Saint Gregory–s Seminary, etc.– and it is all that remains of the University of Seville founded by Maese Rodrigo de Santaella under Royal Letters Patent of King Ferdinand and Queen Isabel dated February 22, 1502, establishing it as a University and at the same time a center for general studies. It was dedicated to Saint Mary of Jesus and occupied the space reaching from this chapel to the corner of the arquillo de la Plata, and behind, the whole length of San Gregorio street. This University had Schools of Law, Theology, Medicine and Arts.

We enter the chapel through an arched door. Inside, the church is Gothic Mudejar, with beautiful ribbed vaulting

Belfry of the chapel at Puerta de Jerez.

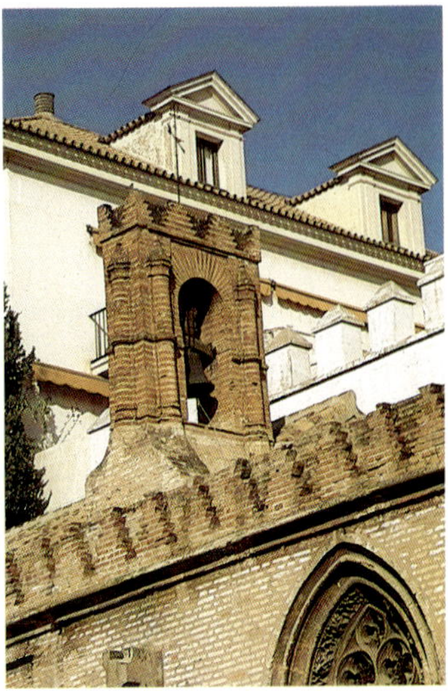

over the chancel. The walls have socles of glazed Sevillian tiles made with the so-called «cuerda seca» technique dating from the time it was founded.

On the high altar a beautiful picture of the Virgen de la Antigua can be seen with Maese Rodrigo de Santaella kneeling in front a model of the University building in order to place it under her protection. The painting, with its charmingly primitive character, was executed by Alejo Fernández at the beginning of the 16th century. To the right of the altarpiece, because this was a University church, there are statues of the Doctors of the Church, Saints Augustine, Jerome, Gregory the Great, and Ambrose. On the altar socle, there are paintings of Saint Isidore and Saint Thomas, an Ecce Homo, Saint Nicholas, Saint Catherine and the Virgen del Pópulo, the latter in Byzantine style. All of them are very valuable due to their fine quality and age.

The rest of the chapel has metallic glazed Triana tiles imitating Persian cloth and an ogival garret. In front of the altar is the tomb of Maese Rodrigo de Santaella, a simple tombstone engraved with fine verses in Latin.

The Mint
Casa de la Moneda

On Constitución Avenue, but on the opposite side from the plaza Puerta de Jerez there is a little street, called Maese Rodrigo, which suddenly leads

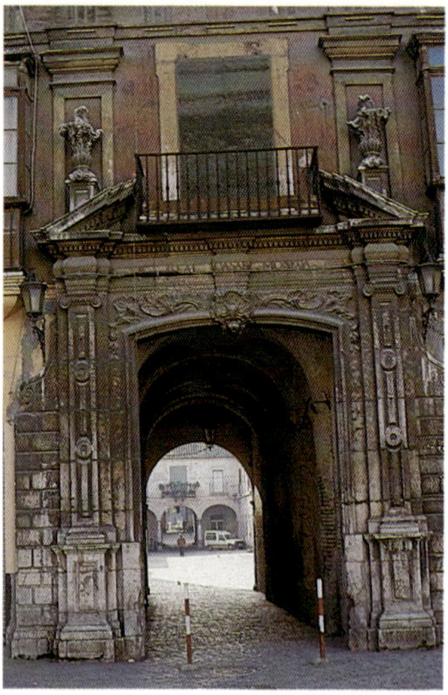

The Mint (Casa de la Moneda)

us into the Casa de la Moneda (Royal Mint), although this building has its main entrance on neighboring Santander street, with a sign over the door informing us of its royal status.

The building is really like a small village, which even had its own wall, part of which can still be seen. There are several large courtyards flanked by buildings containing storerooms, casting furnaces, offices, stables, etc., which formed a world in itself. All the gold that came from Spanish America and the Far East colonies, when Spain and Portugal were one, comprising the greatest empire ever on Earth, was minted here into coins: doubloons, ducats, escudos ; gold coins, which were used to pay for the wars in Flanders, Italy, Germany, and which in the end ruined the Empire. When the shipments of gold came to an end, in the 19th century, the Mint was finally closed down.

The paths inside the Mint bear colonial names, such as Havana, El Jobo, Guines....

Today, merely a shadow of what it was, it displays its empty store-rooms and idle furnaces as a reminder of its glorious past:

Sic transit gloria mundi

(Thus pass the glories of this world).

The Church of San Jorge de la Santa Caridad

We leave by the main gate opening onto Santander street and follow this street as far as Temprado street. In this street, the first thing we find on the right is the Hospital de la Santa Caridad , founded in the 17th century by Miguel de Mañara Vicentelo de Leca, a very wealthy man and »the greatest sinner on earth», as he called himself, but who after being converted to piety and charity, dedicated his last years to helping the poor, the aged, beggars and the sick.

To our left there is a small garden and at the entrance, a statue representing Miguel de Mañara carrying a sick man in his arms. This monument in bronze is the work of sculptor Antonio Susillo.

Opposite the garden is the main door to the hospital over which there is a sign that reads: Domun pauperum scala coeli, «house of the poor, stairway to heaven.»

Miguel de Mañara, from whose life it seems that real

Church of Saint George of the Holy Charity.

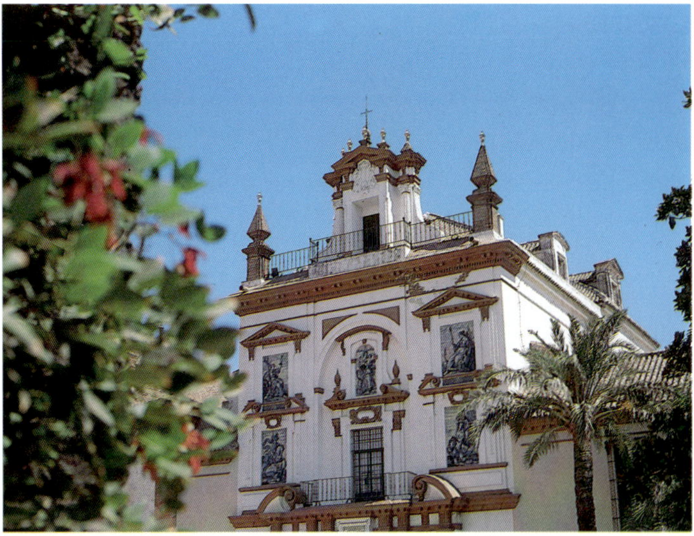

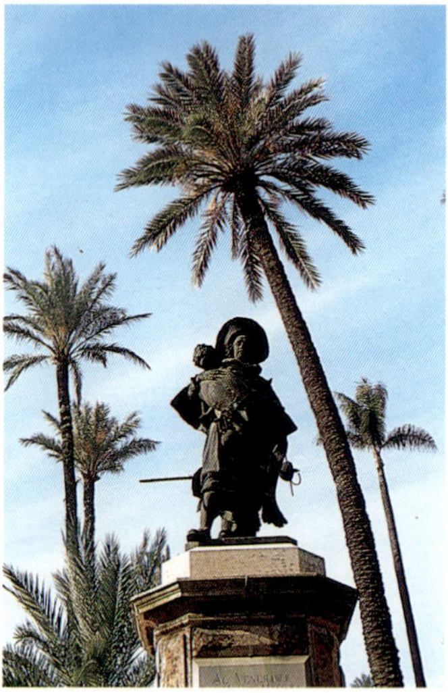

Statue of Miguel de Mañara.

episodes were also borrowed to complete the legend of Don Juan, devoted all his energies to the construction of this hospital, acquiring four buildings from the former dockyards where he set up the hospital. The building is handsome, with sunny courtyards where he personally planted rose bushes which over three hundred years later still bloom. The first one has rich glazed tiles painted with stories and brought over from Italy.

But the most artistic part of all is the adjoining church, called the church of Señor San Jorge. On the façade on Temprado street, we can see glazed tiles painted by Bartolomé Esteban Murillo. Inside the church, everything is of refined taste and profound mysticism, since Miguel de Mañara wished so to honor God and the poor, who represent Him in this world.

The building was designed and built by Bernardo Simón Pineda in 1674. The church has a single nave, with vaulting and a cupola over the chancel with an artistic wrought iron railing.

The main altarpiece is Baroque and rises to Heaven in an apotheosis of glory. It includes a sculpted group, The Burial of Christ, by Pedro Roldán, with images of Saint George and Saint Roch. Other altars have sculptures representing Saint Joseph, Our Lady of Charity and an Ecce Homo, all authentic gems of Baroque art.

But the greatest treasure of this church is the collection of paintings by Murillo, which we have seen reproduced many times in books on Art. Here we have the originals: *The Miracle of Moses*, *The Multiplication of the Bread and Fishes*, *The Annunciation*, *Saint John of God Carrying a Sick Man in his Arms*, *Saint John the Baptist as a Child*, and the amazing *Saint Isabel of Hungary attending the Sick*.

On the side walls of the lower choir two great works by Valdés Leal known as *Los Novísimos* or *Postrimerías*, illustrate the *vanitas* theme better than painting has ever been able to, showing death putting an end to every form of vanity. A bishop and a knight rot side by side in their coffins with terrifying realism, rich silks lie about abandoned while tiaras and crowns have fallen. These paintings by Valdés Leal are masterworks of universal art.

Torre de la Plata and Torre del Oro

We leave Temprado street and, looking back towards Santander street, where we came from, we see a tower rising over the houses. This is the Torre de la Plata (Silver Tower), built during the last years of Moslem rule.

If we now go up Santander street and cross the paseo de Colón, we will be able to see the Torre del Oro (Golden Tower), sister to the previous one, although much more famous.

It was built around 1200 by the Moslem governor Sidi Abu Elola at a time when Seville was a province of Morocco.

The Torre del Oro consists of two sections of Arab architecture, with twelve sides, which makes it look almost round. Above these two sections, a turret with a little cupola was added in the year 1760, which made it more graceful but less authentic in style.

The decoration characteristic of these two parts is, on the lower one, the small arches below the battlements, and in the upper section the slender, divided windows. On the other hand, the large windows in the lower section were opened in the 18th century; previously, the only windows were those under the cornice, since it was a defensive tower and only had embrasures or arrow-slits.

From the Torre del Oro, a strong chain was extended every night across the river, secured to another tower or fortress on the Triana side, thus effectively closing the Guadalquivir to navigation.

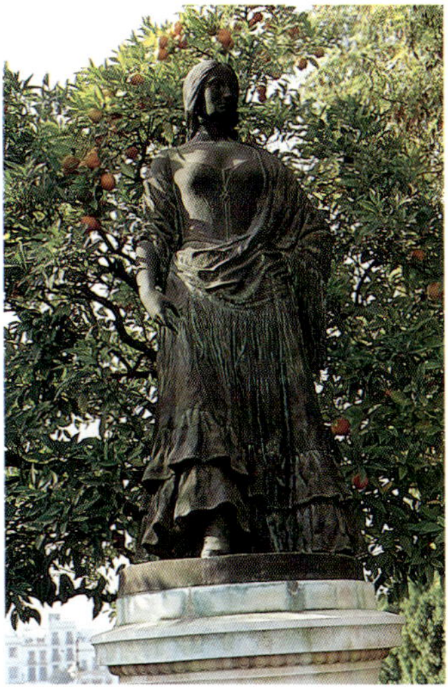

Carmen.

Inside the tower there is a small naval museum, displaying many ship models, cannons, pictures of naval battles, uniforms, nautical charts and many other curious historical objects.

The statue of Carmen

We leave the Torre del Oro and turn left from its door, following the stone wall, contemplating the river and Triana quarter on the opposite shore.

As we stroll along we will soon come to the bullring of La Maestranza. Without crossing the avenue, we will see right opposite the entrance to the arena, almost on the edge of the sidewalk, a bronze statue of a woman dressed as a Gypsy. This is the monument to

«Carmen», the protagonist of the novel by Prosper Merimée, who took the plot from reality. Don José fell in love with Carmen and abandoned his military career to become a smuggler for her sake. But in spite of his sacrifice, she deceived him and joined the bullfighter Escamillo, while Don José, blind with jealousy and pain for his ruined life, waited for Carmen and stabbed her to death in front of the bullring, where her lover Escamillo has just triumphed as a matador.

La Maestranza Bullring

We cross the avenue to reach the bullring. The name Maestranza signifies that this

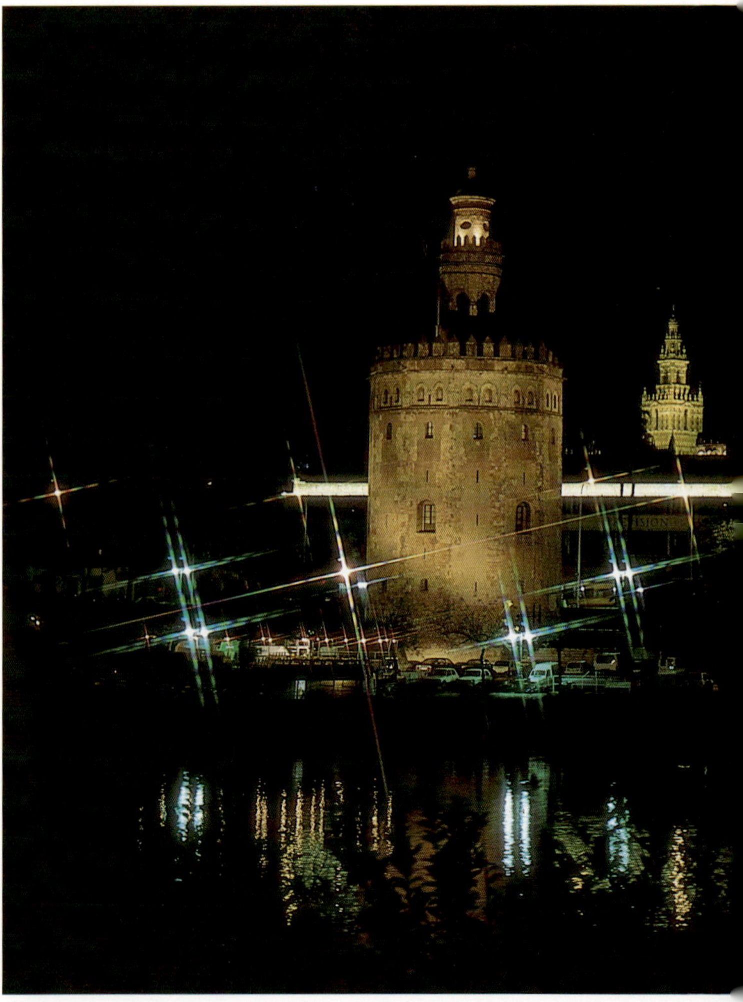

arena was built by and still belongs to a corporation of Sevillian noblemen, and called the Real Maestranza de Caballería. It was founded in 1670 during the reign of Charles II, with the purpose of maintaining horse breeding and the art of horseback riding in Spain, as training for war. Even Today, the members devote their principal attention to social work, including offering scholarships for higher studies. The bullring, as we have said, is their property, but it is run by a commercial enterprise.

The building of the arena is magnificent, designed by architect Vicente San Martín, who started it in 1763. The

Evening view: the Guadalquivir and the GoldenTower.

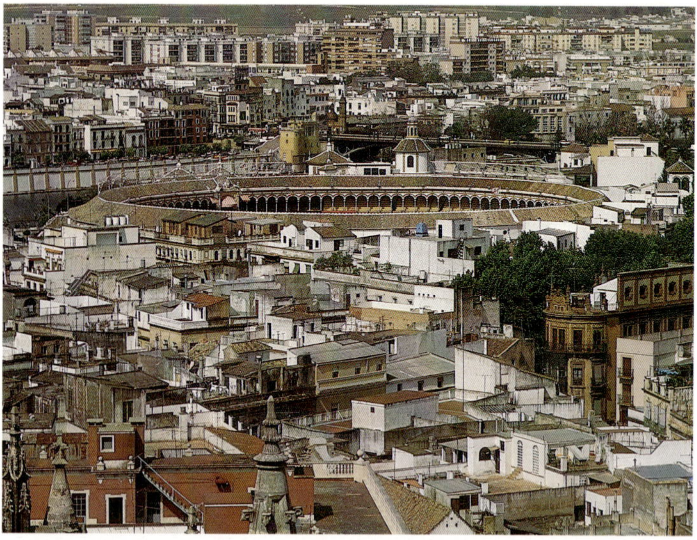

La Maestranza.

Prince's box or balcony is made of marble with a balustrade of little pillars. It is like a small chamber, covered with a large segmented arch flanked by very thin columns with Corinthian capitals, crowned by a Neoclassical pediment with a large royal coat of arms.

All this rests on a lower gallery with a semicircular arch facing the arena, flanked by Ionic pillars supporting the balcony.

The bullring itself is made of stone and the upper part has marble columns. The building was not finished until the 19th century.

A must is the chapel where the bullfighters pray before going into the arena to display their dangerous art. This chapel has an altarpiece that belonged to the Dominican convent of Regina Angelorum on Regina street, demolished in 1927. It has sculptures by Pedro Roldán from the 17th century. The great iron gate under the Prince's box, also designed by Pedro Roldán, came from the same convent.

This arena is considered «the cathedral of the art of bullfighting» and for famous bullfighters it is an honor and the peak of their career to triumph here in an important bullfight and to leave the arena amidst public acclaim on the shoulders of fans through the Prince's Door.

Leaving the bullring, we turn right on the same Paseo de Cristóbal Colón.

The Church of La Magdalena

We walk as far as a street on the right called Reyes Católicos, exactly opposite Triana bridge. We go down this street until we reach a large church on the left which is the former Dominican monastery of Saint Paul, and nowadays the parish church of La Magdalena.

This church was formerly the most important of the monastic churches of Seville, not so much for its size as due to the respect and fear inspired by the powerful Dominican Order, in charge of the Inquisition Court.

nardo Figueroa. It has three aisles, the central one maintaining the Mudejar apse which acts as a crossing, but since several chapels have been added on one side, it appears to have four aisles.

The main altarpiece is Baroque, and contains a figure of Saint Paul and a Mary Magdalene which does not belong to this church, but to the previous parish church which stood on today's Plaza de la Magdalena.

Cupola of the Church of Mary Magdalene.

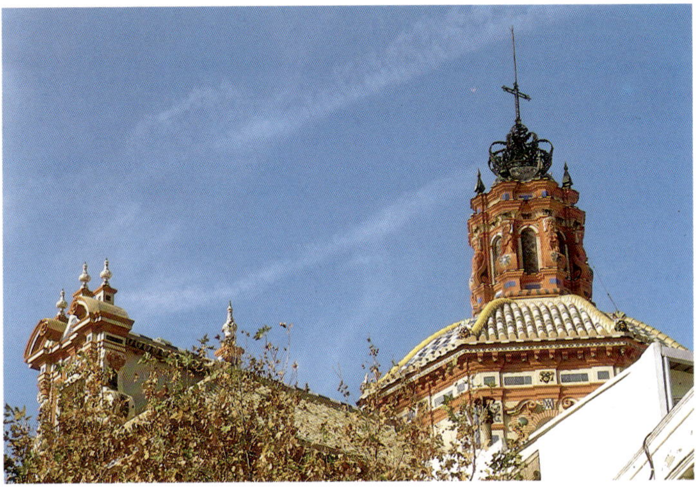

In the façade, next to the door, several slabs recall that in this church the famous Bishop Fray Bartolomé de las Casas was consecrated, known as protector of the natives in the newly discovered teritories in America and bishop in Chiapas, in the Yucatan peninsula.

The building was erected during the last years of the 17th century by architect Leo-

In the presbytery there are two large paintings of Biblical themes by Lucas Valdés. On each side of the sacristy door there are altars, one with Saint Joachim, the Virgin, and Saint Anne, and the other with a Virgen de las Fiebres (Our Lady of the Fevers), who has a large following in Seville, by Juan Bautista Vázquez the Elder, from the16th century.

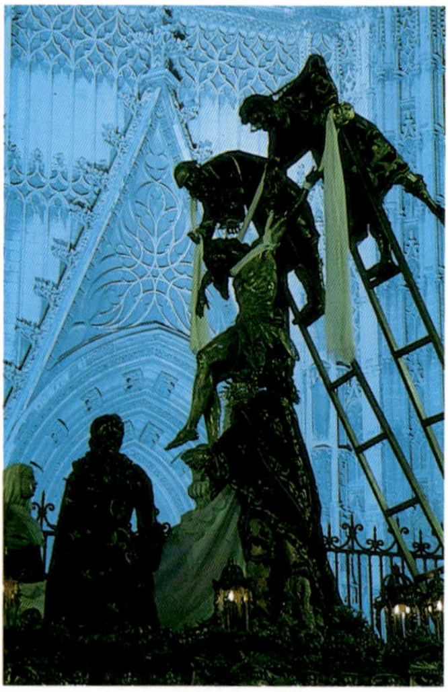

Descent of the Brotherhood of the Fifth Anguish.

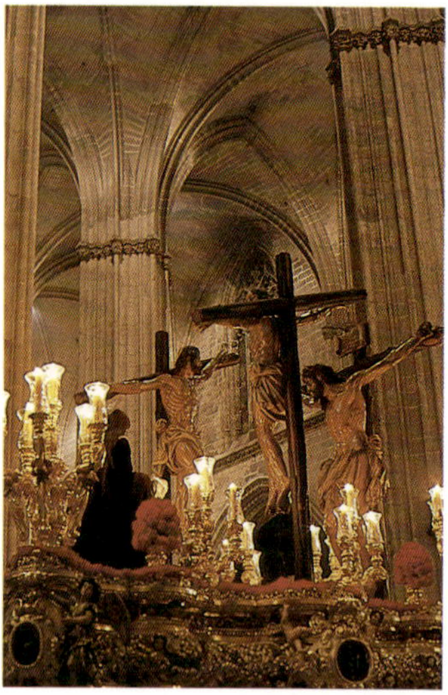

Christ of the Brotherhood of Our Lady of Montserrat.

Among the most important pictures housed in this church are *The Cure of the Blessed Reginald* painted by Zurbarán, and a large fresco representing the *Entrance of King Ferdinand the Saint in Seville*, after defeating the Moors.

In this church the President of the Governing Council, Francisco Arias de Saavedra is buried. This council substituted Ferdinand VII while he was held captive in France and governed Spain during most of the Spanish Peninsular War.

In the chapel of the Brotherhood of the Descent of Christ and the Fifth Anguish of Blessed Mary, there are very beautiful sculptures of the Descent group, where The dead Christ is lowered from the cross by the holy men. The figure of Christ is by Pedro Roldán, while the holy men and women are by Pedro Nieto. The Virgin is by Rodríguez Caso.

After this visit, if we are lucky, maybe the small chapel to the right, on Cristo del Calvario street is open, where we can see images of the Brotherhood of Christ of the Conversion of the Good Thief and Our Lady of Montserrat, a brotherhood founded by the Catalans in the year 1601.

The image of Christ Crucified looking at the Good Thief is the work of Juan de Mesa and bears an extraordinary resemblance to Christ of Great Power as the sculptor used the same model for both. Our Lady of Montserrat is a Virgin of Sorrows, attributed by some to Juan de Mena and by others to Martínez Montañés.

Going down the same street, we reach the plaza de la Magdalena.

Plaza de la Magdalena

On this square, as on others, until recently there were beautiful palaces, which have sadly been demolished to build shopping galleries, which we consider a black and shameful episode in the history of Seville.

On the façade on this side of the plaza, there is a large plaque indicating that until the 19th century this site was occupied by the parish church of Mary Magdalene, and that, somewhere in the square, the famous sculptor Martínez Montañés is buried. However, reality seems to be otherwise. Although it is true that Montañés belonged to this parish, and as such was to be buried here, the sculptor happened to die during the tragic epidemic of the year 1649, on June 18, and due to the extraordinary amount of victims, some were taken to the moat at the city wall, which was turned into a common grave, so that Montañés in reality is buried in this moat, today covered by Santas Patronas street.

Convent of the Santo Angel

From the plaza de la Magdalena, we take Rioja street, and halfway up it we will find the convento del Santo Angel , whose entrance is through an open courtyard. The church was built in 1587 and was open for worship until the friars were secularized in the 19th century. It was used for different purposes until 1904, when the Carmelites returned. Of its three aisles, the only one remaining from the 16th century is the central one, with half barrel vault. The other two were reconstructed in this century. The sculptures were not made for this church, but are replacements, although some are

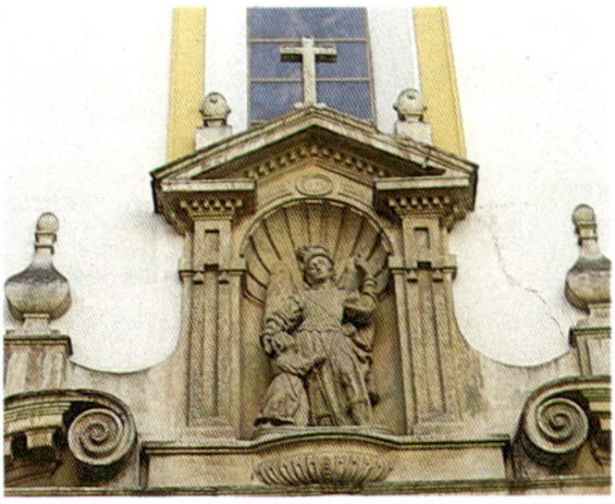

Convent of the Holy Angel. Detail of the façade.

excellent, for example a Saint Anne Teaching the Virgin to Read, by Pedro Roldán, and the Cristo del Amparo attributed to Martínez Montañés.

After visiting the monastery, we continue along Rioja street to the right, which leads us to Tetuán street, in the city center.

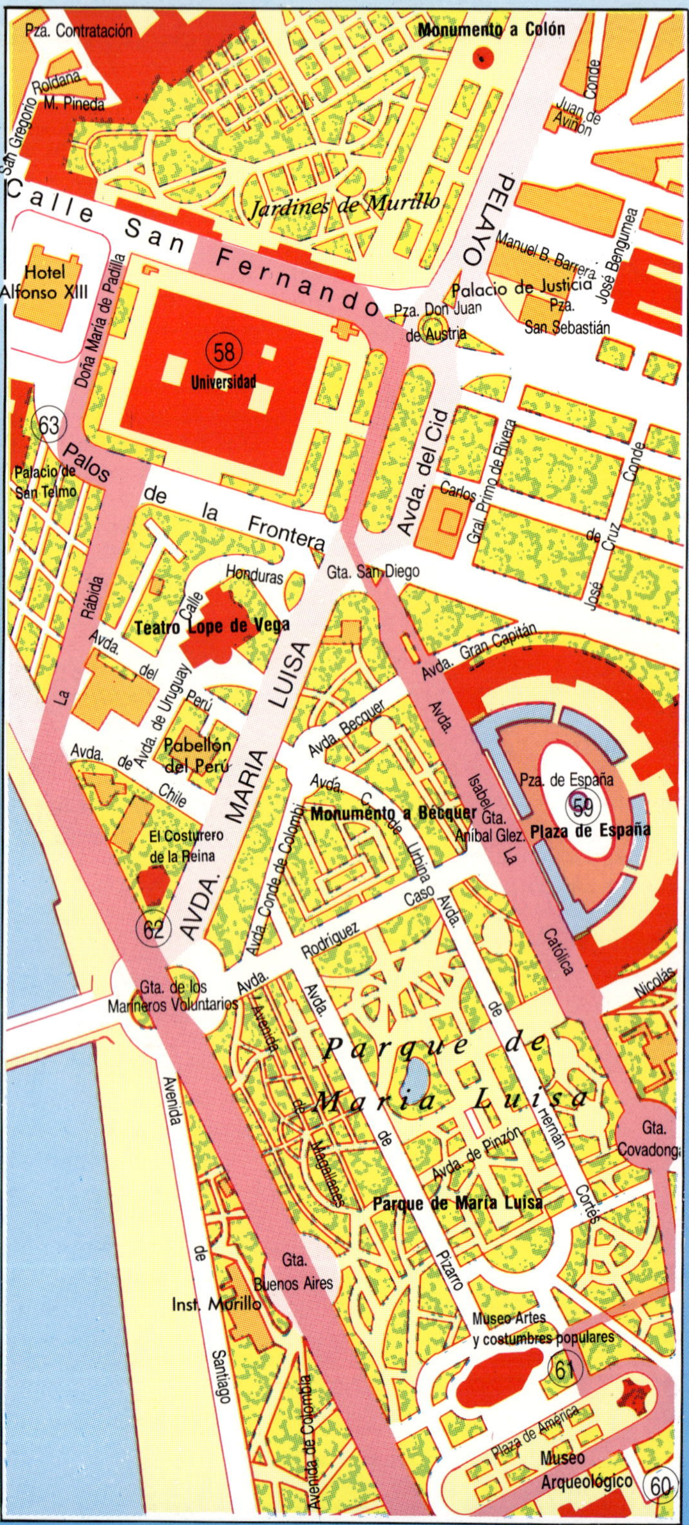

Pza. Contratación
Monumento a Colón
Roldana
M. Pineda
San Gregorio
Conde
Juan de Aviñón
Calle San Fernando
Jardines de Murillo
PELAYO
Manuel B. Barrera
José Bengumea
Hotel Alfonso XIII
Doña María de Padilla
Palacio de Justicia
Pza. Don Juan de Austria
Pza. San Sebastián
58
Universidad
63
Palacio de San Telmo
Palos de la Frontera
Avda. del Cid
Carlos
Gral. Primo de Rivera
Conde de Cruz
José
Honduras
Gta. San Diego
Calle
Teatro Lope de Vega
La Rábida
Avda. del Perú
Avda. de Uruguay
AVDA. MARIA LUISA
Avda. Gran Capitán
Avda. Isabel La Católica
Avda. Becquer
Pabellón del Perú
Avda. de Chile
Avda. C. de Urbina
Monumento a Bécquer
Pza. de España
59
Plaza de España
Gta. Aníbal Glez.
El Costurero de la Reina
Avda. Conde de Colombi
AVDA.
62
Avda. Rodríguez Caso
Gta. de los Marineros Voluntarios
Avenida de Magallanes
Avda. de Pizarro
Avda. de Hernán Cortés
Nicolás
Parque de María Luisa
Gta. Covadonga
Avda. de Pinzón
Parque de María Luisa
Avenida de Santiago
Gta. Buenos Aires
Inst. Murillo
Museo Artes y costumbres populares
61
Avenida de Colombia
Plaza de América
Museo Arqueológico
60

ROUTE 7: MARIA LUISA PARK

PLACES OF INTEREST

(58) **University**
Former 18th century tobacco factory; mixture of civilian and military architecture. Holds the University Library.

(59) **Plaza de España**
Monumental site surrounded by an artificial stream and benches decorated with ceramic tiles representing historic moments from each Spanish province.

(60) **The Archeological Museum**
Unique items from the Carambolo Treasure. Important collection of Roman statues and mosaics from Itálica.
Plaza de América.
Tel: 423 24 01.
Opening hours: 10 to 14. Closed on mondays.

(61) **Museum of Folklore and Art**
Typical costumes, furniture, furnished rooms, ceramic, etc.
Plaza de América.
Tel: 423 25 76.
Opening hours: 10 to 14.

(62) **The Queen Sewing Cabinet**
Alfonso the XIIth's wife, Queen Mercedes, used to sew and embroider here. Tourist office. Avenida de la Constitución, 21.
Tel: 422 14 04

(63) **Palace of San Telmo**
Baroque building which now houses the Palace of the Regional Government Presidency.
Calle Palos de la Frontera, 2.
Tel: 421 38 65.

STARTING POINT	Plaza de la Puerta de Jerez
EXIT TO NEXT ROUTE	From Puerta de Jerez across Puente de San Telmo, to start Route 8.

USEFUL ADDRESSES NEARBY

Chemists:	Avenida de la Constitución next to Puerta de Jerez Avenida Menéndez Pelayo, 31 and 69 Avenida de la Raza, bloque 2 San Fernando
Photo service:	Different stands at M.ª Luisa Park
Restaurante Egeña-Oriza:	San Fernando, 41. Gardens of Murillo. Open air restaurant, typical andalusian cuisine with basque influence. Game dishes when in season.
Restaurante la Raza:	M.ª Luisa Park.
Restaurante Luna Parque:	Avenida de M.ª Luisa, 2 (in the park)
Tapas-Bars	
Bar Citroen:	In the park
Restaurante Los Monos:	Paseo de la palmera
Restaurante Juliá:	Paseo de la palmera

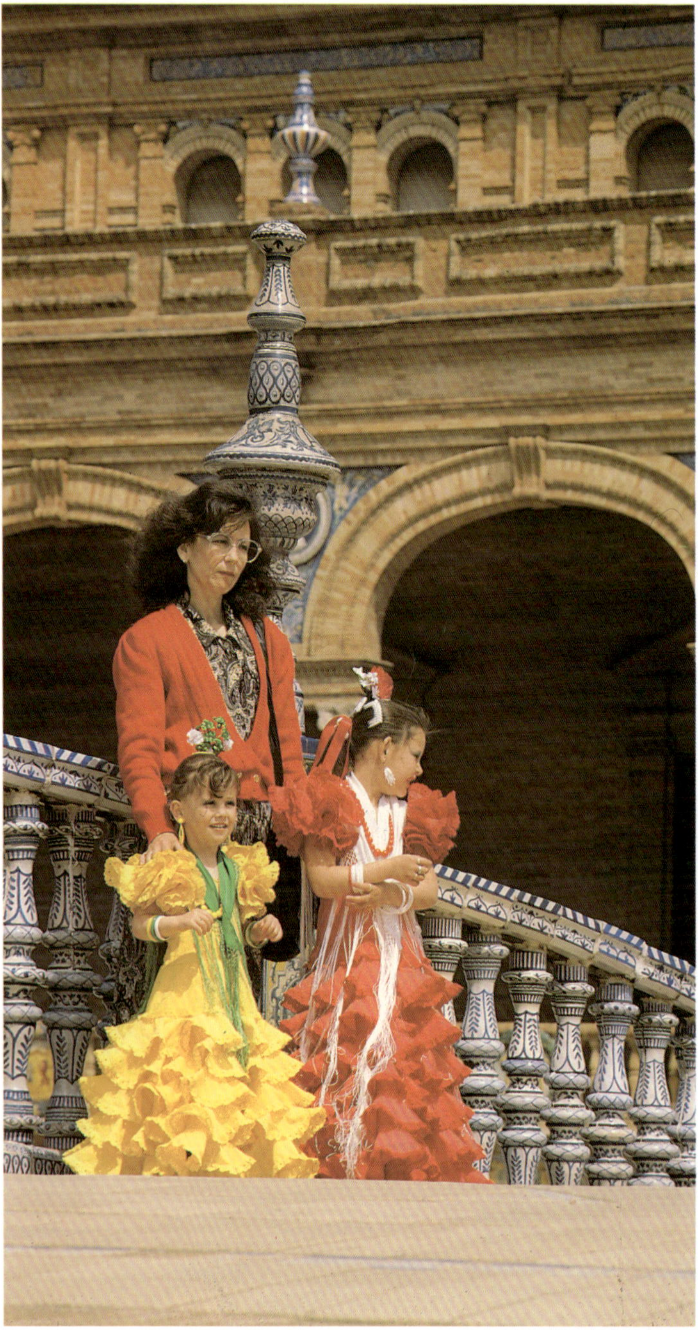

Typical costumes at Plaza de España.

ROUTE 7: MARIA LUISA PARK

If we stand on the plaza Puerta de Jerez, which we visited previously, we will see a long, wide street called calle San Fernando.

Alfonso XIII Hotel

The first building on the right, with a garden in front, is the Alfonso XIII Hotel, a lovely edifice designed by brilliant architect José Espiau Muñoz, for the Iberoamerican Exhibition of 1929. It is a splendid palace rather than a hotel, built in brick, marble and glazed tiles, with tapestried reception rooms and staircases with handrails in noble wood. The furniture, pictures, chandeliers, lamps and tapestries are worthy of a royal palace and this hotel can be counted among the grandest in the world.

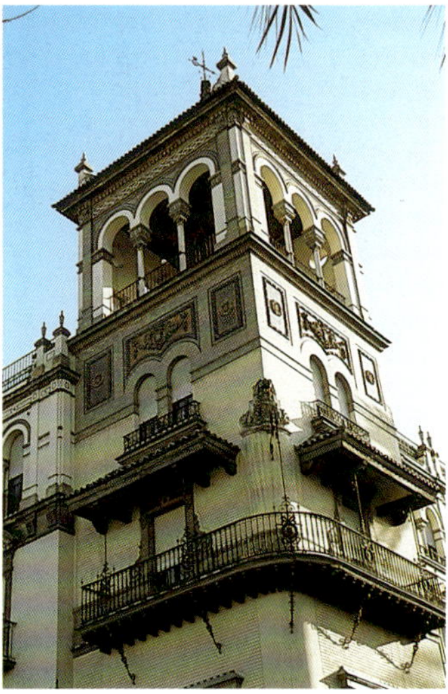

Alfonso XIII Hotel.

The Real Fábrica de Tabacos

On the same sidewalk as the Alfonso XIII Hotel is the beautiful building of the Real Fábrica de Tabacos (Royal Tobacco Factory), now the seat of the University of Seville. In front of it there is a beautiful iron gate, its sections supported by pilasters decorated with Triana glazed tiles, with the words «Real Fábrica de Tabacos».

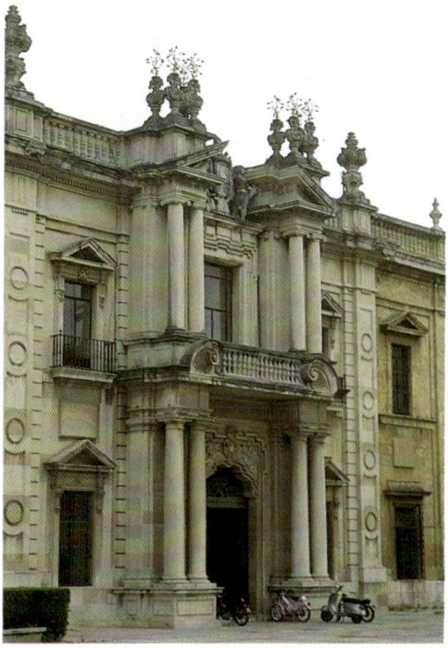

Royal Tobacco Factory.

To understand the grandiosity of this building, which is 250 meters long and 180 meters wide (820 ft. x 590 ft.), we have to bear in mind that in the16th and 17th centuries the Spanish Empire was the largest ever in World History: half of the present-day United

States of America, Mexico, all Central and South America, plus the Pacific Islands, comprising the Philippines, Marianas, Caroline, Palaos, Guadalcanal, etc., plus the coast of Macao in China, the island of Taiwan, which the Spaniards named Formosa, all the western coast of India with Goa as its capital, the islands of the Indian Ocean and Mozambique, the Cape, Angola and Oran in Africa.

When tobacco was discovered in America and Europeans started to smoke, Spain was the only nation with territories whose climate allowed this product to be cultivated, so that until the 19th century Spain held an absolute monopoly over tobacco.

Given the extent of this trade, the first ground tobacco and cigar factory in the world was built in Seville. It was located in what is now the plaza del Cristo de Burgos, opposite the church of San Pedro.

However, although the factory was large, it soon became too small for the growing volume of its products, and thus King Ferdinand VI in the 18th century, decided to build another factory, larger and adapted to the new manufacturing techniques of the times.

In this construction, the architects Juan Vandemberg, Vicente Catalán and Bengoechea participated. Work was interrupted several times and was not finished until 1757, being at the time the building with the largest constructed surface space in Spain. It was surrounded by a military moat for its defense, still in existence except on this street, where it was filled up in the 19th century. The moat is a great piece of engineering and was designed by Vandemberg.

The portal is superb, as is the whole building. Carved in stone with a Roman arch, the door is flanked by two columns supporting the upper-floor balcony. This, flanked by another two columns, is crowned by a triangular pediment with the royal coat of arms, and over this Fame playing the trumpet tops the whole building, with large stone vases containing bunches of bronze lilies on either side.

If the façade is colossal, so is the inside of the building, which has no less than 44 courtyards and huge galleries. The halls where tobacco was ground by means of millstones moved by mules are today lecture rooms and libraries, housing since 1955 the Schools of Law, Science and others of the University of Seville, besides the Rectorate, the Secretariat and the University Assembly Hall.

It is a building of which Seville is proud.

The statue of El Cid

We follow this calle de San Fernando, recalling that in front of this façade the first act of the opera »Carmen» takes place, since Carmen was a cigarmaker in the Tobacco Factory and it was precisely on this street where she met Don

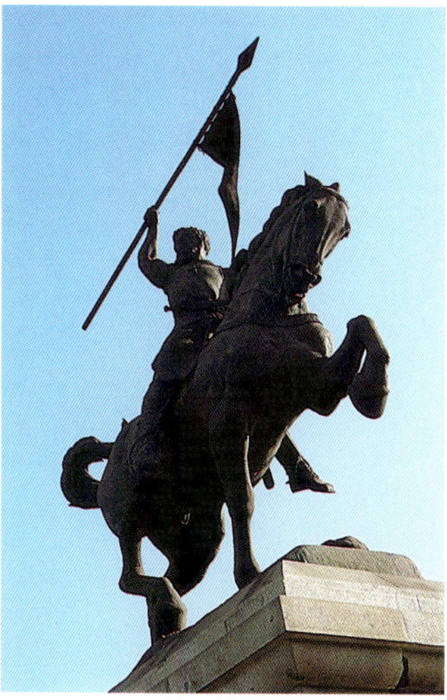

Statue of El Cid.

José, a sergeant in the Dragoon Company guarding the building.

At the end of the street, we turn right, bordering the moat of the Tobacco Factory, where the stone sentry boxes formerly used to guard the Factory can still be seen. And thus we come to the glorieta del Cid.

In the center, with the University on one side and the gardens on the other, there is a magnificent statue of El Cid, Rodrigo Diaz de Vivar, on a heavy stone pedestal.

The statue is extraordinarily vigorous, due to the sturdiness of the horse as well as the warrior's posture, brandishing a spear with banner. Such a vigorous monument was made by a «weak» woman, Anna Huntington, the sculptress wife of the American multimillionaire Huntington, the founder of the Spanish Society in New York.

Mrs. Huntington not only made the monument, but also donated it to Seville as a reminder that El Cid came to Seville as ambassador of King Alfonso VI to Almotamid, the Moorish King. On the pedestal, engraved on stone, is a text from a Moslem chronicle which says that El Cid, terror of Islamism, for his extraordinary courage, was an authentic miracle of God on earth.

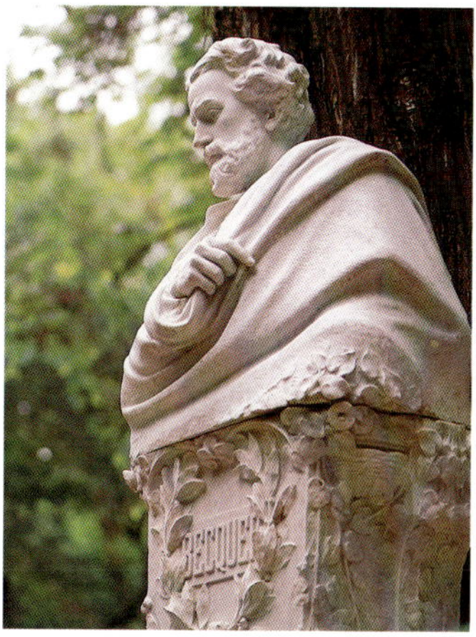

Bust of Bécquer.

The Plaza de España

On Isabel la Católica avenue we enter Maria Luisa park. Part of these beautiful Sevillian gardens formerly belonged to the Palacio de San Telmo (Palace), while the rest was orchards and countryside. At the beginning of this century, the Infanta María Luisa de Orleans donated San Telmo

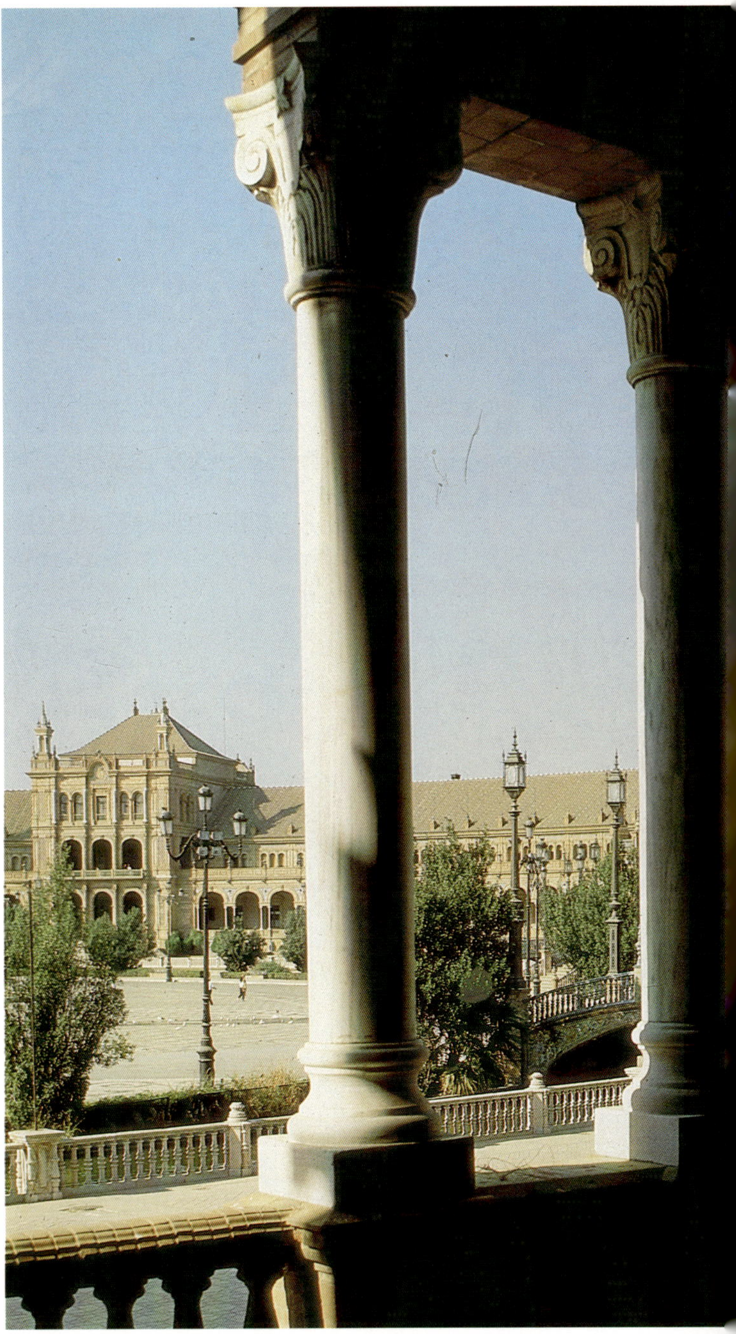

Plaza de España.

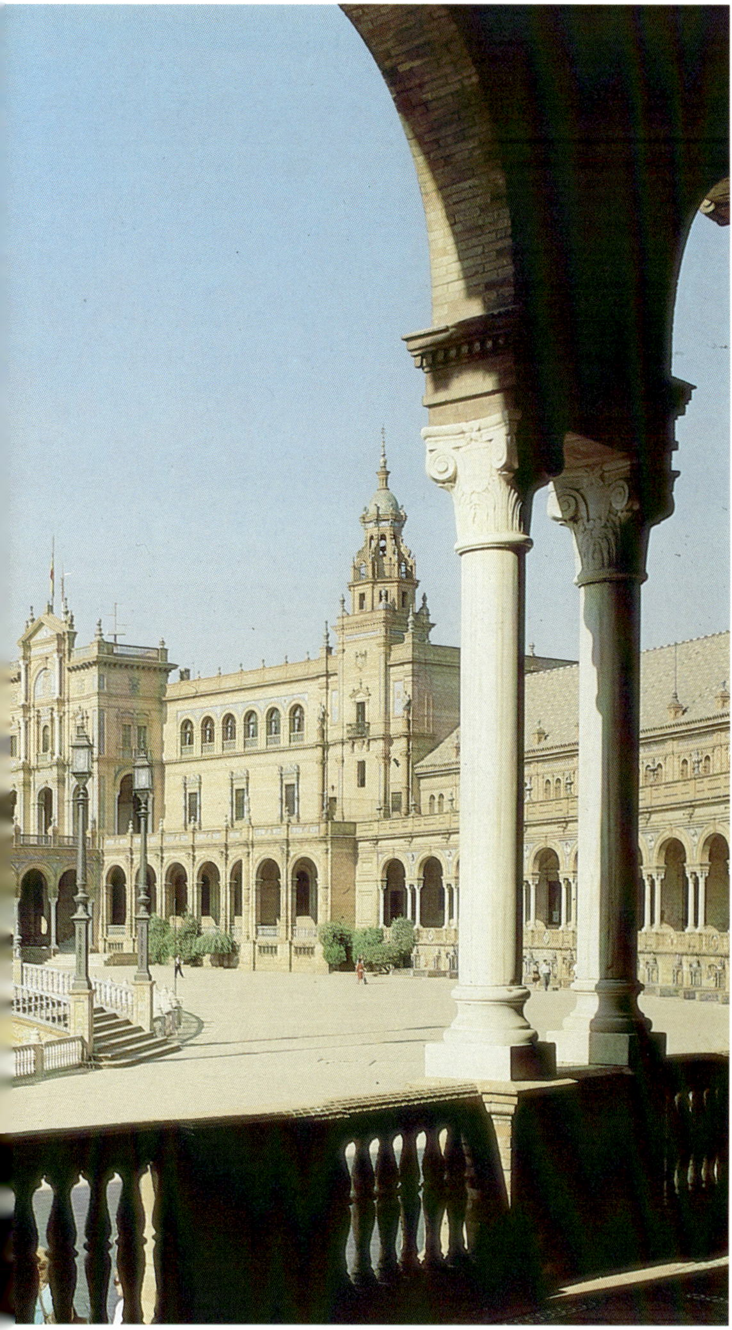

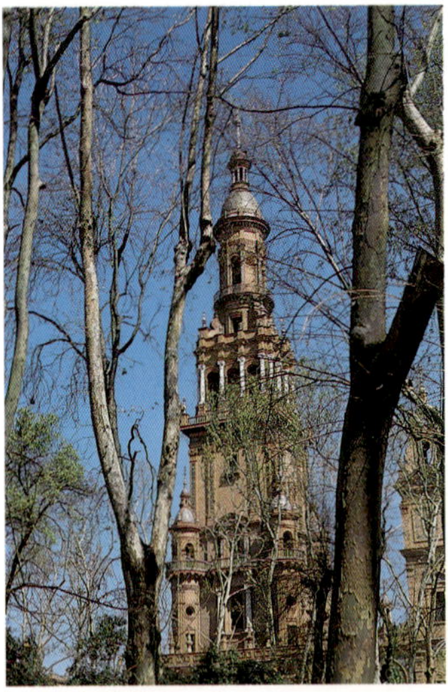

rried out by the Artillery Colonel Luis Rodriguez Caso, while architect Aníbal Gonzalez was responsible for the plans and the construction of the main buildings.

The main structure of the exhibition was the Plaza de España, which we will soon reach and which earned Anibal González his prestigue.

The Plaza de España is a semicircle, with a large fountain in the center. The plaza has a diameter of 220m (656 ft.) and is bordered by a small canal spanned by bridges de-

Two views of Plaza de España.

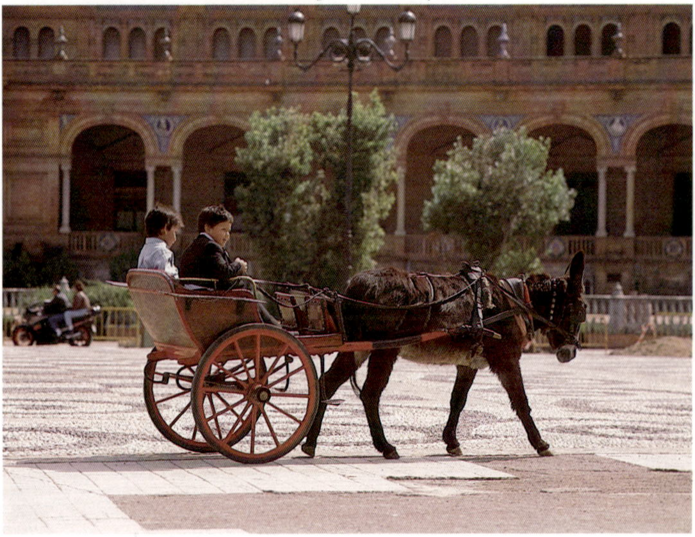

palace to the Church to set up a Seminary, and most of the gardens to the city, as a public park for the people of Seville.

It was decided to install the Iberoamerican Exhibition of 1929 in this park, its general design and layout being ca-

corated with Triana ceramic tiles.

Behind this, the semicircular building stands with two beautiful towers at the northern and southern ends. It has a long two-storied colonnaded gallery with a three-storied

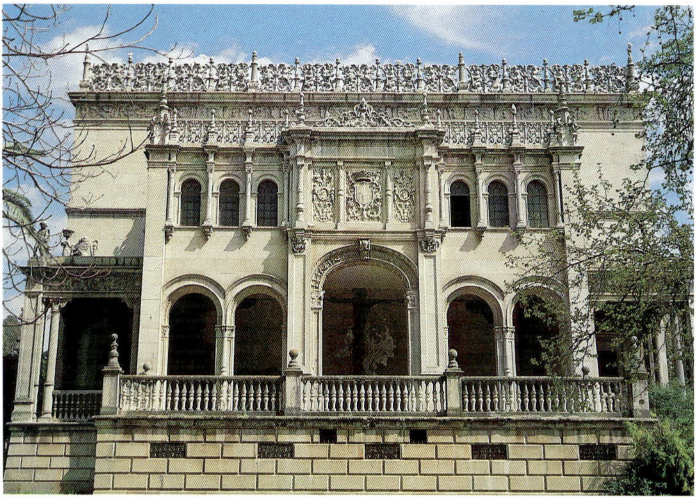

Archeological Museum.

structure in the center topped by two small turrets.

The whole construction is in brick combined with white marble and decorated with ceramic tiles, and it could be regarded as the epitome of Sevillian regional style.

At the foot of the colonnade there is a walk with benches decorated in ceramic tiles and over each of them, a large panel, also tiled, with a historical painting relating to one of the Spanish provinces.

Since the 1929 Exhibition, the Plaza de España has been used for administrative offices.

Plaza de América

Following Isabel la Católica avenue to the glorieta de Covadonga, and then Don Pelayo and La Gomera avenues, we reach the plaza de America, all of it the work of Aníbal González. Here we find the Royal Pavilion, in Gothic style, now the Delegation of the Ministry of Education and Science, the Fine Arts Pavilion, now the Museo Arqueológico Provincial (Provincial Archeological Museum), and the Mudejar Pavilion, today the Museo de Artes y Costumbres Populares (Museum of Popular Arts and Customs).

The Museo Arqueológico

The Museo Arqueológico (Archeological Museum) has one of the best collections of Roman sculpture in Spain, mainly from the ruins of Itálica, including a sculpture of Hermes or Mercury which presides over the Roman Hall, considered the best statue of Roman times in Spain, statues of Trajan and Hadrian and the beautiful Aphrodite, conside-

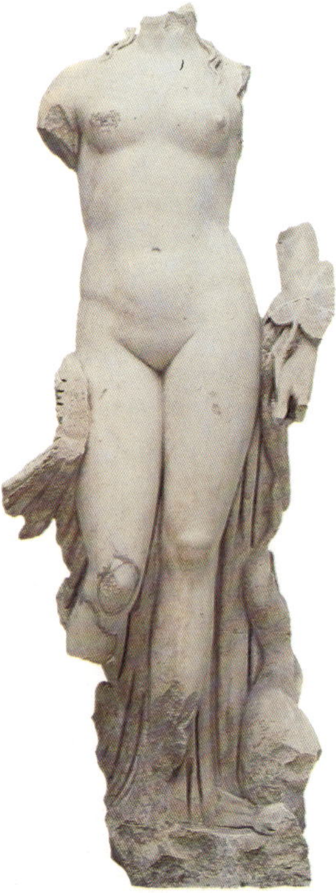

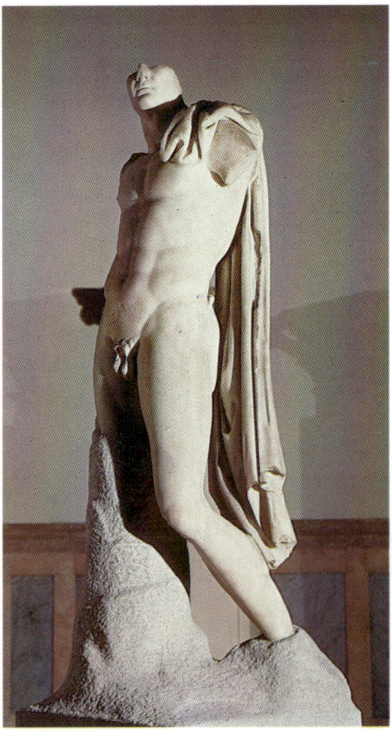

Trajan.

◁ *Aphrodite from Ithaca.*

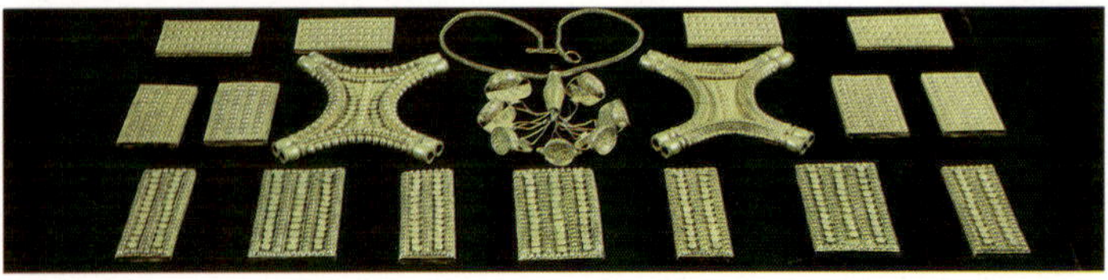

The Carambolo Treasure.

red by many the finest marble body of a woman to be found in Spain.

Other halls show Roman mosaics and sculptures dating from pre-Roman civilizations. Among the most valuable objects, we should mention the «Carambolo Treasure», a set of embossed pieces of gold comprising the ceremonial dress of a Tartessian king and queen or possibly a priestess.

The pieces include a complete belt, wide bracelets, two breastplates and a gold thread from which an ornament of metal disks hangs, a unique piece of gold art from Spanish protohistory.

The Museo de Artes y Costumbres Populares

The Mudejar Pavilion is built in splendid Arab-Andalusian style. It houses the Folklore Museum where the artistic ceramic rooms are worth a visit, as they display very notable pieces. The room containing typical costumes from all the regions of Andalusia is also interesting.

It should be pointed out that Andalusia has a great variety of typical costumes, although in general only the flounced dress seen at the Seville April Fair is well known, along with the men's outfit consisting of short jacket, country boots and wide-brimmed hat. In Andalusia there are over ten different types of men's hats and up to twenty different suits, as well as dozens of women's dresses which bear no resemblance to the fa-

Museum of Folklore and Arts.

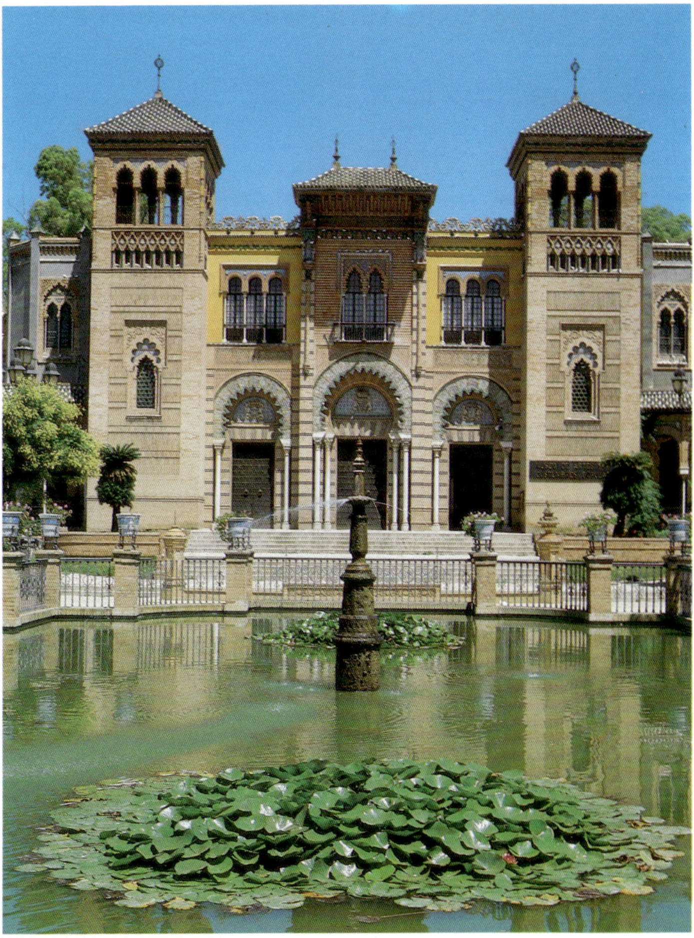

mous Flamenco skirts. This wealth of costumes was on the verge of disappearing and has been saved greatly thanks to this museum.

There is also a collection of farm tools that mechanization has made obsolete, as well as ancient weights and measures and home furnishings. Whole rooms have been kept intact with their furniture of past centuries, among them some very interesting examples from the Romantic age and a lovely collection of needlework, embroidery, crochet work and hand-woven pieces.

All of this, together with paintings by good artists from different times help to grahpically explain uses, crafts and old customs.

The Costurero de la Reina

Leaving the plaza de America on the opposite side, we find the Paseo de las Delicias and keeping right we will see, at the beginning of a wall, a small building with corners like round towers, built of two-colored brick. After this building, a long wall commences.

This little building is known as the Costurero de la Reina (Queen's Sewing cabinet). It was the guard house of the Palacio de San Telmo when members of the royal family where in residence.

According to tradition, around 1875, the daughter of the Duke of Montpensier, Merceditas Orleans y Borbón, used to climb up to the flat roof of this building on winter mornings to sun herself on

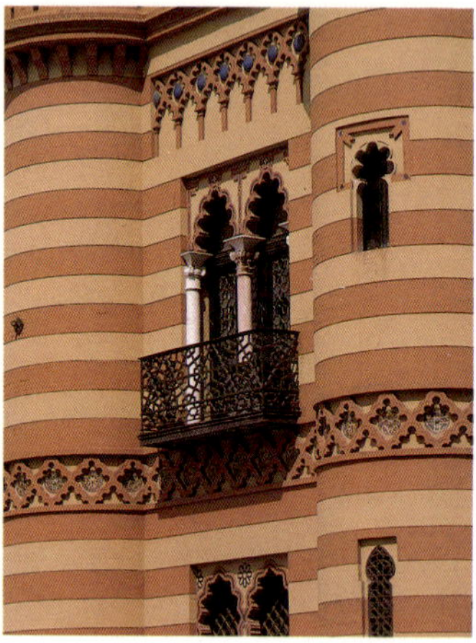

The Queen's Sewing Cabinet.

doctor's orders and spend her days sewing and embroidering. Merceditas married King Alfonso XII, her cousin, who during the courtship also often went up onto the roof terrace of the tiny building to keep his fiancée company.

When they married, she became Queen of Spain, but died shortly afterwards of tuberculosis, which she had suffered from adolescence. During the last months of her life, the doctors made her leave Madrid to escape from the cold weather of the capital, and she came to Seville in the hope that the more temperate climate would cure her. As when she was child, she again used to sit in the sunshine on the flat roof of the guard's pavilion. This is why the building, today a tourism office, is known as the «Queen's Sewing Cabinet».

Palacio de San Telmo

The wall that starts here borders the jardines de San

Telmo (gardens) and following it we reach the magnificent palace of San Telmo.

This building was constructed at the end of the 17th century as a Nautical School for navigators sailing the Route to the Indies, known as the Seminary of San Telmo. Actually the patron saint of seamen is not Saint Telmo, but Saint Elm, apparently a Catalan saint.

The building was possibly designed by the architect Antonio Rodríguez, who started it in 1682. Construction work lasted all through the 18th century, with the participation of the Figueroa family of architects: Leonardo, his son Matías, and his grandson Antonio. The portal is by Leonardo in late Baroque style, abundantly decorated, in three courses. The first is the entrance flanked by six very elaborate pillars. The second is the grand balcony, under a flat arch, and also flanked by six columns. The third course consists of a belfry with a central arch, four pillars on the sides and a graceful pediment.

Under an arch doubling as a niche, a statue of Saint Telmo can be seen with a small boat in his hand. The building became purposeless when Spain lost her Empire and the colonies, which included all of South America, Mexico, and half of the United States. Navigators were no longer needed to sail to the Indies and the impoverished nation could not afford to keep up the school. Therefore, in 1850, the State sold the building to the Duke of Montpensier, Antonio de Orleans, who was married to the infanta doña María Luisa

Façade of the Royal Pavilion.

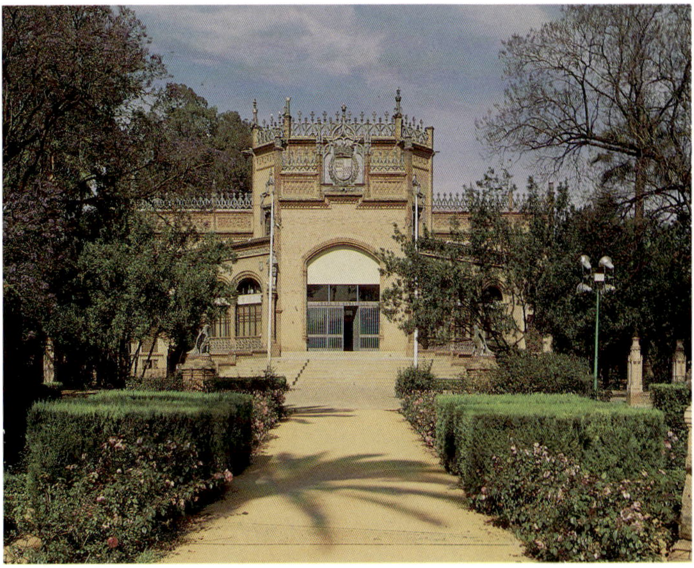

de Borbón, sister to Queen Isabella II.

The Montpensiers turned what had been a nautical school into a very handsome palace and rivalry between the two sisters made the Montpensier household compete with the Court in Madrid in luxury and splendour of their palace, as well as in the brilliance of

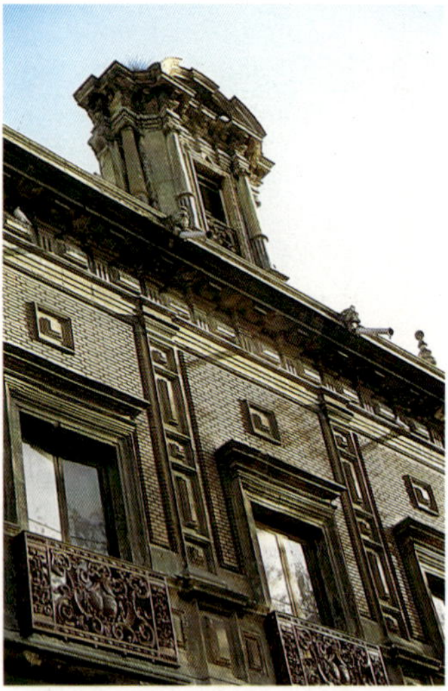

Palace of Saint Telmo.

their parties, concerts and receptions.

As a patron of the arts, the Infanta María Luisa commissioned Antonio Susillo to make sculptures of the most famous personalities in the history of Seville, which we can admire today on the balustrade to the left of the main entrance.

These statues, from left to right, represent Fray Bartolomé de las Casas; the soldier Pedro Afán de Ribera; the painter Murillo; the linguistic scholar Benito Arias Montano; Captain Luis Daoiz; poet Fernando de Herrera «the Divine»; the historian Luis Ortiz de Zúñiga; the dramatist Lope de Rueda; the founder of the Hospital de la Caridad, Miguel de Mañara;the painter Velázquez ; the soldier Ponce

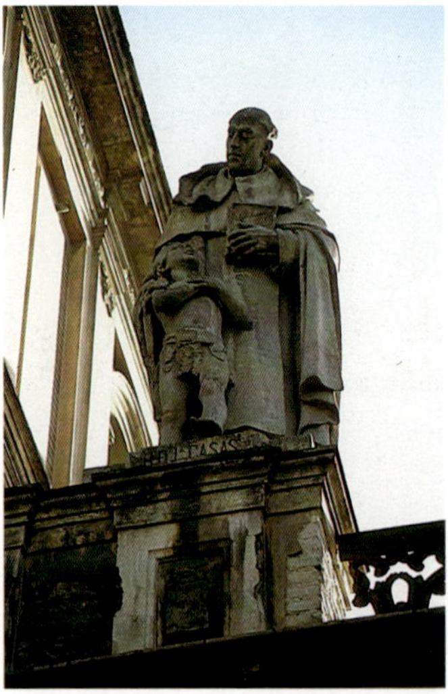

Bust of Fray Bartolomé de las Casas.

de León, who conquered Granada, and the sculptor Martínez Montañés, all of them Sevillians, either by birth or in their lives and works.

The palace of Saint Telmo now belongs to the Council (Regional Goverment) of Andalusia and is the president's residence.

And now we return to puerta de Jerez via the avenida de Roma.

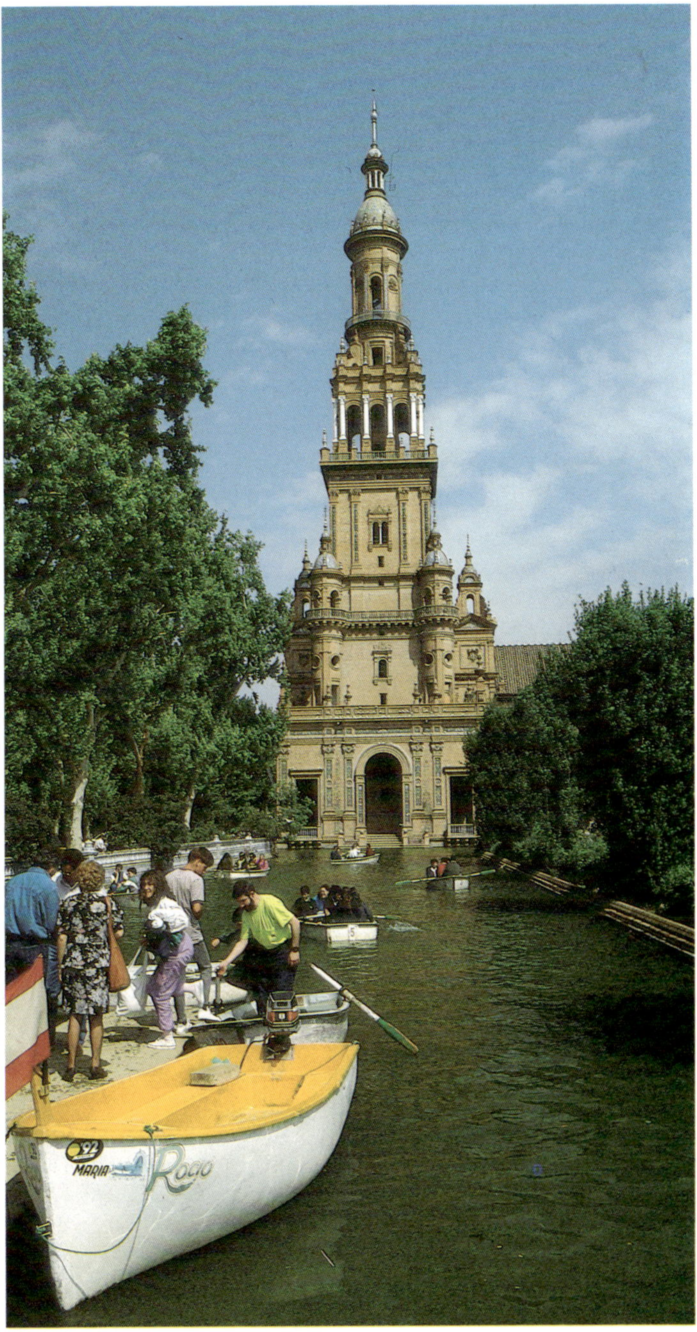

Boats at Plaza de España.

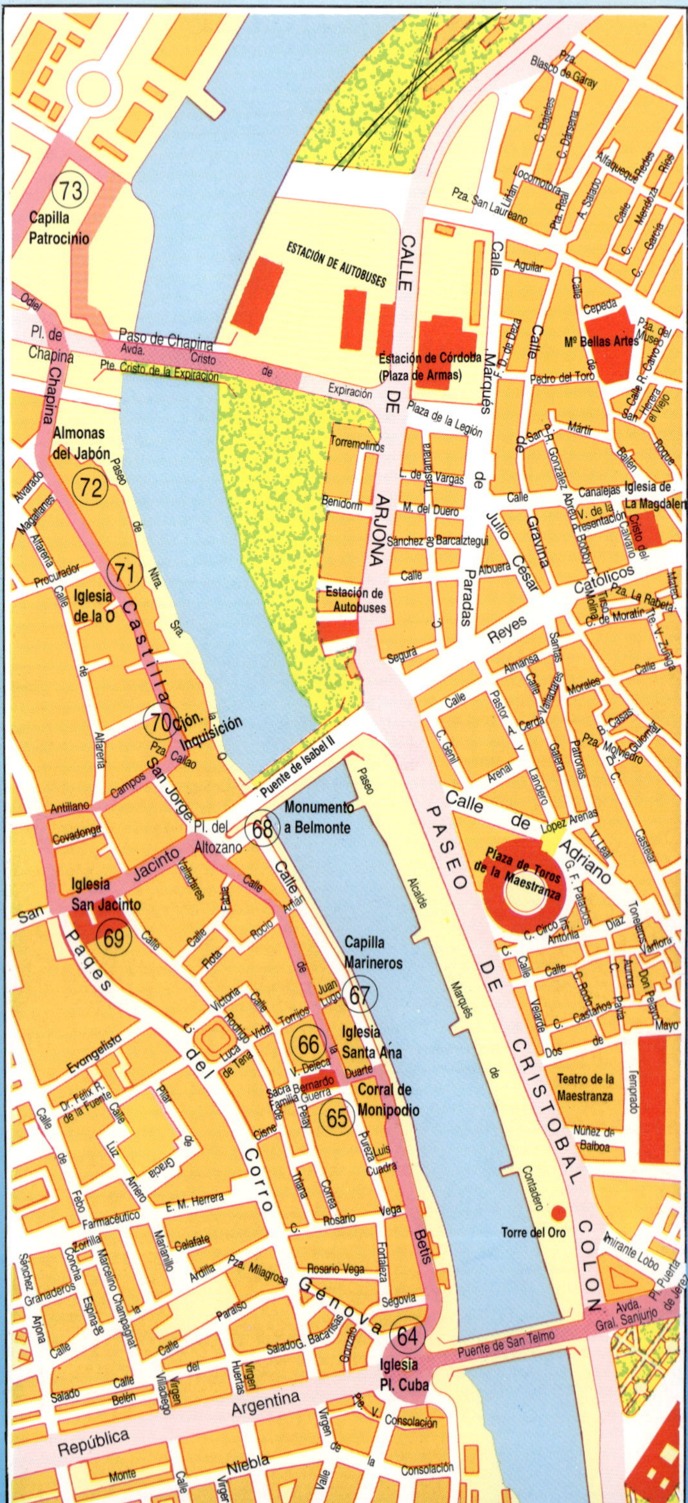

73
Capilla Patrocinio
Odiel
Pl. de Chapina
Paso de Chapina
Avda. Cristo de Expiración
Pte. Cristo de la Expiración
Chapina
Almonas del Jabón
72
Alvarado
Magallanes
Alfarería
Procurador
71
Iglesia de la O
Castilla
Paseo de Ntra. Sra. de la O
70
Cjón. Inquisición
Pza. Callao
Campos
San Jorge
Antillano
Covadonga
Pl. del Altozano
68
Monumento a Belmonte
Puente de Isabel II
Jacinto
Iglesia San Jacinto
69
San Jacinto
Pagés del Corro
Valladares
Fabié
Calle
Pinta
Rocío
Victoria
Rodrigo
Vida
Torrijos
Calle Antillano Campos
Callejón de Juan Lugo
Capilla Marineros
67
66
Iglesia Santa Ana
V. Deleca
Duarte
Sacra Familia
Bernardo Guerra
Corral de Monipodio
65
Pelay
Cisne
Pureza
Luis Cuadra
Evangelista
Dr. Félix R. de la Fuente
Pilar
Gracia
Luca de Tena
Luz
Arriero
Febo
Farmacéutico
E. M. Herrera
Calafate
Marianillo
Ardilla
Pza. Milagrosa
Triana
Correa
Rosario
Vega
Rosario Vega
Fortaleza
Segovia
Betis
Génova
Paraíso
Salado
G. Bacarisas
Gonzalo
64
Iglesia Pl. Cuba
Puente de San Telmo
Sánchez
Granaderos
Concha
Zorrilla
Marcelino Champagnat
Espinel
Arjona
Calle Salado
Calle Belén
Villadiego
Virgen del Huertas
Virgen
Argentina
República
Monte
Niebla
Virgen
Valle
Virgen de la Consolación
Consolación
ESTACIÓN DE AUTOBUSES
CALLE DE ARJONA
Estación de Córdoba (Plaza de Armas)
Expiración
Plaza de la Legión
Torremolinos
Benidorm
L. de Vargas
Trastámara
M. del Duero
Sánchez Barcaiztegui
Estación de Autobuses
Segura
Paseo Alcalde Marqués de Contadero
Torre del Oro
PASEO DE CRISTOBAL COLON
Calle de Adriano
Plaza de Toros de la Maestranza
López Arenas
G. F. Palacios
C. Circo
Ins. Antonia Díaz
Calle Valarde
Dos de Mayo
C. Castaños
Teatro de la Maestranza
Núñez de Balboa
Temprado
Almirante Lobo
Avda. Gral. Sanjurjo
Pl. Puerta de Jerez
Pza. Blasco de Garay
C. Bajeles
C. Dársena
Locomotora
Pza. Real
Lirio
Pza. San Laureano
Alfaqueque
Redes
Ríos
A. Salado
Calle Mendoza
C. García
Aguilar
Calle Cepeda
Mº Bellas Artes
Pza. del Museo
R. Calvo
Calle Marqués de F. de Deza
Pedro del Toro
San Vicente
Herrera el Viejo
Mártir
Bailén
Roque
San P. R. González Abreu
Calle de Julio César
Gravina
Canalejas
Iglesia de La Magdalena
V. de la Presentación
Cristo del Calvario
Bobby
Molini
Tirso de Molina
Católicos
Reyes
Pza. La Rabeta
Moratín
Te. V. Zúñiga
Albuera
Calle Paradas
Almansa
Santas Patronas
Morales
Calle Pastor y Landero
A. Cerda
C. Genil
Arenal
Galera
Valladares
B. Casas
Pza. Molviedro
Gulomar
Castelar
V. Leal
Toneleros
Varflora
Aurora
Don Pelayo
C. Pavía
C. Bolo

ROUTE 8: TRIANA QUARTER

PLACES OF INTEREST

(64) **Church at Plaza de Cuba**
Former chapel of the Convent of Los Remedios, today office for the Expo'92.

(65) **Corral de Monipodio**
Meeting point for the Sevillian picaresque

(66) **Church of Santa Ana**
Vázquez de Leca, 12.
Opening hours: 9 to 10 and 19.30 to 21.
Closed in the mornings in summer.

(67) **Chapel of the Sailors**
Ancient 17th century chapel in which the Virgen de la Esperanza de Triana is venerated.

(68) **Monument to Belmonte**

(69) **Church of San Jacinto**
Convent of the Dominics.
San Jacinto, 47.
Opening hours: 9 to 10 and 19 to 20.30.

(70) **Inquisition Alley**
Remains of the building of the prisons of the Inquisition Tribunal, in which many famous people died, among them Torrigiano, the sculptor.

(71) **The Church of la O**
Contains images of the brotherhood of Our lady of la O.

(72) **Almonas del Jabón (Ancient soap industry)**
Main soap industry in Europe in the 16th century.

(73) **The «Cachorro» Chapel**
Contains the Christ of «el Cachorro».

STARTING POINT	Puerta de Jerez
EXIT TO NEXT ROUTE	By calle Pedro del Toro to the Plaza del Museo.

USEFUL ADDRESSES NEARBY

Chemists:	Castilla, 5 and 109 San Jacinto, 13 and 65
Photo Service:	Calles Asunción, Pza. de Cuba
Restaurante El Mero:	Betis, 1 and 3
Restaurante Ezcarray:	Salado, 57
Restaurante La Cala:	Salado, 11
Restaurante Banco del Salmón:	República Argentina, 13
Restaurante La Dorada:	Virgen de Aguas Santas, 6
Restaurante La Manola:	Virgen de Aguas Santas, 15
Restaurante La Montanera:	Sebastián el Cano, 16
Restaurante El Candil:	Almirante Carrero Blanco, 14
Restaurante Las Flores:	Plaza del Altozano
Restaurante La Encina:	Virgen de las Aguas Santas, 6
Bodega Jerezana:	Virgen de las Montañas, 1
Restaurante Rincón de Curro:	Virgen de Luján, 45
Restaurante Sebastián:	Virgen de las Montañas, 17
Restaurante San Marco:	Betis, 68. 18th century palace. International cuisine.
Tapas-Bars	
Bodega la Albariza:	Betis, 6. Especiality: shrimp omelette.
Casa Anselma:	Pagés del Corro, 49. Life sevillanas dance.
Bar Las Golondrinas:	Antillano Campos, 26. Typical tapas.

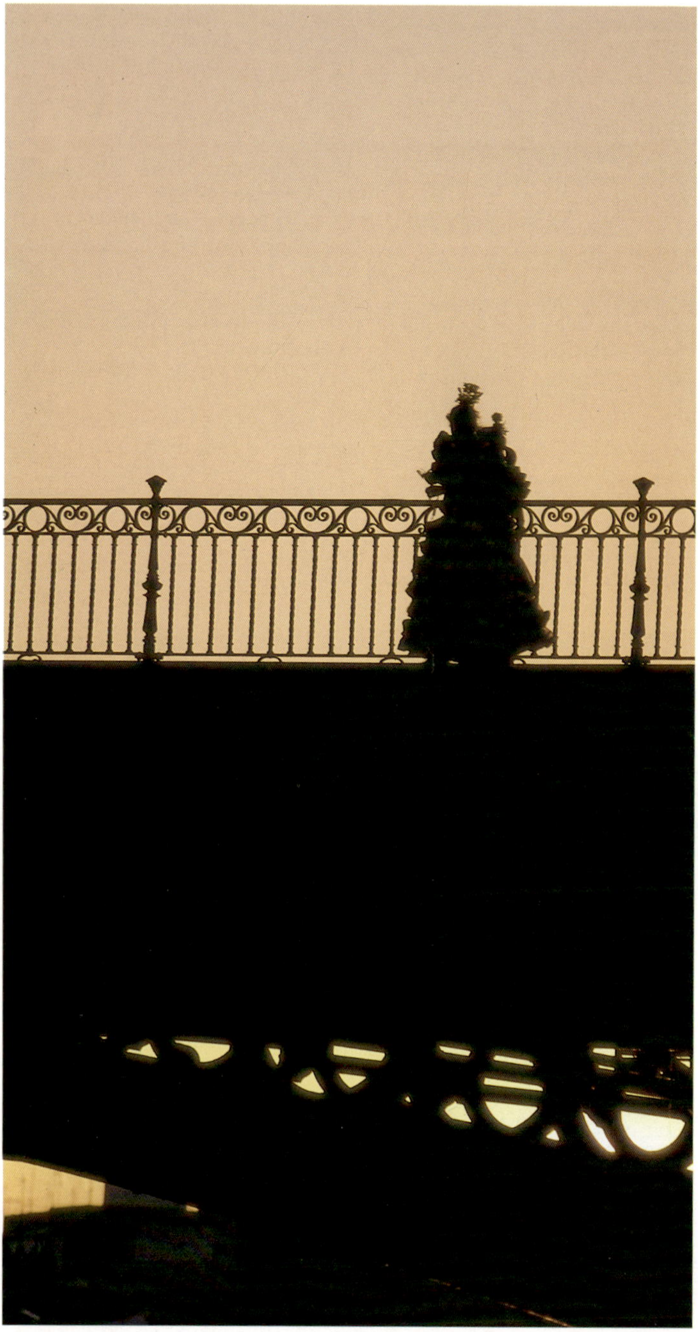

Triana Bridge.

ROUTE 8: BARRIO DE TRIANA

We start this route in plaza Puerta de Jerez, as before. Following Sanjurjo avenue, we cross the river by San Telmo bridge to reach Plaza de Cuba.

Plaza de Cuba

This is a universally known historical site. Even though its architecture is modern, since the buildings were constructed only twenty five years ago, the land they stand on was in the 16th century the Muelle de las Mulas, from where the first ships sailed for the Indies and to where they returned.

To our left, we have a small religious-looking building, the chapel of the former convent of Nuestra Señora de los Remedios, which after the secularization of the monasteries was acquired by a prominent citizen, Rafael González Abreu, who turned it into the Spanish-Cuban Institute. More recently it has been used to house the offices of Expo '92. On one of the side walls, facing the river, there is a large plaque recalling one of the great exploits of mankind, comparable then to what was

Expo '92 Offices.

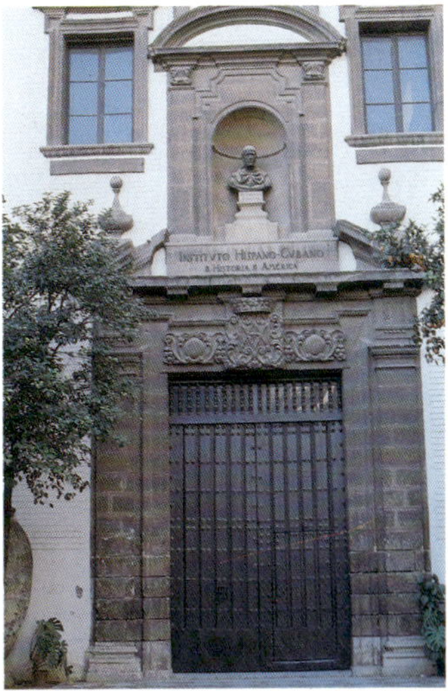

Plaza de Cuba.

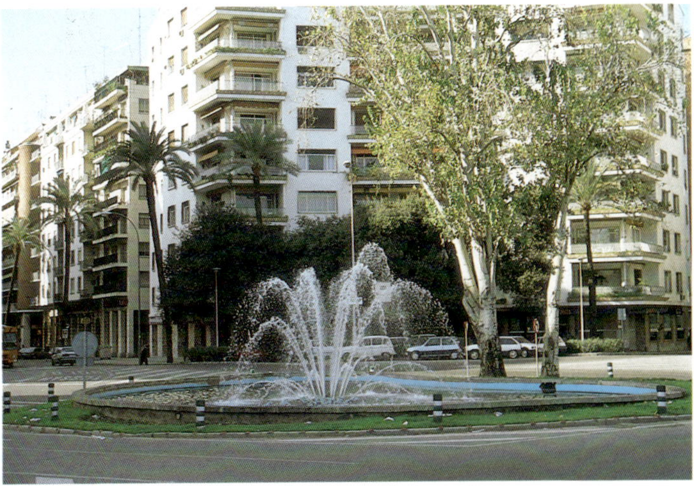

the first trip to the Moon in our days. Let us read the text:

«On the 10th day of August of the year 1519, there sailed forth from this shore of the Guadalquivir and site known as the Wharf of the Mules, the ships Trinidad, San Antonio, Concepción, Santiago and Santa María de la Victoria, commanded by Hernando de Magallanes (Magellan), with the purpose of finding the Strait which joined the South Sea and the North Sea.

«On the 8th day of September of the year 1522, having achieved that glorious enterprise, the Santa María de la Victoria, steered by Juan Sebastián Elcano, returned alone and battered to the same quay of the same port, after having sailed around the world for the first time».

Here was the first practical confirmation that the Earth was round, together with information concerning the size of our planet.

Calle Betis

On the opposite side of the plaza, that is, to the right as we cross San Telmo bridge, is calle

Night over the river bank.

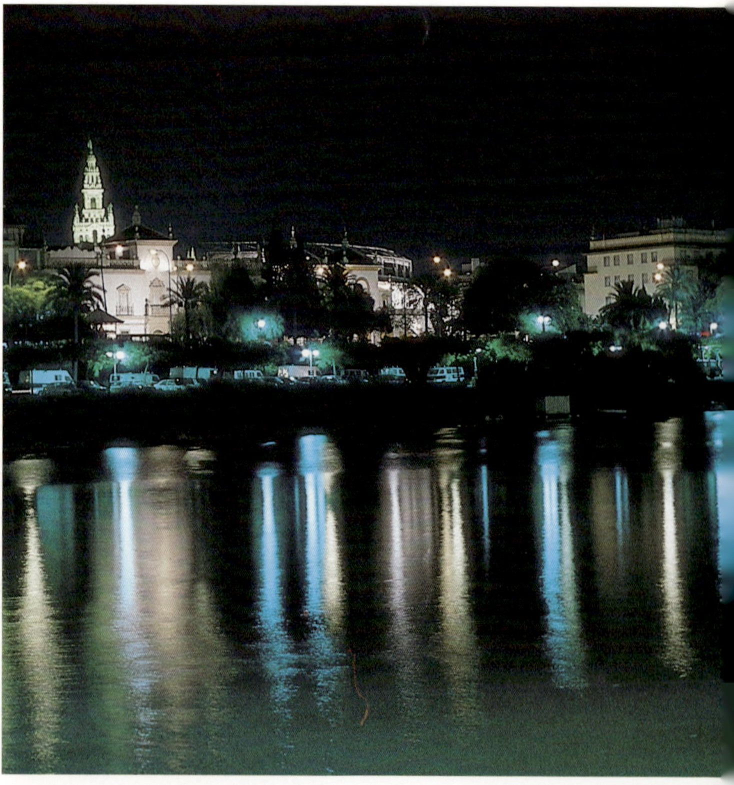

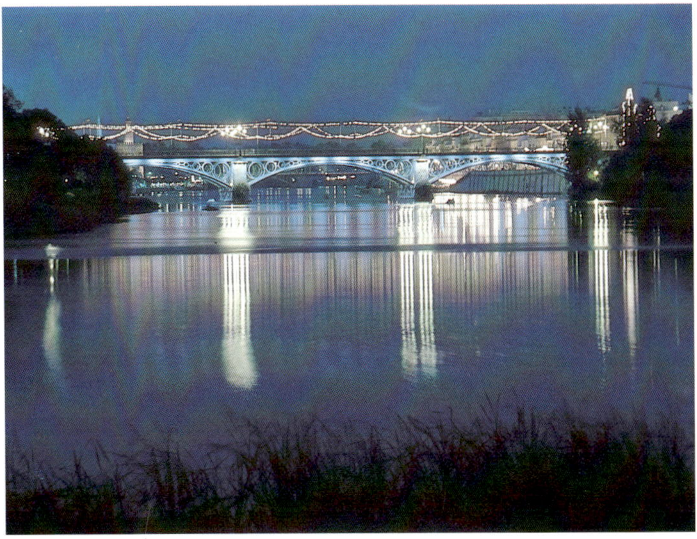

Triana Bridge.

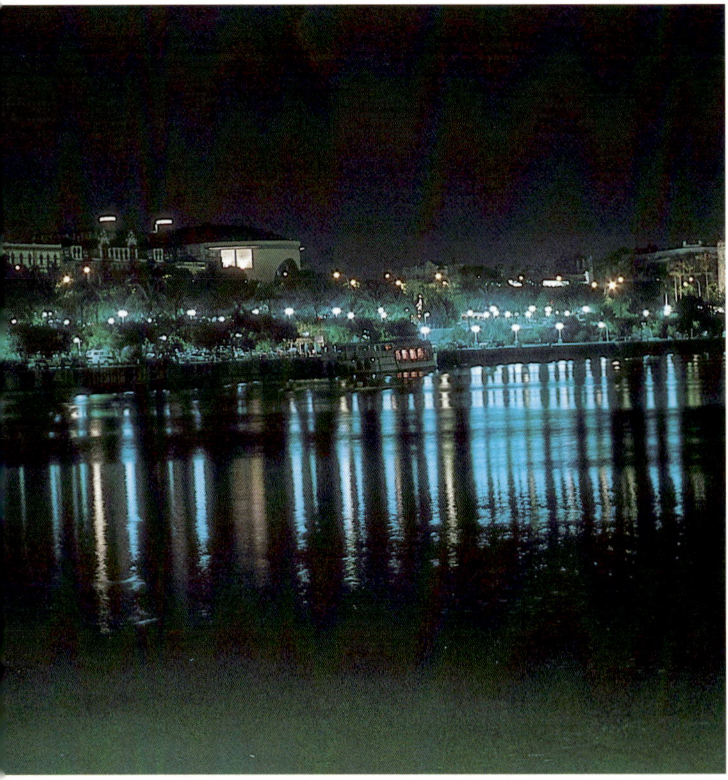

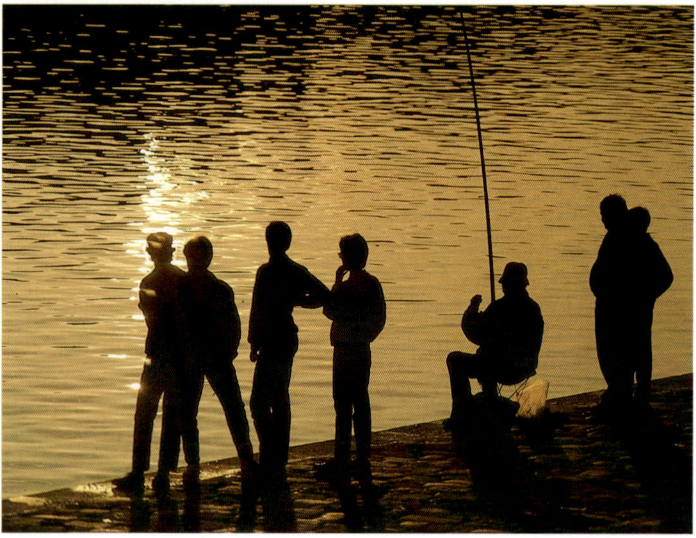

Fishing in the Guadalquivir.

Betis, so called because in ancient times, Betis was the name of the river, until the Arabs changed it to Guadalquivir. It is the street bordering the river from San Telmo bridge to Triana bridge.

From the railing we can observe at leisure the Torre del Oro and the old houses of Seville, with the Giralda and spires of convents and churches emerging from among them.

A few boats sail the river and it is easy to imagine what this place was like during the 16th and 17th centuries, when frigates, corvettes, vessels and ships of all types crowded its banks twice a year when the Fleet of the Indies sailed in.

Thus Lope de Vega writes:

Y aún otro mundo está en ella
y esto no es cuento ni engaño,
que dos veces al año
se entran las Indias por ella
(And there is still another world in it and this is neither tale nor lie that twice a year the Indies come through it.)

The Guadalquivir was also a place of leisure when the fleet was not in. The young people of Seville used the river for their entertainment, turning it, as Torres Naharro says, into «a jovial Guadalquivir» (gay Guadalquivir). Lope de Vega also alludes to it in a famous poem:

Ay río de Sevilla
que bien pareces
lleno de velas blancas
y ramos verdes.

Barcos engalanados
van a Triana
el primero de todos
me lleva el alma.

(Oh river of Seville how well you look full of white sails and green boughs Vessels bedecked sail to Triana the first of all takes my soul along).

To the left we have Gonzalo Segovia street, and a bit further Troya street. The space in between these streets was a fortress in Moslem times, of which there were ruins until the 19th century, and so strong was its mortar that the street behind it was called Argamasón street. Today it is called Fortaleza street. From the Torre del Oro to this fortress, a sturdy chain was stretched out at night by means of a boat, closing the port and preventing ships from entering. This chain, together with a pontoon bridge situated where Triana bridge is today, was broken by the ship that Admiral Bonifaz smashed into it, in order to incommunicate Seville and Triana, and thus capture the port, which enabled King Ferdinand to conquer Seville.

A tile on the corner of Troya street tells us that this is where Miguel de Cervantes situated his «corral de Monipodio», a meeting place of rogues and beggars. Maybe Cervantes was referring to the ruins of the fortress, which was used as a shelter by vagabonds. We follow Betis street and two streets beyond we find Duarte street. We take this one to reach the church of Santa Ana.

The church of Santa Ana

This church is known, and it is no exaggeration, as the cathedral of Triana. A beautifully proportioned church, it was built about 1260. Historians Ortiz de Zúñiga and Morgado both say that King Alfonso X the Wise raised this church in

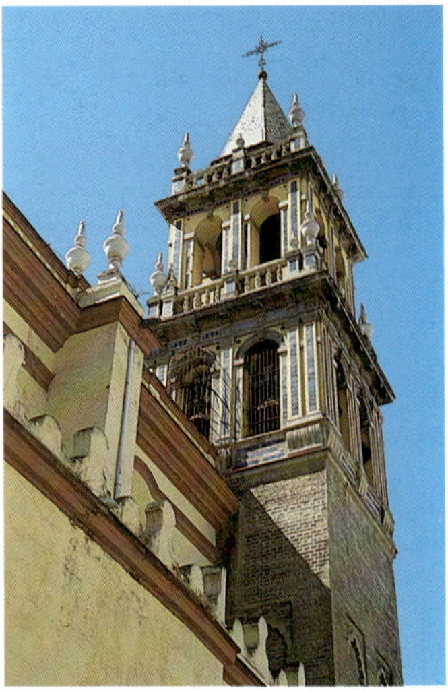

Church of Saint Anne.

thanksgiving for having been cured of a tumor he had in an eye. This version of both historians coincides with what the King himself narrates in his Cantigas , of having been miraculously cured of such an illness.

The church's style is transitional between Romanesque and Gothic. It has three aisles, the central one with an apse reinforced with buttresses and Gothic vaulted ceilings with ribbing. A beautiful church if it had not been somewhat spoilt when the choir was built across the nave. As in so many cathedrals and major churches, the choir was added in the 17th century.

The reredos in the chancel is splendid, with architecture in Renaissance style, decorated with heads of angels, small statues and volutes.

The sculpture was made by Nicolás Jurate and Nufro Orte-

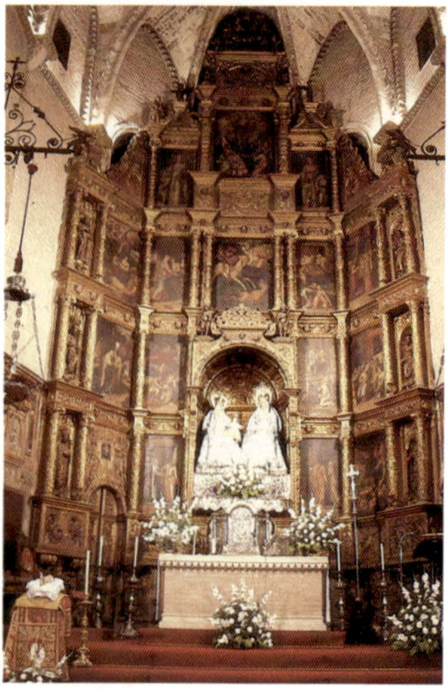

Altarpiece of Saint Anne's Church

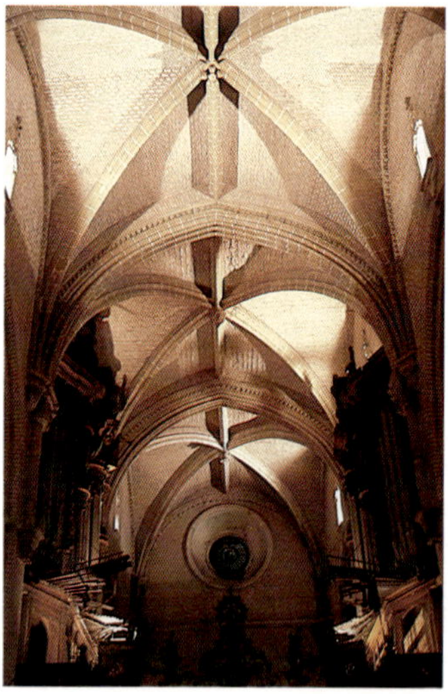

Vault of Saint Anne's Church.

ga in 1542. In the central niche, there is a group formed by Saint Anne, the Virgin and the Child Jesus, popularly called in Triana «God's grandmother, with her daughter and grandson».

The figures of Saint Anne and the Virgin date from the time of the construction of the church, that is, the 13th century. The Child Jesus is possibly from the 17th or 18th century.

The paintings in the 24 panels of the altarpiece are by Pedro de Campaña, Andrés Ramírez, Andrés Morín, Antón Pérez, Antón Sánchez and Pedro Jiménez in 1557. There are other interesting altarpieces in the chancel and also a small bas-relief, in alabaster, representing Saint Jerome, attributed to Torrigiano.

In the left hand aisle, the altar of Saints Justa and Rufina is very interesting, with dressed images dating from the 18th century. These are the patron saints of Triana, for they lived in this quarter in Roman times and suffered martyrdom under Diocletian.

In the right hand aisle there is, among other paintings, a polyptych of Saint Catherine, painted by Hernando de Sturmio in 1553. In several chapels there are valuable old Triana glazed tiles.

Among the most interesting works we should refer to a tomb in the right hand aisle, made of tiles representing the reclining body of a man, dressed in a loose yellow robe, green stockings and black shoes. This glazed tile tomb was the first one of this kind in Spain and it was made by the famous Italian ceramist Nicolás de Pisa, «Niculoso Pisano», in the year 1503. Pisano is, believed to have been the artist who raised tiles from their humble decorative function in socles and inlays to apply them artistically to painted altarpieces, incorporating them into Renaissance art.

There are also many interesting signs with information about the founders of different chapels, patrons paying for the altarpieces, etc.

This church has a magnificent silver mostrance made by Mateo Ximenez in the 17th century, which is taken out in procession on the eighth day after Corpus Christi, called the minor Corpus Christi.

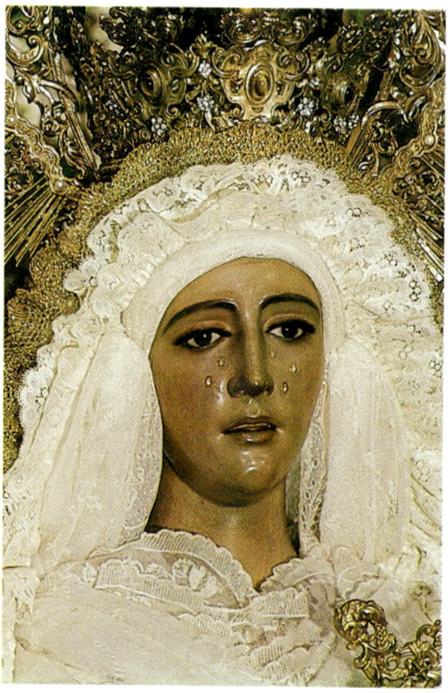

Our Lady of Hope of Triana.

Chapel of los Marineros

We leave the church of Santa Ana and turn into Pureza street, where the chapel of the Brotherhood of La Esperanza de Triana, also known as the capilla de los Marineros (chapel of the Sailors), is located.

Here the Cristo de las Tres Caídas and La Virgen de la Esperanza are venerated. The figure of Christ dates from the 17th century, and is attributed to Marcos Cabrera, a disciple of Jerónimo Hernández.

La Esperanza de Triana and Nuestra Señora de la Macarena are the two popular devotions in Seville. This Virgin is by an unknown artist, which casts a mysterious charm. We only know that Juan de Astorga restored it in the 19th century and that Castillo Lastrucci, redid her face in this century, as it had deteriorated in the course of time.

The remaining figures here are by Castillo Lastrucci.

The Brotherhood was founded in the 17th century when the two brotherhoods, that of the Christ of the Three Falls and that of Our Lady of Hope merged. The chapel also dates from the 17th century and has been restored.

Plaza del Altozano

Following along Pureza street we reach the plaza del Altozano. This is a place with memories of various ages in history. From the Moslem era, we are reminded of the pontoon bridge broken by Admiral Bonifaz, substituted in the 19th century by today's Isabel II or Triana bridge. Every year during Holy Week, this bridge is crossed by the procession of the Esperanza de Triana and the Cristo de la Expiración, called el «Cachorro», the waters of the

Guadalquivir reflecting the light from thousands of candles.

But the dramatic and sinister memory of the Inquisition also lurks here at plaza del Altozano. All the land today occupied by the market was formerly the Castle of Saint George, where the Holy Inquisition had its prison.

Altozano was during the 19th century one of the meeting places of Flamenco singers, mainly at the «Taberna de Berrinche» on the corner of San Jacinto and San Jorge streets. Bullfighters also gathered here. That is why, on one side, there is a monument to the famous matador Juan Belmonte, a modernist statue in bronze, not particularly successful.

We will take San Jacinto street down from Altozano, which leads us to the Chapel of La Estrella (The Star) on the left a bit below the corner of Juan Romero street.

The chapel of La Estrella reminds us of a circumstance repeated throughout the history of Sevillian brotherhoods. The brotherhoods were usually first set up in a parish church, but in time, they became troublesome to the parish priest with their religious services and the relative familiarity with which the members went about the church, altering the accustomed life of the parish. The result was that in time the brotherhoods built their own churches and left the parishes where they has been established.

This chapel of the Brotherhood of The Star is very new, hardly twenty years old. The beautiful image of Our Lady of the Star, used to be in the church of San Jacinto. The figures venerated in this chapel are those of the Brotherhood: Christ of Sorrows, seated, waiting while the executioners prepare His cross, by the famous sculptor Jerónimo Hernández, and Our Lady of the Star, attributed to Martínez Montañés.

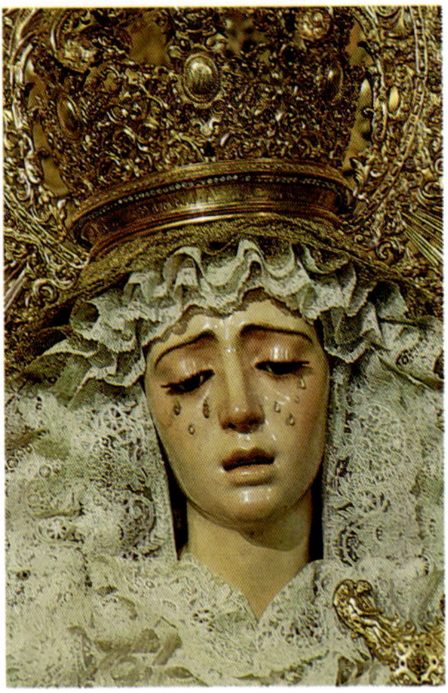

Our Lady of the Star.

Church of San Jacinto

Following the same left sidewalk of San Jacinto street, a bit further down, we find the grand monastery of San Jacinto, whose church we will visit.

The grandiose church has three aisles, with a high chapel and sacristies. The construction dates from the 18th century and was raised by architects of the Figueroa family. The style is proper of the 18th century, with ribbed vaulting.

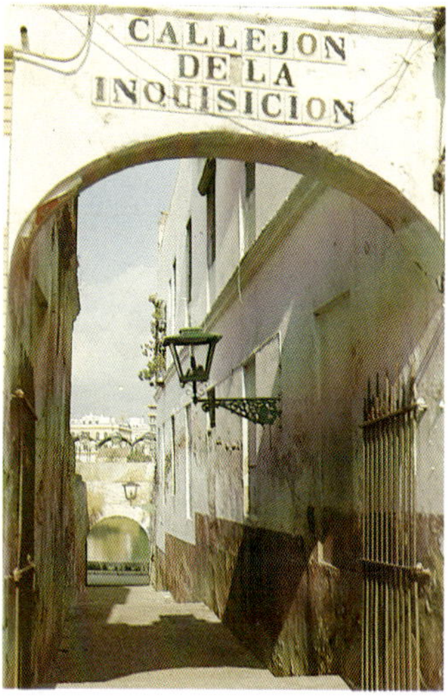

Inquisition Alley.

The images in this church date from the 18th century, the best of them being Our Lady of the Rosary on the main altar and a Saint Anthony of Padua on one of the side altars.

There are good frescoes on the pendentives in the transept, representing Saint Thomas and other Dominican saints. The loss of documents when the friars where secularized in the 19th century, makes it impossible to identify the artists.

Callejón de la Inquisición

On leaving the church of San Jacinto by the street of the same name, we cross to the other side and enter Pages del Corro street. The second intersection to the right is Antillano Campos, which will lead us to the plaza del Callao, where we find the Callejón de la Inquisición (Inquisition Alley), with a sign over its entrance archway.

The callejón de la Inquisición is all that remains of the prisons of the Inquisition Tribunal. The present buildings on the right were erected on land where the Inquisition jails stood. Famous personalities died here, such as Torrigiano the sculptor, and a confessor of Charles I, a theologian and prebendary of the Cathedral of Seville. The Inquisition claimed that both had committed suicide in prison to avoid being burned at the stake.

The Castillo de San Jorge (castle of Saint George) where the Court had its headquarters was completely demolished when the Inquisition was abolished in the 19th century, leaving only this alley as a reminder.

The church of La O

Going down Castilla street, on our right we will come to the Church of La O, from which each year during Holy Week the procession of the Brotherhood of Jesus of Nazareth and Our Lady of O leaves. The church was built in 1697, designed by the late Baroque architects Félix and José Romero. It has three aisles, and its ceiling rests on lovely red marble columns. The main altar dates from before the construction of the church and its niche contains the figure of Our Lady of O, property of the Brotherhood, by Castillo Lastrucci. At the foot of the niche there is a group formed by Saint Joachim, Saint Anne and the Virgin as a Child in the middle, a splendid work by Pedro Roldán. The figure of-

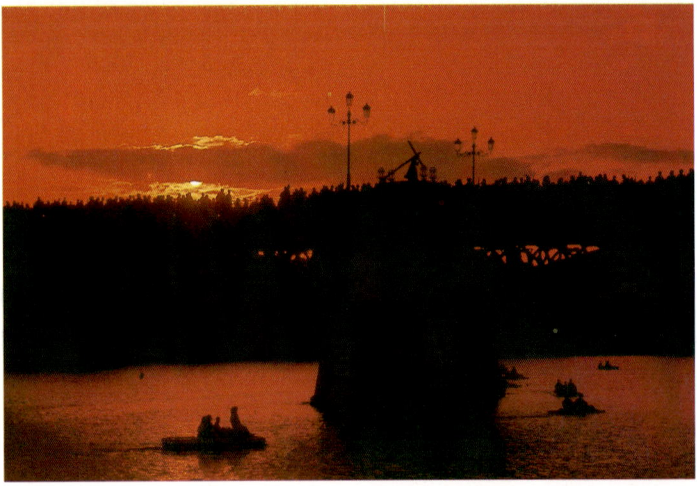

A penitent of the Brotherhood of O crossing Triana bridge.

Jesus of Nazareth, which belongs to the Brotherhood, has its own chapel and was also made by Pedro Roldán in 1685. The cross is covered with tortoise shell and the story goes that sailors who had survived a shipwreck in the Indies deposited at the foot of Christ several bundles containing tortoise shell, which was used to cover the cross. It is edged with embossed silver.

We also find in this church an 18th century image of Our Lady with the Child, by Pedro Duque Cornejo. Since it is the second parish in Triana, it is natural for this church to be embellished inside with Triana tiles, as well as outside on the tower.

Las Almonas del Jabón

Nearby, on the same side and at number 24 of this street, the ruins of the old Almonas del Jabón (Ancient soap industry) of the Dukes of Alcalá can still be seen. This was one of the most flourishing industries in 16th-century Seville, as it possessed technical secrets for making soap, specially toilet soap, which was exported to Germany, France and curiously, also to England, which was an enemy nation, during the 16th century. Such was the quality of this soap, unique in the world at that time.

On this same spot, 24 Castilla street, there is a small arch which communicated the street and the river, over which we can see an old slab with a curious text.

The «Cachorro» Chapel

If we go down Castilla street to the end, we will find the Chapel of the Brotherhood of Cristo de la Expiración and María Santísima del Patrocinio, which houses these two images belonging to the Brotherhood. The

Cristo de la Expiración is also known popularly as the «Cachorro», because sculptor Antonio Ruiz Gijón , also known as Francisco Antonio Gijón, according to tradition, modelled it on a dying gypsy nicknamed «el Cachorro», to give his Christ a realistic expression. It is one of the best Baroque sculptures of the 17th century, commissioned in the year 1682.

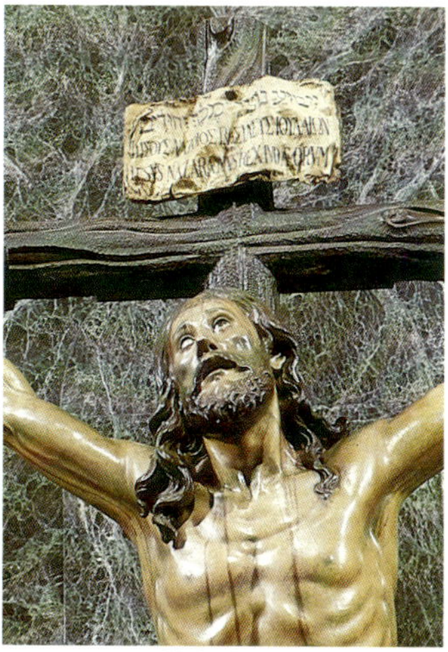

«El Cachorro».

The image of the Virgen del Patrocinio is modern, as an accidental fire destroyed the earlier one. It was made by the young sculptor Luis Alvarez Duarte in 1973.

After visiting the Patrocinio chapel, we return by Castilla street to Chapina bridge, which leads back to the old city center.

With this itinerary we conclude our visit to the historical and artistic parts of Seville. However, this city does not only consist of monuments, but also of picturesque streets, stately mansions, courtyards overflowing with plants and the unexpected glimpse of a tower or a belfry over any number of secluded convents.

Therefore, apart from all the monuments we have mentioned in the previous chapters, it is also called for to stroll about the streets, so as to soak our spirit with the intimate essence of immortal Seville.

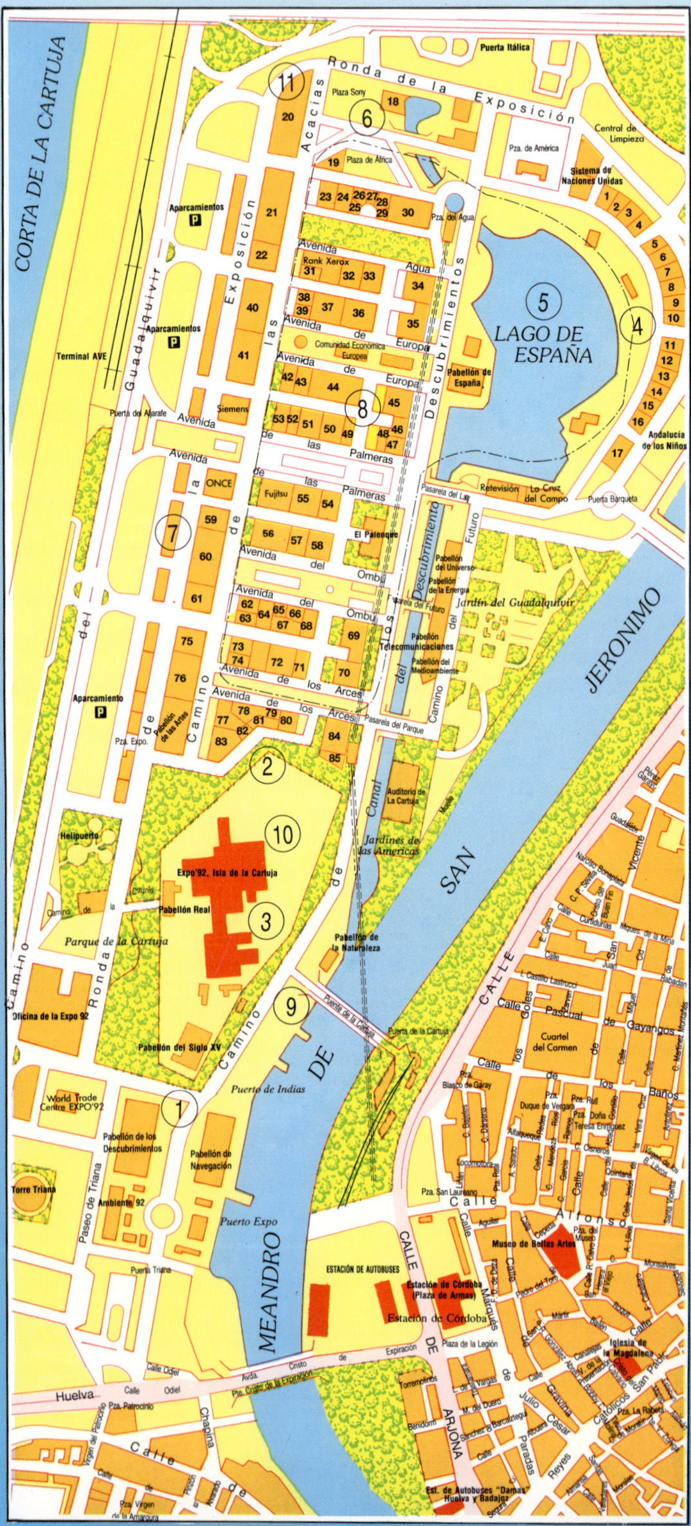

CORTA DE LA CARTUJA
Ronda de la Exposición
Puerta Itálica
Plaza Sony
Plaza de África
Pza. de América
Central de Limpieza
Sistema de Naciones Unidas
Pza. del Agua
Avenida de las Acacias
Camino de los Descubrimientos
Aparcamientos
Terminal AVE
Avenida Rank Xerox
Agua
Avenida de Europa
Comunidad Económica Europea
LAGO DE ESPAÑA
Pabellón de España
Andalucía de los Niños
Puerta del Aljarafe
Avenida
Siemens
Avenida de las Palmeras
ONCE
Fujitsu
Retevisión
La Cruz del Campo
Puerta Barqueta
Pasarela del Lago
El Palenque
Avenida del Ombú
Pabellón del Universo
Pabellón de la Energía
Pasarela del Futuro
Camino del Futuro
Jardín del Guadalquivir
Canal de los Descubrimientos
Pabellón Telecomunicaciones
Pabellón del Medioambiente
Avenida de los Arces
Pasarela del Parque
Aparcamiento
Pabellón de las Artes
Pza. Expo.
Camino de las Artes
Ronda del Guadalquivir
JERONIMO
Auditorio de La Cartuja
Helipuerto
Expo'92, Isla de la Cartuja
Jardines de las Américas
Camino de la Cartuja
Pabellón Real
Parque de la Cartuja
Pabellón de la Naturaleza
SAN
Oficina de la Expo 92
Camino de los Descubrimientos
Pabellón del Siglo XV
Puente de la Cartuja
Puerta de la Cartuja
Puerto de Indias
World Trade Centre EXPO'92
Pabellón de los Descubrimientos
Pabellón de Navegación
Torre Triana
Ambiente '92
Paseo de Triana
Puerto Expo
Puerta Triana
MEANDRO DE SAN JERONIMO
ESTACIÓN DE AUTOBUSES
Estación de Córdoba (Plaza de Armas)
Estación de Córdoba
Plaza de la Legión
Calle Odiel
Avda. Cristo de la Expiración
Pte. Cristo de la Expiración
Huelva
Pza. Patrocinio
Calle Chapina
Calle de Arjona
Calle Marqués de Paradas
Calle San Vicente
Calle Goles
Calle Pascual de Gayangos
Cuartel del Carmen
Calle Baños
Calle Alfonso XII
Museo de Bellas Artes
Pza. del Museo
Pza. San Laureano
Iglesia de la Magdalena
Julio César
Reyes Católicos
San Pablo
Pza. La Rabeta
Torremolinos
Benidorm
M. del Duero
Est. de Autobuses "Damas" Huelva y Badajoz
Pza. Virgen de la Amargura

ROUTE 9: WORLD EXPOSITION EXPO'92

PLACES OF INTEREST

① **Area of Discoveries**
② **Onimags**
③ **Royal Pavilion: former 14th century Charterhouse**
④ **Pavilions of the Autonomous Communities of Spain:**
1. Basque Country
2. Catalonia
3. Galicia 4. Asturias
5. Cantabria 6. La Rioja
7. Murcia 8. Valencia
9. Aragon 10. Castile La Mancha 11. Canary Islands
12. Navarre 13. Extremadura
14. Balearic Islands
15. Madrid
16. Castile and León
17. Andalusia
⑤ **Visit Artificial Lake**
⑥ **Pavilions of the Future**
⑦ **Area of the National Pavilions:**
18. Concessionaire 19. South Pacific Islands 20. Concessionaire
21. U.S.A. 22. New Zeland
23. Cyprus 24. Paquistan
25. Thailand 26. Singapore
27. Malaysia 28. Indonesia
29. The Philipins 30. Australia
31. Turkey 32. South Korea
33. Puerto Rico 34. Mexico
35. France 36. Belgium
37. The Netherlands 38. Ireland
39. Luxembourg 40. United Kingdom 41. Germany
42. Denmark 43. Greece
44. Italy 45. Portugal 46. Israel
47. India 48. Vatican
49. Hungary 50. Austria
51. Sweden 52. Finland
53. Norway 54. Czechoslovakia
55. Switzerland 56. Canada
57 and 58 concessionaires
59. Venezuela 60. CEI
61. Concessionaire 62. Monaco
63. Sri Lanka 64. Cuba
65. Concessionaire 66. Rumania
67. Concessionaire 68. Chile
69. Caribbean 70. Arab Countries
71. Poland, Bulgaria 72. China
73. Papua-New Guinea
74. Concessionaire 75. Saudi Arabia 76. Japan 77. Algeria
78. Tunisia 79. Kuwait
80. Oman 81. Mauritania
82 and 83 Concessionaires
84. Morocco 85. Concessionaire.
⑧ **Beer Factory at work**
⑨ **Monorail train**
⑩ **The Charter House building:**
Remains of the old Pickmann china factory
⑪ **Musement Area**

STARTING POINT	Court of Arms. Entrance to the Exposition.

USEFUL ADDRESSES NEARBY

Information office for Expo'92:	Tel: 462 87 00
Inside the precinct all kind of services can be found:	police station, Red Cross first aid, chemists, shops, photo services, restaurants, bars and hotels. It is like a small city inside the city.

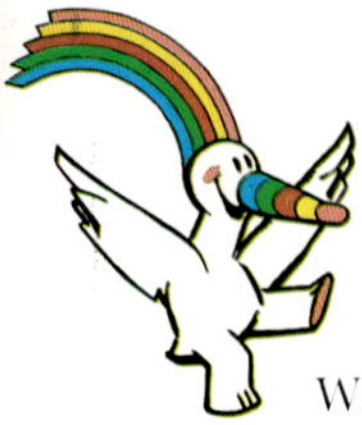

ROUTE 9: WORLD EXPOSITION EXPO '92

When the International Expositions and Fairs Commitee chose Seville as the venue of the 1992 UNIVERSAL EXPOSITION, or EXPO '92, it was decided to install the fair on the island of La Cartuja, so called because it is indeed an island, between two arms of the Guadalquivir river and has in its centre the ancient building of La Cartuja de las Cuevas. This monastery is a Gothic construction dating from the end of the 14th century, built under the initiative and patronage of Archbishop Gonzalo de Mena.

In order to host this important event, which is expected to attract so many visitors, estimated in 17 millions, the city has undergone important improvements as to services, new hotels, street and roadwork, etc.

Particular mention should be made of transport facilities, such as road improvement, a new railroad station and a new airport, plus the construction of five new bridges over the Guadalquivir, assuring traffic flow over the river between the Island of La Cartuja and City Center, although this is also within walking distance. The Exposition has five entrances.

Among the new accesses to Seville for motorists it should be mentioned that the Madrid and Mediterranean Highways have been connected. There are direct flights from Seville – Barcelona –Bern – Vienna – Prague – Luxembourg – Bonn – Berlin, and Seville – Madrid – Paris, Brussels – Amsterdam with connections from Paris to Germany and the United Kingdom.

Expo '92: The Fairgrounds

The fairgrounds of Expo '92 encompass an area of 215 hectares, of which 350,000 square meters are buildings and 1,800,000 square meters are open space.

An artificial lake has been created with a canal that connects it with the river. There is also a sports marina.

Outside the grounds, but staging events related to the Expo, an opera theater, sports stadiums, water sports areas, a bullring and other entertaintment facilities are to be found.

Contents of the Exposition

The Exposition is divided into the following areas:

Area of Spain

This includes the Royal Pavilion, the Government Pavilion and the Pavilions of the Autonomous Communities of the different Spanish regions, plus the Seville Pavilion.

These pavilions are for official events and public relations. They also exhibit works of art related to the region of each pavilion.

Area of Discoveries

This area encompasses a series of installations where not

only geographical discoveries are exhibited, but all kinds of discoveries made in the world from 1492 onwards in different areas of human knowledge, technological acumen of each age and world culture during this period, including European as well as American scientific

Model of Expo'92.

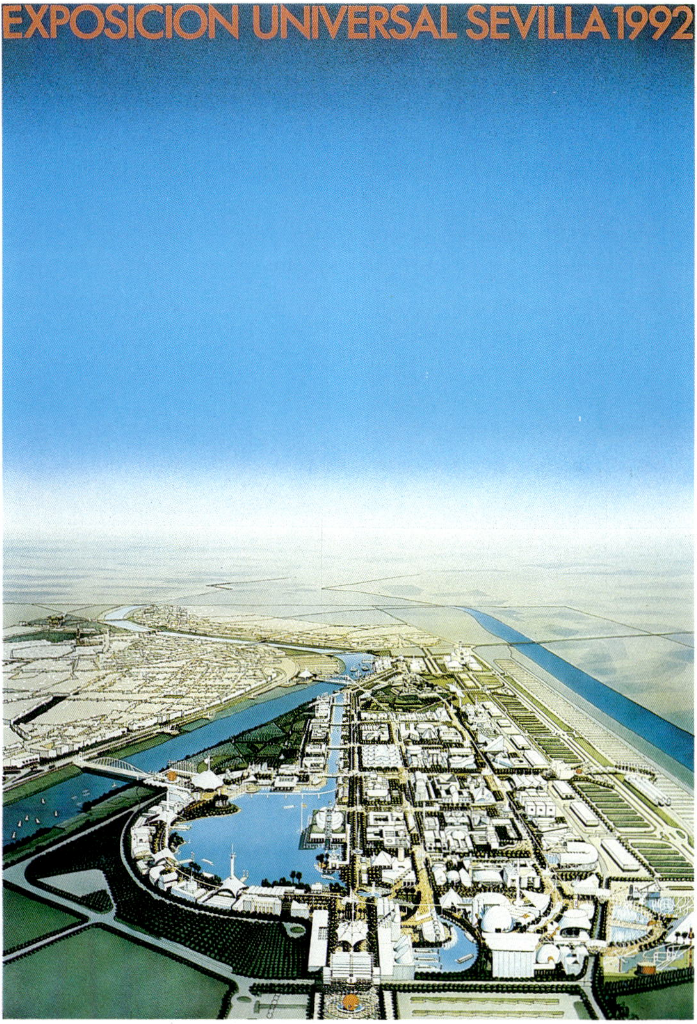

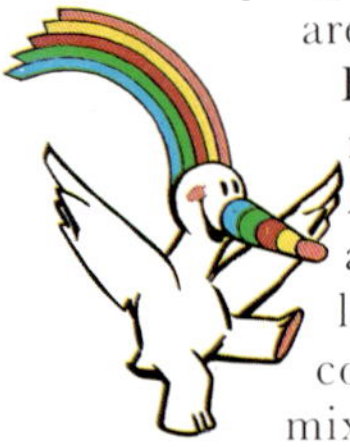

progress. Also included are the cultures of Asia, Black Africa, Oceania and the Latin American countries as they developed politically from the Discovery on, with the mixture of native elements and Spanish civilization from the 16th to the 19th centuries.

Area of the Future

This includes the present state of science and technology and their projection into the future, such as computer science, spatial navigation, genetic engineering, etc., including all types of apparatus and materials, together with film projections, etc., in such a manner that visitors may acquire truly valuable information on life in the coming century.

Area of the National Pavilions

This comprises the pavilions of the different nations participating, which are over one hundred. Each exhibits in its pavilion a sample of its industrial production, art and progress. The Vatican Pavilion is showing masterpieces from its famous museum.

Docking area.

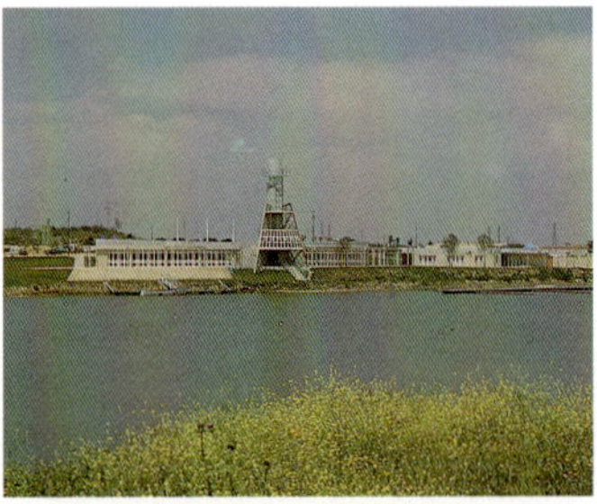

Convention Palace.

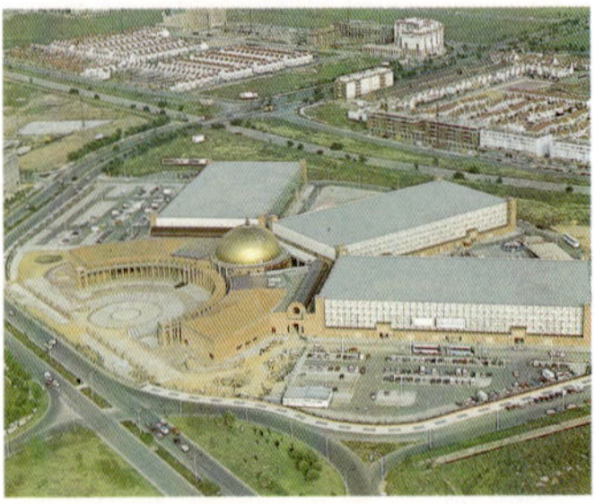

Communications Tower.

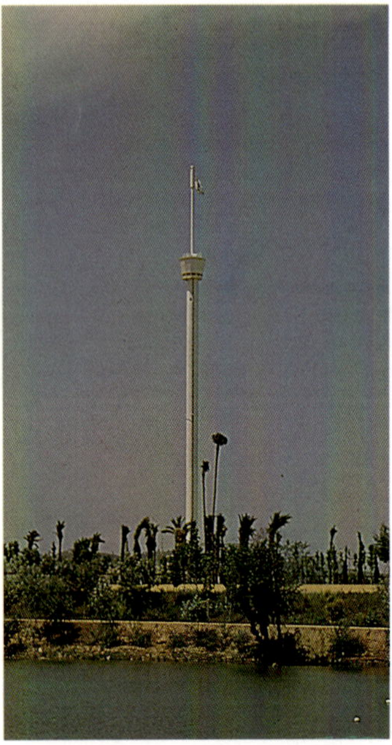

Entertainment Area

This includes daily ballet performances, concerts, folklore from the different countries, etc, within the Exposition grounds as well as in installations outside.

Amusement Area

This area includes a gigantic Fun Fair, with all types of amusements, as well as cultural attractions, such as a bird house, a botanical garden, an aquarium and a planetarium.

Curiosities

Among other things a beer factory in operation can be visited, where the public can see the complete process of making beer.

Museums

Inside the fairgrounds of Expo '92 there are museums showing masterworks of universal painting and sculpture which are on loan for this exceptional occasion from the principal Spanish museums, galleries of other countries, the Royal Spanish Heritage and other entities.

EXPO'92 SEVILLA

Opening and closing dates

Official inauguration of Expo '92 was on April 20, 1992, coinciding with the end of Holy Week in Seville.

It will be open for 176 days, officially closing on October 12th of this same year.

Different bridges into the Expo.

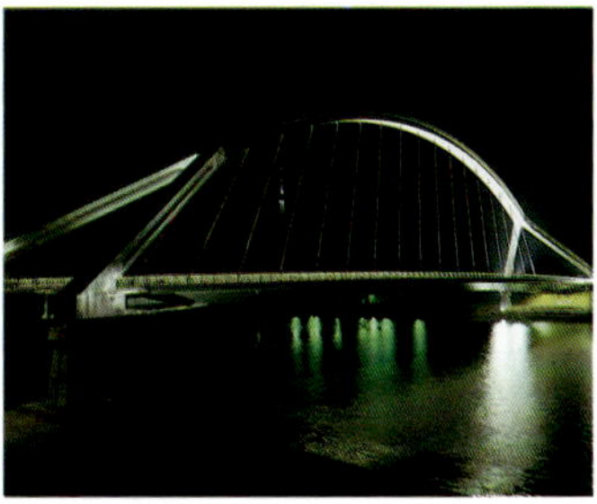

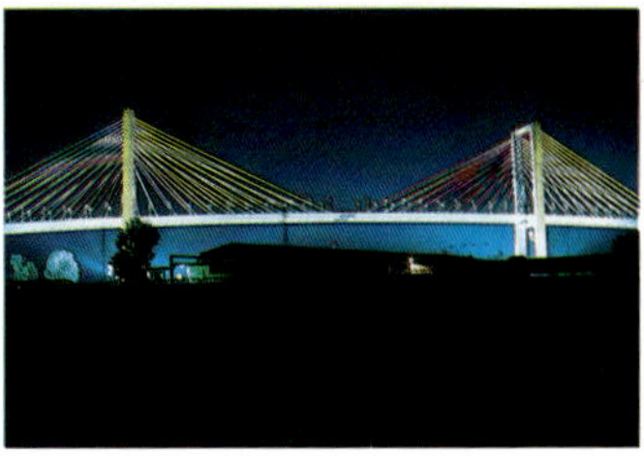

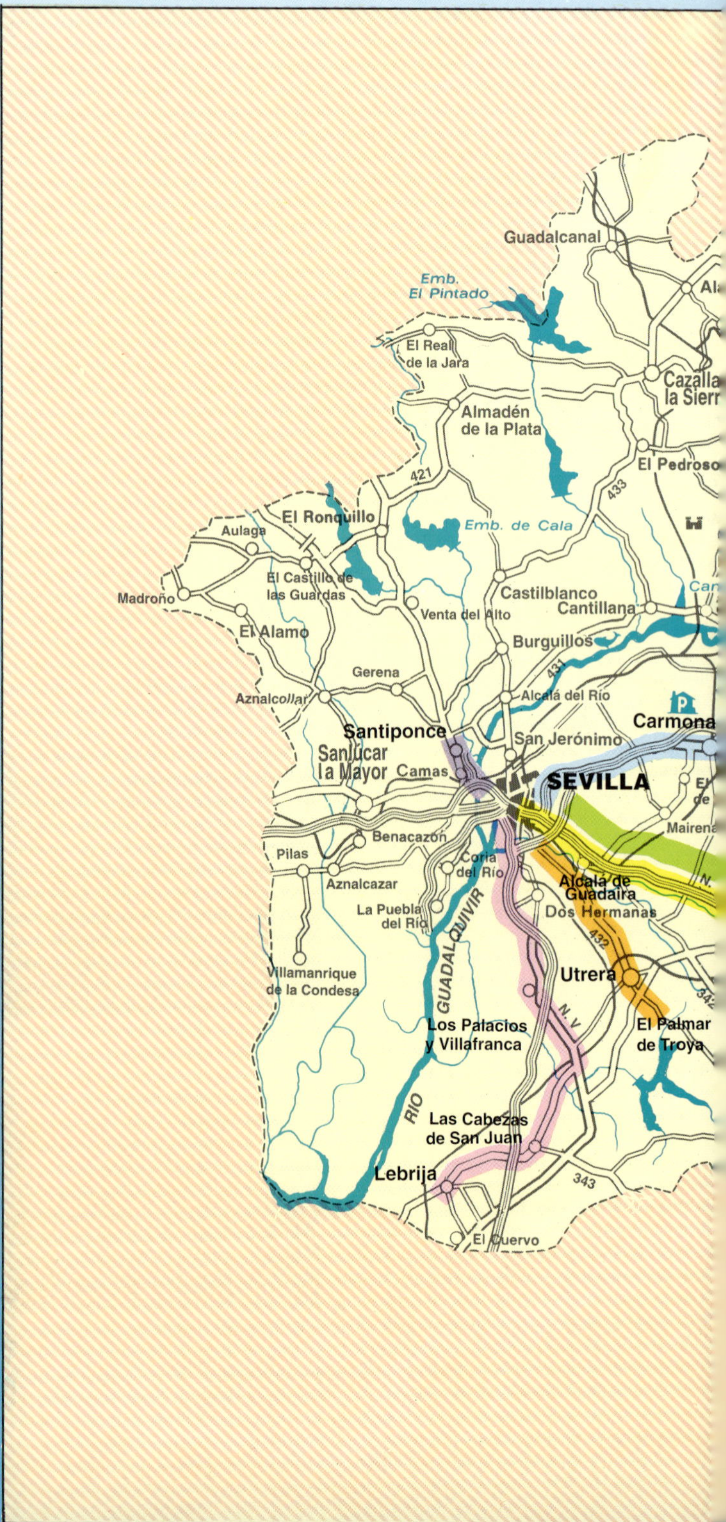

Guadalcanal
Emb.
El Pintado
El Real
de la Jara
Cazalla
la Sierr
Almadén
de la Plata
El Pedroso
421
433
El Ronquillo
Aulaga
Emb. de Cala
El Castillo de
las Guardas
Madroño
Venta del Alto
Castilblanco
Cantillana
El Alamo
Burguillos
Gerena
431
Aznalcollar
Alcalá del Río
Carmona
Santiponce
San Jerónimo
Sanlúcar
la Mayor
Camas
SEVILLA
Mairena
Benacazón
Pilas
Coria
del Río
Aznalcazar
Alcalá de
Guadaira
La Puebla
del Río
Dos Hermanas
432
Utrera
Villamanrique
de la Condesa
GUADALQUIVIR
N. V
Los Palacios
y Villafranca
El Palmar
de Troya
RIO
Las Cabezas
de San Juan
Lebrija
343
El Cuervo

ROUTE I.–SEVILLE-SANTIPONCE

ROUTE II.–SEVILLE-CARMONA-ECIJA

ROUTE III–.SEVILLE-ALCALA DE GUADAIRA-ARAHAL-MARCHENA

ROUTE IV.–SEVILLE-LOS PALACIOS-LAS CABEZAS DE SAN JUAN-LEBRIJA

ROUTE V.–SEVILLE-UTRERA-EL PALMAR DE TROYA

ROUTE VI.–SEVILLE-OSUNA

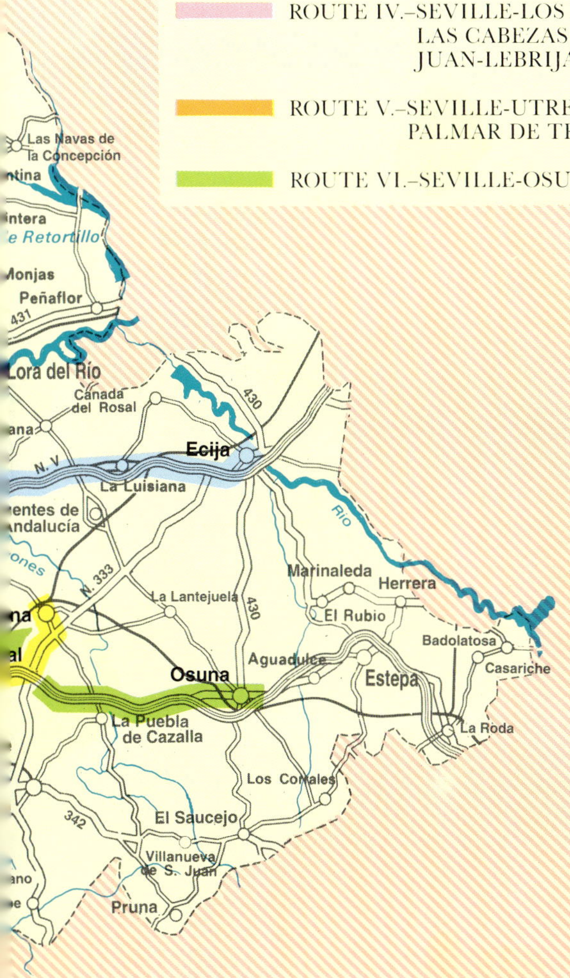

EXCURSION ROUTES

SEVILLE

SCALE 1: 1.000.000

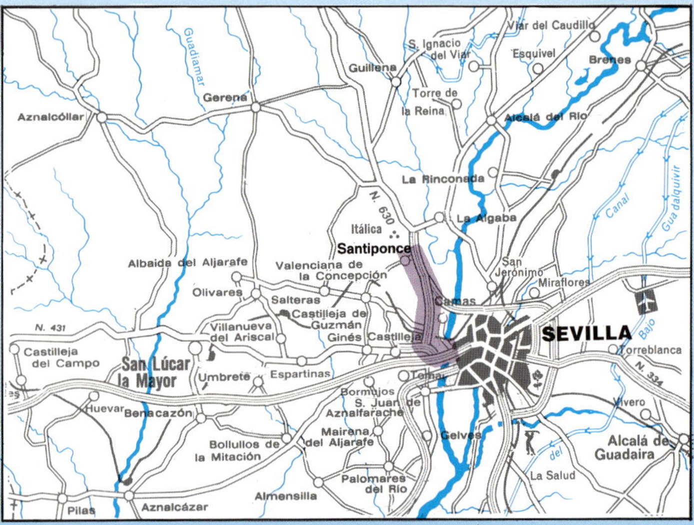

ROUTE 1: SEVILLE-SANTIPONCE • PLACES OF INTEREST

PLACES OF INTEREST

- **Camas:** Parish Church of the 18th century.
- **Santiponce:** Monastery of San Isidoro del Campo, 13th century.

ACCESS	Road N-630, 7 km from Seville
END OF ROUTE	Take N-630 back to Seville

ROUTE 1: SEVILLE · CAMAS SANTIPONCE

CAMAS

We leave Seville on N-630. About two and a half kilometers from Seville, at the foot of Santa Brígida hill, lies the town of Camas. Until recently, this was a town on its own with a flourishing agricultural life, but now it is almost part of Seville due to continuous construction and the extension of Triana quarter.

The town is of Moslem origin, from Almoravid times, and its name is derived from that of the owner of this alcarria or plateau, Ebn Alkama, who apart from farmer and politician was also a historian of Arab Spain and Andalusia, with his two works: *Ixbania and Ard-Andalus*.

The parish church of Camas is dedicated to Our Lady of Grace, a Baroque building dating from the 18th century, with three aisles and vaulted ceiling. The altarpiece is Neoclassical from the end of the same century. The image of Our Lady of Grace occupies the center of the altarpiece and can be dressed. It is accompanied by other saints of the Order of the Holy Trinity.

The reredos of the Vera Cruz altar contains sculptures of Christ Crucified and Our Lady of Sorrows, and the altar of Our Lady of La Antigua, an attractive relief. There is an interesting image of Saint Brigitte which until recently was kept in the shrine of Saint Brigitte, located on the hill that bears her name. This image, together with that of Our Lady of Candlemas, were taken to Seville to the chapel of Patrocinio when the shrine disappeared, but the people of Camas demanded them back so energetically that the Archbishopric of Seville was forced to authorize the return of both images to the parish of Camas.

During the 17th and 18th centuries, the town was under the jurisdiction of the all-powerful royal favourite Count-Duke of Olivares, of the Guzmán lineage.

SAN ISIDORO DEL CAMPO

Three kilometers ahead, in the municipality of Santiponce and on our left we come across a splendid building. This is the monastery of San Isidoro del Campo, which was founded in the year 1298 by a gentleman from León, Alonso Pérez de Guzmán «the Benevolent». A hero in the defense of Tarifa, he preferred to sacrifice his son captured by the Moors rather than surrender the stronghold the King had entrusted him with and turn over its defenders to the knives of the attackers.

The monastery was built with a church intended as a burial place for Alonso Pérez de Guzmán and his wife, excluding anyone else, even their descendants. After it was finished, Alonso Pérez de Guzmán handed it over to the Cistercian Order, one of the great religious orders of the Middle Ages, which came from France to establish itself in Spain, because

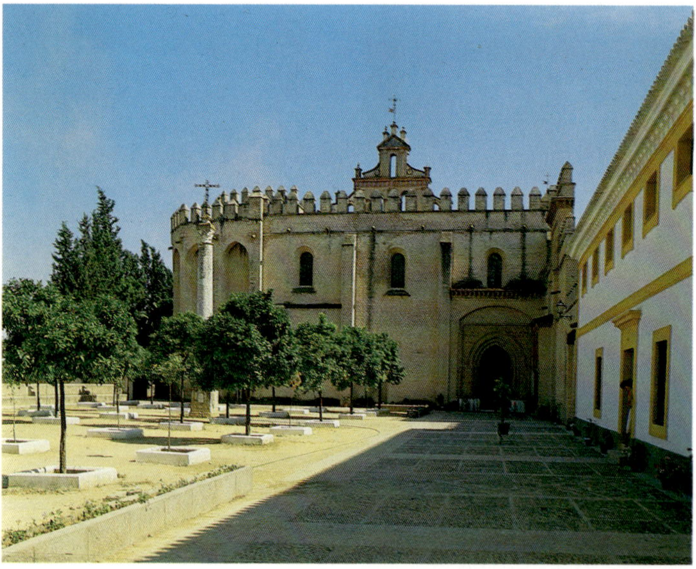

San Isidoro del Campo. Apse and entrance to the church.

the Pope distrusted the Spanish clergy, suspecting that they could have been influenced by Moslem beliefs. Thus, the Cistercian Order was assigned the task of preserving the Catholic dogma in all its purity. Later, through arrangement with the Duke of Niebla, the transfer was cancelled and the monastery made over to the Hieronymite Order.

The building was erected over an ancient Visigothic church, where, according to tradition,the body of Saint Isidore was found in the 9th century, under Moslem rule. It was delivered to the Christian King of León by the Moorish King of Seville Almotahdi. This is why Saint Isidore is buried in León.

This monastery was built at the beginning of the 14th century and is therefore in the purest ogival Gothic style, although its aspect is that of a fortress because due to the proximity of the Moors, it was still necessary to provide isolated buildings in the countryside or in small towns with some sort of military architecture.

Inside the monastery there are two churches: the first one is the oldest, Gothic from the 14th century, but reformed to Baroque taste in the 17th century. In this church there is a grand altarpiece by the sculptor Juan Martínez Montañés about 1610, with sculptures of Saint Jerome, Saint Isidore and relief scenes of the Nativity, the Adoration of the Magi, the Resurrection and the Ascension, together with Saint John the Evangelist, Saint John the Baptist, and the Assumption of Our Lady. It is really a magnificent altarpiece and on either side are the tombs of Alonso Pérez de Guzmán »the Benevolent» and

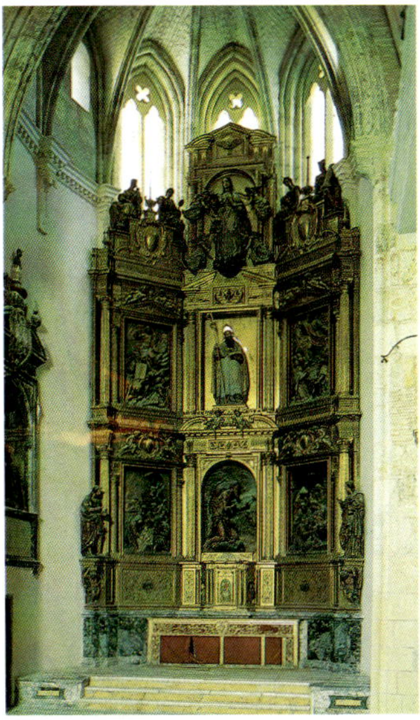

Main altarpiece of the church.

his wife doña María Alonso Coronel, with praying statues on the tombs, in niches also by Martínez Montañés.

On the right hand wall there is an 18th century Baroque altar, with images of Saint Joachim, Saint Anne, the Virgin, and the Child Jesus, sculpted by Martínez Montanés.The remaining images are by an anonymous 18th century artist.

The second church, which is really a twin aisle joined to the former one by an arch, has in its main altarpiece a Gothic Crucified Christ accompanied by images of Our Lady and Saint John the Evangelist, all dating from the 16th century. Since the descendants of Guzmán «the Benevolent» could not be buried in the first church, they are buried here in fine tombs from the 14th to the 16th century. It is curious that this second church was built precisely due to this prohibition and the dispute maintained in Rome between the Guzmans and the Archbishop of Seville, Gonzalo de Mena, which the latter won.

In the sacristy there is yet another altarpiece, also by Martínez Montañés, and valuable paintings by followers of Zurbarán.

Adjoining the sacristy is the chapter house where the monks used to meet, and its splendour reveals the large number of friars living here at its most brilliant time. Among its treasures, there is a large ivory crucifix (large for its kind), carved by Pedro Roldán, as well as a series of paintings on the life of Saint Jerome, replicas of those kept in El Escorial.

The so-called Patio de los Muertos (Courtyard of the Dead) is very interesting. This is where the monks were buried and it still has many tombstones, some of these with interesting inscriptions.

The refectory, whose size also conveys a good idea of the number of monks, is presided over by a large 15th century fresco representing The Last Supper.

The community of friars of the Hieronymite Order were under the protection of Charles I, who chose this order for his retreat in the Monastery of Yuste, and Philip II, who founded the Monastery of El Escorial with Hieronymites. They were cruelly persecuted by the Inquisition, partly because the monastery had taken on the spirit of the Protestant reform and partly because the Tribunal

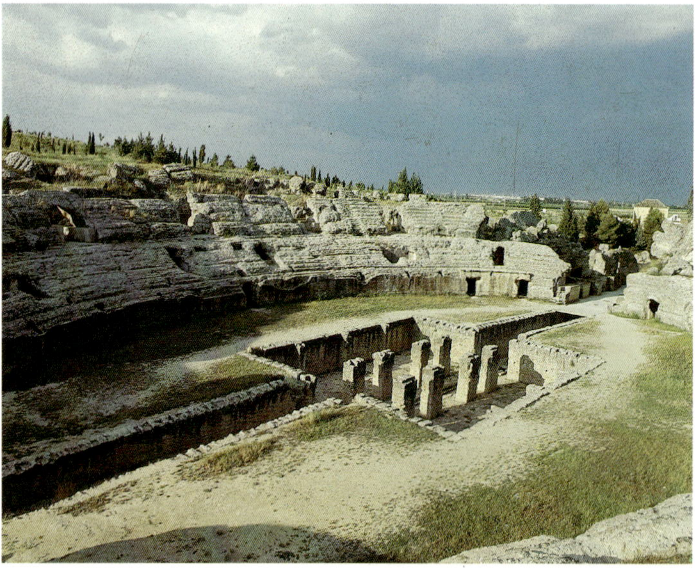

Ruins of Italica.

wanted to make it clear to all that even if kings protected an order, the authority of the Inquisition was over and above royal patronage. The outcome was that the prior of San Isidoro del Campo, fray García Arias, and twenty of the Hieronymite friars were tortured and sentenced to the stake. Others were condemned to prison. Only twelve managed to escape, among them two who later became famous: Casiodoro de Reina and Cipriano de Valera. The former found refuge in England, where he carried out very important philological work translating the Bible directly from Hebrew and Greek manuscripts. This translation was later revised by Cipriano de Valera, a task which took him twenty years, this being the most perfect translation of the Bible into the Spanish language to date, as another great scholar, Menéndez y Pelayo, affirmed in spite of the fact that it was made between 1557 and 1590.

THE TOWN OF SANTIPONCE

At the foot of the monastery of San Isidoro del Campo is the bridge of Santiponce, a name derived from San Geroncio, because the town was built next to a shrine dedicated to this saint. However, the Santiponce of today is not the original one, since when the Guadalquivir flooded and overflowed its banks at the end of the 16th century, the villagers were forced to move away from the riverbank.

To build this new village, the people used stones from the ruins of nearby Italica, which was partly the reason for its ever greater destruction, but it also served to attract attention to this very important archeological site and thus scholars started studying it. Thse ruins also inspired the famous poet Rodrigo Cano to write his immortal poem *A las ruinas de Itálica (To the ruins of Italica)*.

THE RUINS OF ITALICA

Estos, Fabio, ay dolor, que ves [ahora
campos de soledad, mustio collado
fueron en un tiempo Italica famosa...

(These, Fabius, oh grief, that you [now
see fields of solitude,
withered slope, were once so famous [Italica..)

The city of Italica was founded in the year 206 B.C. by the Roman general Publius Cornelius Scipio, who after defeating the Carthaginians wanted his wounded soldiers to recover here, a place with such an excellent climate. So Italica was not originally a city, but a convalescent camp for the disabled, what was known in the Roman army as a *castra valetudinaria*.

However, precisely due to its good climate and proximity to Seville, only twelve kilometers away (7.5 miles), Italica soon became a favourite leisure spot for Sevillian patricians, so that the invalid soldiers were replaced by a wealthy class who built beautiful palaces, temples, theaters and a circus or amphitheater here, amongst the most important in the entire Empire. Italica was the residence of notable families and two Roman emperors were born here: Trajan and Hadrian, while some claim that Theodosius was also born here.

After centuries of splendor, Italica declined in the 4th century, coinciding with the decadence of Rome, and the luxurious city was abandoned after the invasion of the Goths, so that in the 6th century it ceased to exist. The dust of centuries, vegetation, rain, earthquakes and plundering destroyed it so completely that after the 7th century it was known as «Campos de Talca» (Fields) without any recollection of there ever having been a city there.

When Santiponce was being built on its present site in the 1600s, ruins came to light, which caused the first excavations. Then, in the 18th century, painter Lucas Valdés became interested in the amphitheater, and later in the century, the politician and archeologist Francisco Bruna, who was at the head of the Audiencia of Seville, excavated the most important pieces discovered in Italica to date: a statue of Diana as a huntress and a bust of Trajan, besides several other sculptures and mosaics.

In the 19th century, Demetrio de los Ríos was in charge of the excavations and studied for the first time the amphitheater, ascertaining its first measurements: 156,5 meters (512 ft) for the principal axis, and 134 m (440 ft) for the minor axis, the only larger ones in all the Roman Empire being the Coliseum in Rome, with 188m (617 ft.) and 135 m (443 ft), and the one in Capua 162m (532 ft) and 132 m (433 ft.).

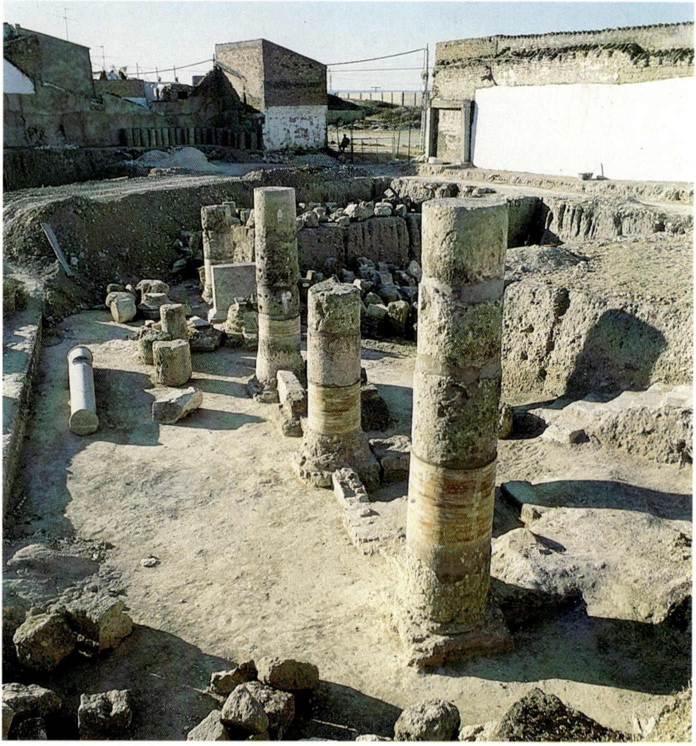

Itálica. Roman amphitheater.

The amphitheater in Italica was therefore considerably larger than the one in Nîmes, which measures 133m (436 ft.) and 38m (125 ft.), or the one in Pompeii with 130m (427 ft.) and 102 m (335 ft.) Nowadays Italica is accessible to visitors, with signs throughout, while several of its spacious streets are transitable. Under these streets run large sewers, visible at some points. In the highest part of the excavations the ruins of mansions with magnificent mosaics can be seen, including one of a tiger attacking a gazelle, another depicting fishes and others also preserved on the site. The most important building excavated is that of the thermae built in Hadrian's time.

The amphitheater is magnificent, with a large part of its tiers of seats still in place, the vomitories and galleries intact, as well as the cavea for the wild animals, and the gladiators' and prisoners' cubicles, all of which are visible and worth a visit. The arena has in the center a large pond which some erroneously supposed was used for naval battles. In reality, the columns in it would have hampered any movement even of the smallest boats. The pond was used to collect rain water in the event of a sudden storm, so that in a few minutes the whole arena was dry thanks to this magnificent drainage system, more effective than that of any football field or bullring today.

In the last few years, since 1975, great discoveries have been made in Italica, excavating a beautiful theater unknown until then.

A visit to the Roman ruins of Italica is a must for history-lovers and antique fans, and an eye-opener for young people and students.

From Santiponce we return to Seville by the same road.

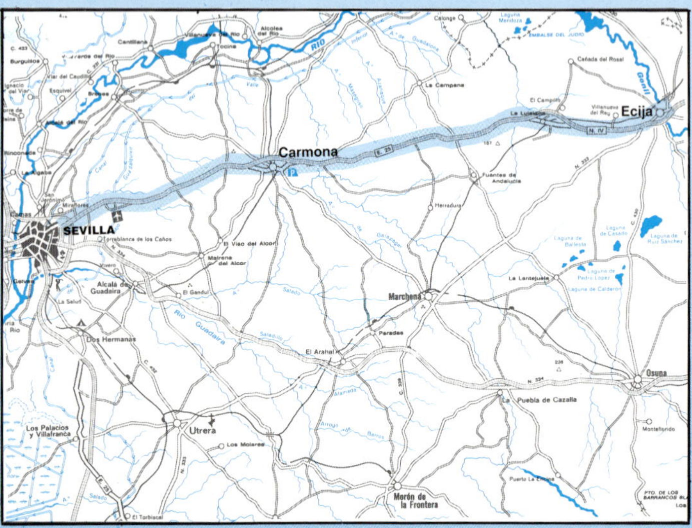

ROUTE 2:
SEVILLE • CARMONA • ECIJA

PLACES OF INTEREST

- **Carmona:** Roman necropolis and amphitheater.
Walls and fortresses (Alcázares)
Church of Santa María
Church of San Felipe
Church of San Blas
Church of San Pedro
Convent of Santa Clara
Municipal Archives
- **Ecija:** Palace of Peñaflor
Palace of Benamejí
Plaza Mayor (Square)
Archeological Museum of Ecija
Church of Santa María
Church of Santiago
Church of San Gil

ACCESS

Take N-IV towards Madrid.
93 km away from Seville.

PRACTICAL INFORMATION ALONG THE ROUTE

Carmona:
Useful addresses and telephones:
- Tourist information office. El Salvador, 2. Tel 414 00 11

Accommodation:
- Parador Alcázar del Rey don Pedro****. Tel: 414 10 10
- El Potro. Sevilla, 78. Tel 414 14 65. Home-made food.

Ecija:
Useful addresses and telephones:
- Tourist information office. Avda. de Andalucía, s/n. Tel: 438 30 62.

Accommodation:
- Astigi Sol**. Road Madrid-Cádiz, km 450. Tel: 483 01 62
- Ciudad del Sol**. Miguel de Cervantes, 50. Tel: 483 03 00/04

Restaurants:
- Casa Pirulas. Miguel de Cervantes, 48. Tel: 483 03 00/04
- Bodegón El Gallego. Rda. Arcipreste Aparicio, 3. Tel: 483 26 18

END OF ROUTE

Take N-630 back to Seville

ROUTE 2: SEVILLE · CARMONA ÉCIJA

CARMONA

We leave Seville on N-IV, driving towards Madrid.

After about 32 kilometers (20 miles) we reach Carmona from an artistic point of view one of the most important towns in Spain, since it contains interesting remains from all the civilizations that have passed through Spain.

From afar we are impressed by its walls, which have witnessed so many battles of Goths against Romans, Goths against Goths, Moors against Christians, Christians against Christians and Moors against Moors, in a unique raveling and unraveling of the warring tangles of History.

Roman necropolis and amphitheater

If we want to visit the town in chronological order so as to appreciate historical events, we will go in the first place to the Roman necropolis, right next to the city, over two kilometers of which have already been excavated.

Like the chief necropolis in Rome, it was divided into two sectors: the Field of Mars for the upper classes, and the Esquiline for plebeians. Here in Carmona the tombs of the wealthy are impressive, specially those that have been identified by name or symbols.

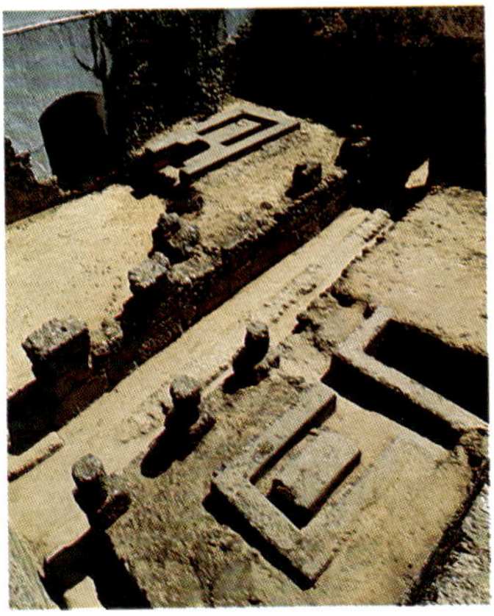

The Elephant Tomb.

They are solid in their architecture, with underground rooms to celebrate funeral banquets, where slabs have been found written in Latin and some in Greek, giving details of the lives of the personalities buried here.

Specially interesting are: the tomb of Prepusa, the Elephant Tomb, so called after the elephant sculpture adorning it, the Colonnade Tomb, the Postumius Tomb, the Circular Tomb and the Columbarium-Triclinius tomb.

There are two different types of tombs, for internment or cremation, with their own characteristics. Various funerary effects have been found, such as small receptacles, in which relatives from other cities sent their tears to be placed in the tomb next to the deceased, as well as coins, jewels, vessels, etc.

The most curious tombstone is written in Greek and reads as follows: «Memory consecrated to the Manes gods. Philometor, native of Tarsus, son of Athenedorus, cananitane stoic, traveling on account of his philosophical passion, died under the Consulate of Crassus and Piso. His soul is seated among the immortal. His body is buried in this sarcophagus. He lived, forty eight years, eight months and four days. May the earth be light upon him.» This stone from the necropolis stood for sometime at the Marchena gate, from where it has been retrieved.

The rich patrician class that had these pantheons made received visitors, as can be deduced from this text, by philosophers and travelers from all over the world.

Another important Roman ruin discovered a few years ago is the amphitheater, which was similar in size to that of the city of Otricoli and somewhat larger than the military amphitheater in Rome. It has the particularity that it was not built upwards, but dug deep into the stone. It is one of the oldest ones in Spain, dating from the 1st century. Here we can still see the lower seats, several *cavea ferarun*, where the beasts were locked up, the *carceres* (enclosures), from where gladiators or the prisoners emerged, and the *editoris munera* box, where the personality who sponsored the games or show sat.

This amphitheater ceased to be used for games in the 4th century, when Christianity spread, rejecting the death of men for entertainment. It was later used as a cemetery towards the end of the Roman empire, and several tombs and tombstones have been discovered from those times.

The walls and fortresses

Today, the walls still stand almost completely surrounding the city of Carmona, and provide us with a magnificent example of military architecture under the Romans, the Visigoths, the Arabs, and in the Early Middle Ages.

In general it can be said, that the foundations of the walls, the base and first stage are Roman, built at the time of the first Barbarian invasions. The crenellated battlements date from Arab times or from after the Reconquest. The «alcázars» are proper castles with solid fortifications. There are two gates in the wall which deserve especial attention: the Seville gate, where we see overlapping architectural styles from the principal eras: Roman, Arab and Renaissance, and the Córdoba gate, which was embellished in 1668 with a superb portal, already Baroque in style.

The walls of Carmona are worth a visit, as well as the castle, now a Parador hotel.

The Church of Santa María

This church was the principal mosque under Moslem rule. After the town had been reconquered, King Ferdinand made it a church with the name Santa María de la Asunción.

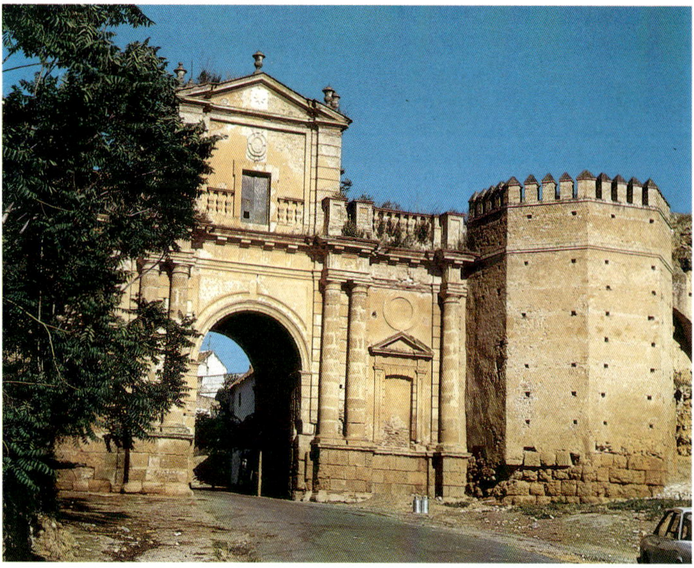

Old city gate

There are still remains of Arab architecture in the Court of the Orange Trees, but there is also a very interesting liturgical calendar from the time of the Visigoths carved on the shaft of one of the columns, which goes to show that before

Alcázar (fortress) of Don Pedro.

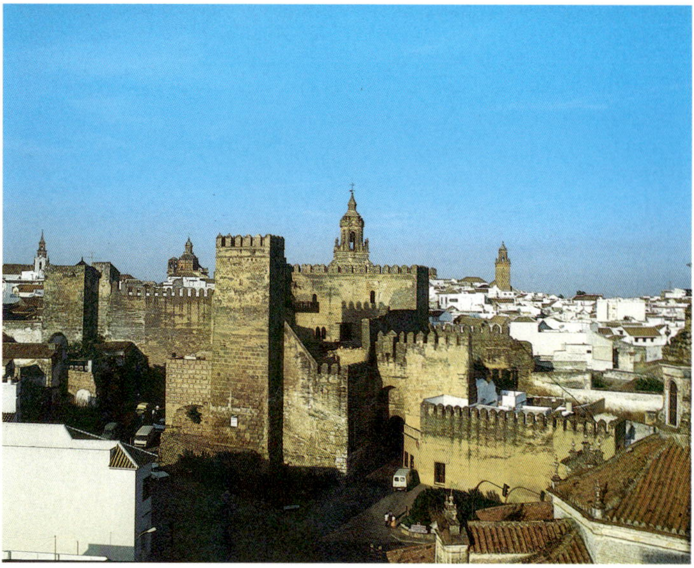

the Arab invasion this was a Christian church. This calendar, allows us to deduce that this was a monastery or prior, where the monks had to keep a series of religious feast-days throughout the year.

The church was reconstructed in the 15th century in Gothic style, other alterations and improvements having been carried out later. It has three aisles, with Gothic ribbed vaulting resting on pillars and buttresses.

The tower dates from the 16th century. In the main altarpiece there are scenes from the Coronation of Our Lady, the Calvary, the Birth of Jesus and other images and reliefs by Juan Bautista Vázquez and Nufro de Ortega.

In the chapel of Nuestra Señora de Gracia the image of the patron saint of the city is venerated, a very old image from the church of the Hieronymite friars. The church has an *Apostolado* (Series of Apostles) by Zurbarán.

Church of San Felipe

This is the oldest church in Carmona, built in the 13th century over the site of a former mosque, of which remains can still be seen. In the 15th century, the tower was added, in Mudejar style, at the foot of which a Gothic portal adorns the entrance to the church.

Inside we find three aisles with Mudejar ceilings in wood, alternating Mudejar ornamentation with the coats of arms of Archbishops Hurtado de Mendoza and Deza.

The main altar has remarkable images of Saint Philip, Saint John Nepomucene and Saint Joseph.

Church of San Blas

This church was constructed in the 14th century under the patronage of King Pedro I, who also founded the Sacramental Brotherhood in it, to which he himself belonged until his death.

The architecture is Mudejar with vaulted ceilings. The tower dates from the beginning of the 18th century. The main altarpiece is Jesuit Baroque and Saint Blas appears flanked by two saints of the Company of Jesus: Saint Louis Gonzaga and Saint John Berchmans. Over the central niche there is an image of the Virgin and Child, made at the beginning of the Baroque period. The rest of the church, all in Baroque style, corresponds to Jesuit taste.

Church of San Pedro

Beautiful inside, this church has a tower inspired in the Giralda of Seville and lovely cupolas.

It was built over a period of time reaching from the 15th to the18th century, with traces of the various different styles predominant over these centuries. Specially important is the chapel of Virgen de la Merced,

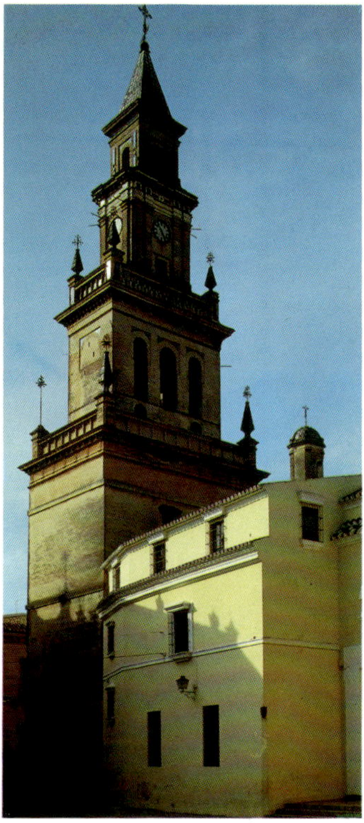

Church of Santa María.

with an altarpiece by Francisco Ocampo, and the Sacramental chapel, built by architect Ambrosio de Figueroa, which follows the style of the Figueroa family, reminding us of the Church of San Luis in Seville.

Convent of Santa Clara

It was founded in the 15th century by the Duchess of Arcos, at a time when the Franciscan order and its female branch, the nuns of St. Clare, were under the protection of kings and nobles. It is therefore a monumental, ornate church. The architectural style is Mudejar, with ogival apse and main arch, ribbed vaults and carved wooden ceilings.

The main altarpiece is the work of Felipe Ribas in the 17th century and carries images of saints of the Franciscan Order. In the presbytery there are paintings representing religious scenes, among them The *Adoration of the Magi* and *Saint Dominic in Soriano*. Many paintings and altarpieces enhance this church, which also has extremely beautiful glazed tiles from the 16th century.

In the presbytery crypt the Duchess of Arcos, its founder, is buried.

Other monuments in Carmona

It is not possible to visit all the churches in Carmona, among them Santiago and el Divino Salvador, but they all house interesting works of art. The Archivo Municipal (Municipal Archives) are also important, with documents from the Middle Ages and later, Royal Letters Patent, privileges, codes of laws and other historical documents.

The Parador has become in recent years a meeting place for politicians and political parties, and in its rooms the Statutes of the Autonomous Region of Andalusia were drafted, so that this document is known as the Carmona Statutes.

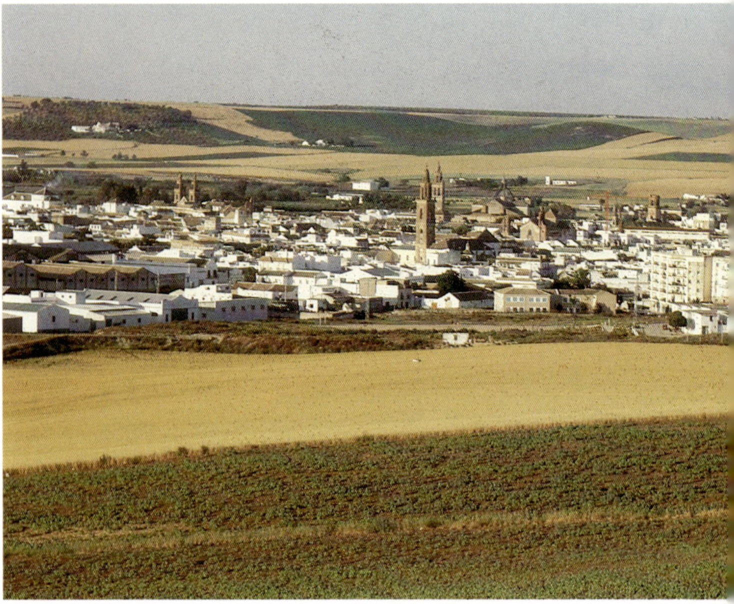

Panoramic view of Ecija.

ÉCIJA

We continue our itinerary towards the town of Ecija, 50 kilometers away (31 miles) and 84 kilometers (52 miles) from Seville.

Owing its warm climate, Ecija is called «the frying pan of Andalusia», in summer the highest temperatures in Spain are recorded here. As can be seen from a distance, it well deserves the name of «the town of towers», thanks to the large number that crown its buildings. It is a very typical Andalusian town as regards its architecture and layout.

The famous geographer Pomponius Mela, in his work *De situ Orbis*, grants this town the classification of *clarissima* and says that it can compete with *Corduba* (Córdoba) and *Hispalis* (Seville).

In comparison to other Andalusian towns, where the only monuments are religious ones, Ecija has a large number of architecturally interesting civil buildings.

Palace of Peñaflor

Built at the start of the 18th century in bonded brick, plastered and covered. The portal is of stone, made in 1726. Outstanding is the grand wrought-iron balcony, which runs from end to end of the façade, and amazes all who contemplate it for the first time.

The portal is very beautiful, with a balcony boasting a rich wrought-iron balaustrade, flan-

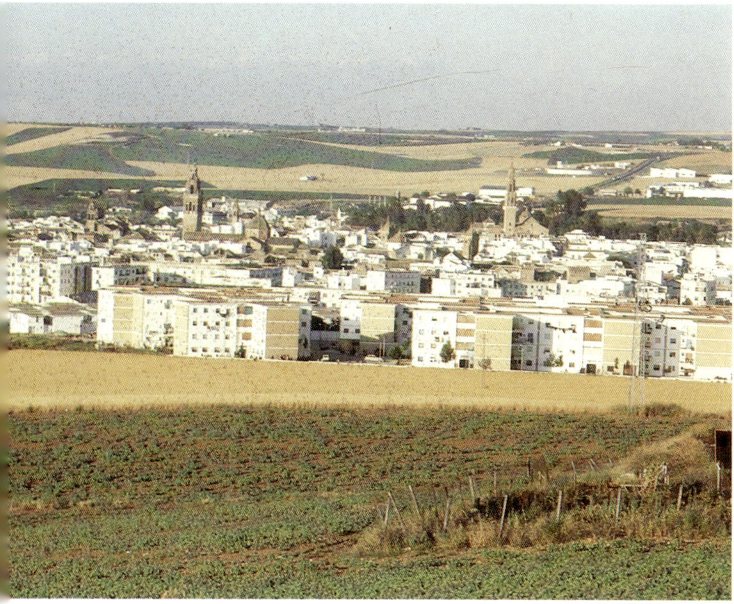

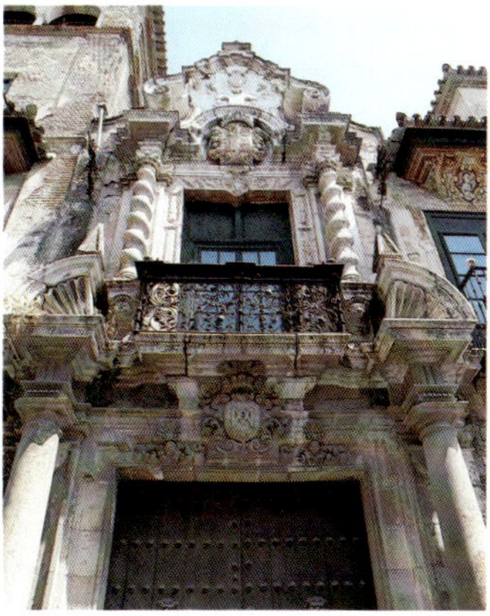

Peñaflor Palace.

ked by two Solomonic pillars and over it, the coat of arms of the Villasis family, who bore the title of Count of Peñaflor.

Next to the entrance stands a watch-tower, which was used in country estates to keep a look out over the property.

Inside we have a colonnaded patio, and in the center a fountain which could well be previous to the construction of the palace, brought here from some older building.

Palace of Benamejí

This is also a very handsome noble house. The portal has four Corinthian pillars sustaining the main balcony and a noble coat of arms flanked by pillars above this. On the façade there are other balconies with stone ornamentation.

The gateway is decorated with a great arch and the start of the double staircase is splendid. The patio has a colonnade

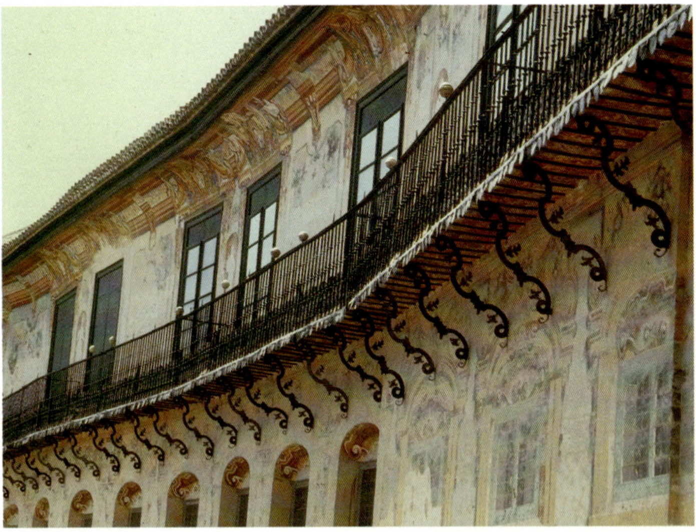

Peñaflor Palace. Balcony on the façade.

with marble pillars supporting the upper gallery.

This palace of the Marquis of Benamejí is also known as that of the Count of Valverde, as in the past both titles coincided in the same family.

Plaza Mayor

Ecija's Plaza Mayor is considered to be one of the most beautiful in the province of Seville, with arcades below and living quarters above. It was built in the 18th century probably under the influence of the new architectural ideas imposed by the chief officer of Seville and superintendent of Sierra Morena, Pablo de Olavide. The extreme temperatures are the reason for these arcades to protect people from the sun.

Other stately homes and public buildings

Also worth seeing are the houses of the Orduñas and the Albornoz, with coats of arms and handsome patios, as well as those of the Count of Aguila and the Count of Puerto Hermoso. The entrance to the palace of the Count of Vallehermoso de Cárdenas dates from the 16th century, with a grand arch and Baroque interior.

From among the public buildings, we must mention two fine ones from the 16th century, both by Hernán Ruiz, who built the belfry on La Giralda in Seville. These are the Carnicerías (Meat Market) and the Arca Real del Agua , whose façades are still standing.

The two towers of the original wall, called Albarrana and Quintana, both of Roman origin are also noteworthy.

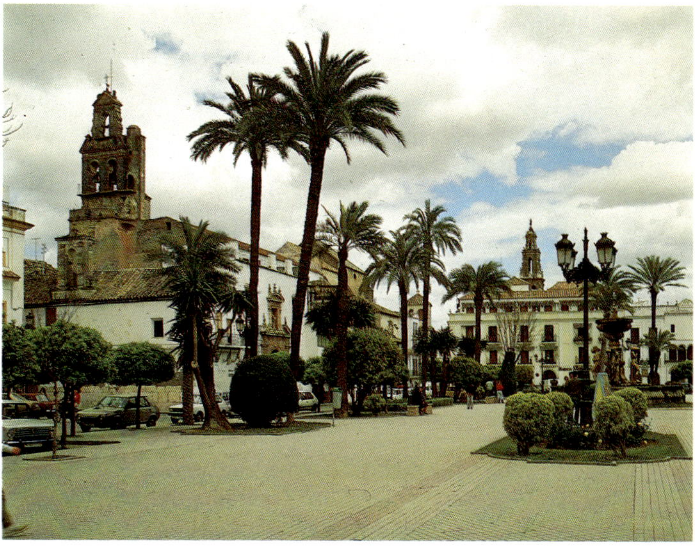

Vallehermoso Palace. *Plaza Mayor.*

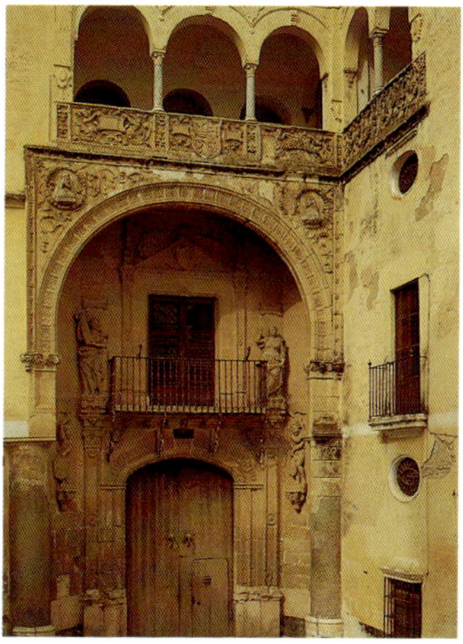

Archeological Museum of Écija

Installed in the courtyard of the Church of Santa Maria, this museum exhibits lovely Roman statues,including an excellent head of Germanicus.

Church of Santa María

Religious architecture in Ecija reflects the wealth of this town from the 16th to the 19th centuries, when not only stately palaces, but also the most notable churches and convents were built.

The church of Santa María, although it already existed in the Middle Ages, was restored in the 18th century, partly by the brothers Antonio and Ambrosio Figueroa, who are responsible for the Baroque style, and partly by José Alvarez, who commenced the transition to the Neoclassical style. It has three aisles and a tower. The monumental façade is in marble, with a niche above containing the Virgen de la Asunción, patron saint of the church.

In the presbytery there is a 16th century painting by Villegas Marmolejo, representing the Virgen de La Antigua. In the center a beautiful tabernacle stands, with carved figures and a Baroque Virgin. Notable are the images of Jesús Cautivo and the Virgen del Pilar, each in a separate altarpiece, made by Cayetano González.

As a whole, the church is adorned with numerous altarpieces from the 18th century, paintings and images many of which date from before the restoration of the church, from the 16th and 17th centuries. In the sacristy there is a Medieval Virgen de la Pera , and a sleeping Child Jesus.

The church furniture, chests in the sacristy, chairs, lecterns, etc., are artistically valuable, as well as the liturgical vessels, including pieces signed by the most famous silversmiths from the 16th to the 18th centuries.

Church of Santiago

This is a lovely church, with a tower whose the belfry bears a certain resemblance to the Giralda in Seville. This tower was built in the 18th century, after the earlier one had been destroyed by the famous earthquake of November 1st, 1755, which destroyed the city of Lisbon.

The style of the church is Mudejar with ogival portal and windows. With the exception of the tower, the rest dates from the 15th century. Inside there are rich paintings with episodes from Our Lord's Passion, by Alejo Fernández. Another series of paintings in the baptism chapel are by Luis Antonio de Morales. There is a Crucified Christ by Pedro Roldán, named Cristo de la Expiración, and in this altarpiece, we can see paintings by Pedro Campaña from the best years of the Renaissance.

Church of San Gil

This is a Mudejar church with a mixture of pointed Gothic from the 15th century, with extensions and restoration in the 18th century, probably to repair damages from the earthquake of 1755.

It houses important 16th century paintings, including the *Miracle of Saint Giles* by Alejo Fernández, and paintings by Villegas Marmolejo. The rest of the sculptures and paintings are fine 18th-century works.

Another ten churches, all similarly adorned, belonging to parishes and monasteries, provide the visitor with the opportunity of spending several days contemplating and studying them.

We will return to Seville by the same road, N-IV.

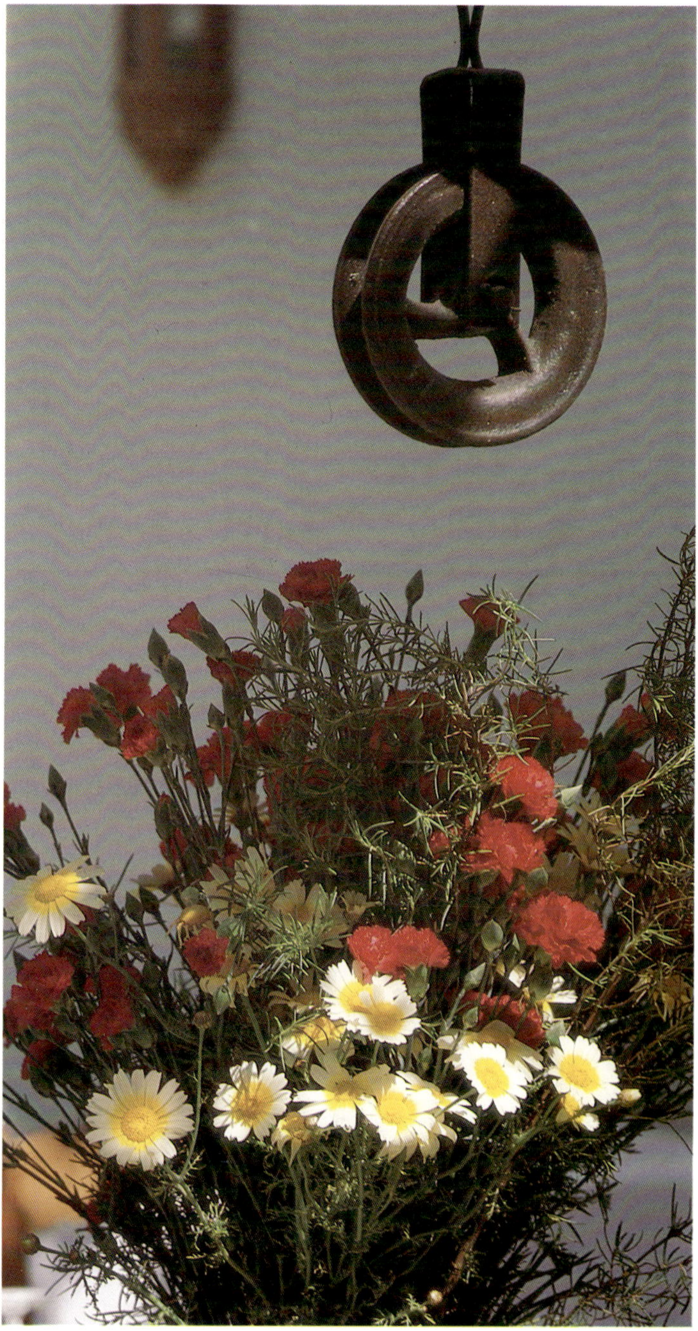

Window box full of flowers in Écija.

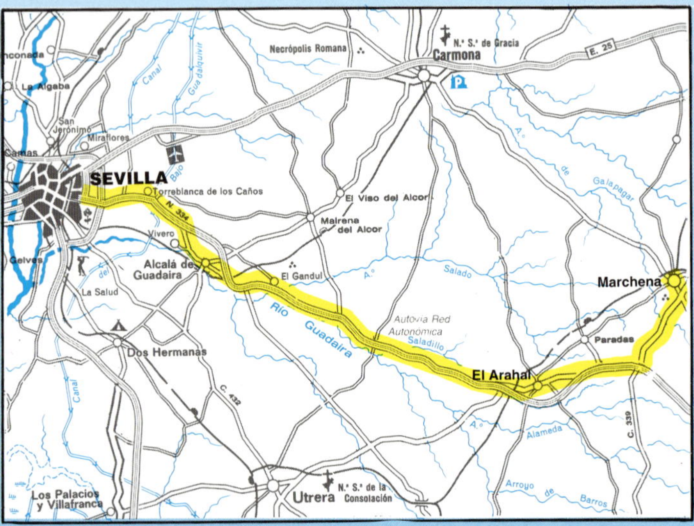

ROUTE 3: SEVILLE • ALCALA DE GUADAIRA • EL ARAHAL • MARCHENA

PLACES OF INTEREST

- **Alcalá de Guadaira**

Church and Sanctuary of Nuestra Señora del Aguila
Marchenilla Castle
Church of Santiago
Church of San Sebastián
Gates of the old city

- **El Arahal:**

Church of la Magdalena
Church of San Roque
Hospital of la Misericordia
Town Hall Chapel of the Vera Cruz
Convent of the Dominican Nuns

- **Marchena:**

The Ducal Palace
Church of Santiago
Church of Santa Maria de la Mota
Church of San Juan
Convent of San Agustín
Convent of San Andrés
Convent of La Inmaculada
Convent of Santa Clara

ACCESS

Take road A-334; after El Arahal turn left to take road A-333. 60 km away from Seville.

PRACTICAL INFORMATION ALONG THE ROUTE

Alcalá de Guadaira

Useful addresses and telephones:

- Town Hall. Tel: 70 10 30
- Red Cross. Tel: 70 57 11

Accommodation:

- Oroma***. Avda. de Portugal, s/n. Tel 470 08 04

Marchena

Useful addresses and telephones:

- Town Hall. Tel: 484 34 00
- Red Cross. Tel: 484 33 79
- Archeological Museum. Calle San Francisco, s/n. Tel: 484 42 89

END OF ROUTE

Take the same route back to Seville from Marchena.

ROUTE 3: SEVILLE · ALCALÁ DE GUADAIRA · ARAHAL MARCHENA

We leave Seville by road 334, which begins to slope gradually up hill, after the last industrial estates outside Seville, commencing the climb up to Sierra de los Alcores, a region of small hills where most towns bear the word Alcor as part of their name, such as Mairena del Alcor and El Viso del Alcor.

Fifteen kilometers from Seville, at the foot of a fortified castle, we find Alcalá de Guadaira.

Alcalá de Guadaira

The name of this town comes from the Arab word *Al-Calat*, which means fortress. However, the castle of Alcalá was not built by the Arabs, nor even by the Romans: it dates back to Phoenician times, 3000 years ago. Reinforced by the Romans when the Barbarians invaded, and fortified by the Moslems in the 10th century, it was one of the most important fortresses in Arab Andalusia, to defend Seville from the Christians. However, the King Ferdinand finally conquered it after a long siege in 1244.

The castle had six towers, but only one stands today, known as Homage Tower because here the Christian banner was raised after it surrendered. This castle continued to play an important role in Spanish history during the war between Pedro I and his illegitimate brother Enrique de Trastamara. It was used as a prison and several personalities were held here, such as the Master of the Order of Calatrava, Diego García de Padilla, and the third Duke of Osuna, Pedro Girón.

Alcala de Guadaira, castle.

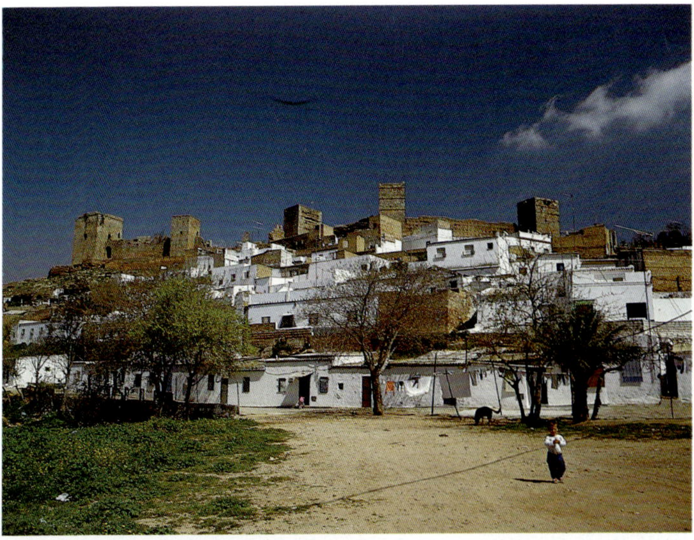

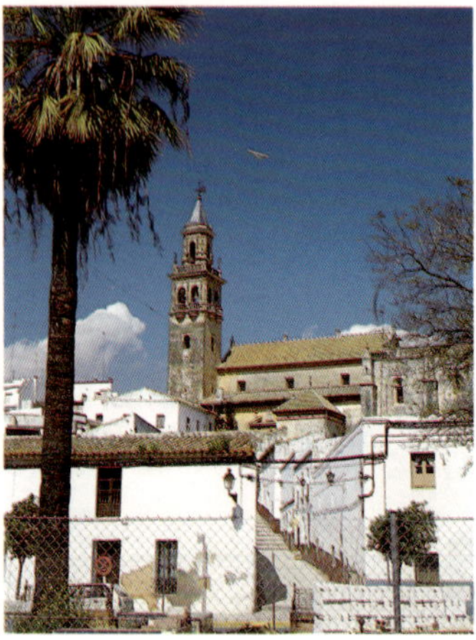

Church of Saint James.

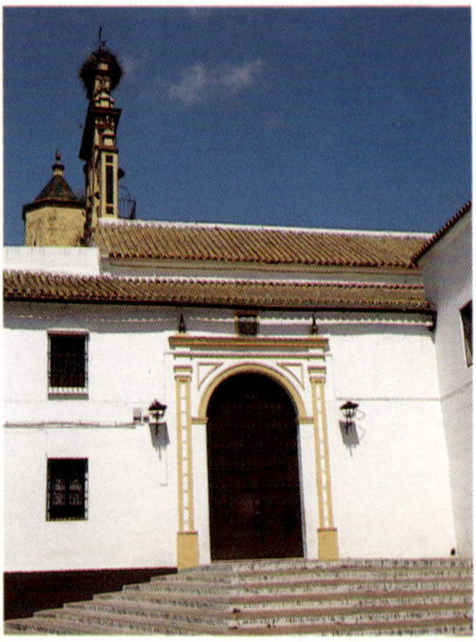

Church of Saint Sebastian.

Church and Sanctuary of Nuestra Señora del Aguila

Within the castle precints, as was customary in the Middle Ages, stands the sanctuary of the patron saint of the town, Nuestra Señora del Aguila. This church is Mudejar in style and was built in the 14th century, with three aisles and an apse. This was the first parish church after the town had been reconquered until the parish of Santiago was built.

In this sanctuary, the image of Our Lady of the Eagle is venerated, a sculpture only eighty centimeters (32 inches) high, a copy of the original Medieval image made by Antonio Illanes in 1937 after the old one had been destroyed in 1936.

Marchenilla Castle

Leaving Alcalá de Guadaira we can see Marchenilla Castle, a solid military structure, with large fortified round towers and battlements.

Church of Santiago

This 16th century Gothic church has three very wide aisles and was reformed in the 18th century, when the aisles were extended. The ceiling is vaulted and coffered over the presbytery. Some authors found these 18th-century reforms in bad taste, although nowadays they are considered acceptable.

The main altarpiece was carved by Miguel Adán in 1589, and the sacrarium was made by Cristóbal de Guadix in the 17th century. In the left hand aisle, the Altar of the Souls has a painting attributed to Pacheco and several sculpted angels attributed to Luisa Roldán de Mena, «La Roldana». In the Chapel of Jesus the images are by Antonio Illanes.

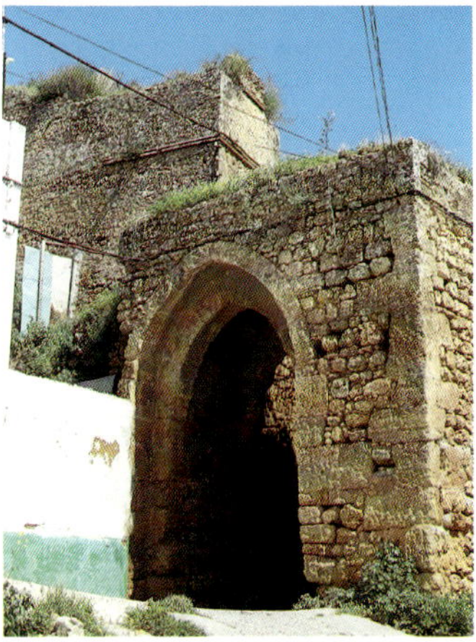

Gateway in the city walls.

The rest of the sculpture dates from the 18th century.

Church of San Sebastián

This church is Mudejar, from the 14th century, and has three aisles. A valuable Mudejar ceiling was lost in a fire in 1936 and the present one is by the Sevillian architect Gómez Millán. The main altarpiece has a painting representing *Saint Sebastian*, by the artist E. Blanco, substituting the Saint Sebastian painted by Pacheco, which was also lost when the church was burnt.

The images in the right hand aisle are all new, by the sculptor Poneda Calderón. There are two old paintings representing the Holy Family and Saint Anthony of Padua, both from the 18th century.

Streets and gates

In Alcalá de Guadaira, the gates of the old city walls are worth seeing, specially the puerta de Santa Catalina (gate), as well as typical streets, such as P. Lafita street and Méndez Bajarano street, both with steep steps and lovely views.

El Arahal

Following this same road 334, we reach the locality of El Arahal, located thirty kilometers (19 miles) further on, or 45 kilometers (28 miles) from Seville. This was the ancient Roman city of Calúcula, but the Arabs changed its name to *Ar-ahal*, which means «land of pastures».

Church of La Magdalena

The main church is that of la Magdalena, built at the end of the 18th century, at the height of the Neoclassical period. The principal façade is severe, rising upwards in straight lines, at the expense of the plain pillars supporting the lintel over the door, repeated above it by other pillars topped by a rectangular pediment and above it, another triangular one. The adjoining tower, on the right is square with a two-stage belfry, the upper one octagonal and closed by a tiled pyramid. The interior of the church is equally Neoclassical with beautiful vaulting. The image of the saint presiding the main altar is by Antonio Mar-

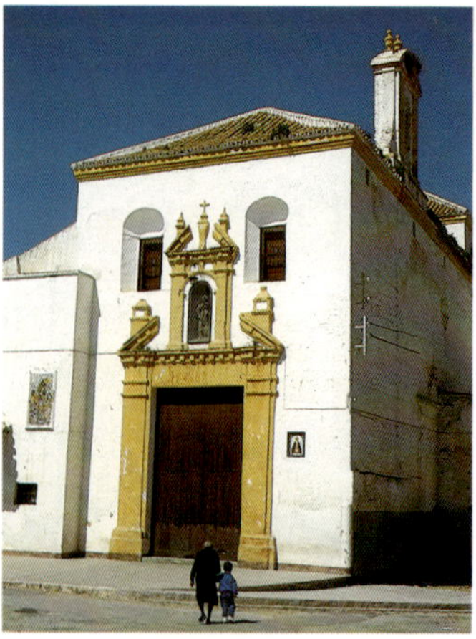

Church of Saint Roch.

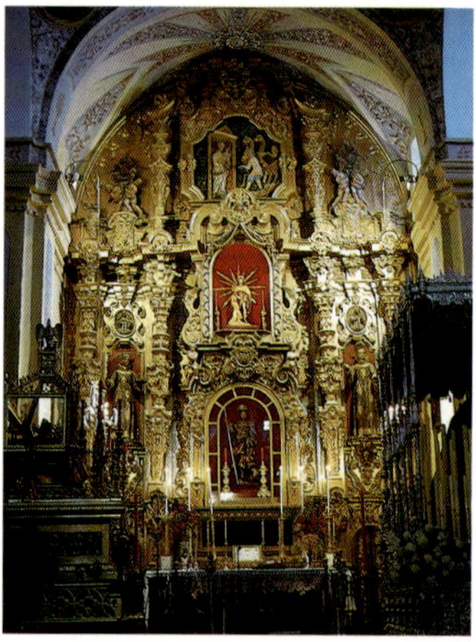

Saint Roch: Main Altar.

zal, dating from the late 18th century; the choir stalls date from the same time and were made by José Antonio Casaus.

All the images, as well as the wrought iron pulpit, and the furniture harmonize with the rest in time and style.

Church of San Roque

This church belongs to a Franciscan monastery, and the images venerated here are therefore those of Franciscan saints, the most important being Saint Francis of Assisi, Saint Roch and Saint Anthony. The church itself, as well as the portal are from the 17th century, as it was founded during the first half of this century.

Quite interesting and curious from the point of view of iconography is a very large painting in a chapel located next to the cloister, representing the Tree of Life: with Jesus on one side and Death with a scythe on the other.

Hospital of la Misericordia

The only thing left of this hospital founded in the 15th century is the portal in Mudejar style with ogival arch. The present church dates from the 18th century with a lovely square tower and a belfry in three sections, the two upper ones in beautiful Baroque style.

The main altar has images of Saint Christopher and Saint Anthony, a relief of the Eternal Father from the 18th century, and the Christ of Mercy, by Antonio Castillo Lastrucci, copied after an earlier Medieval one.

Civil Architecture

El Arahal Town Hall is a beautiful two-story building, the upper one with a colonnade

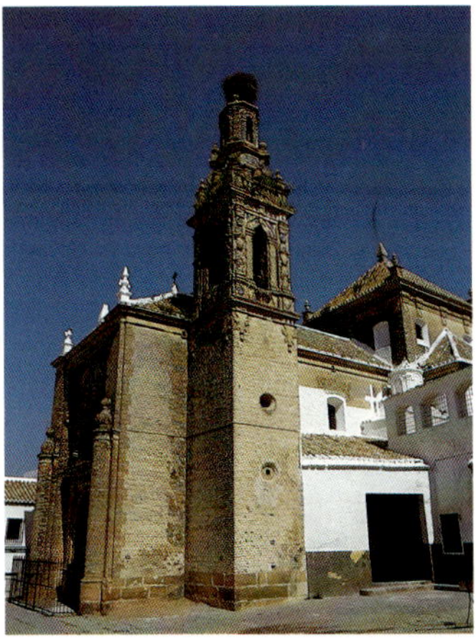

Hospital of Mercy.

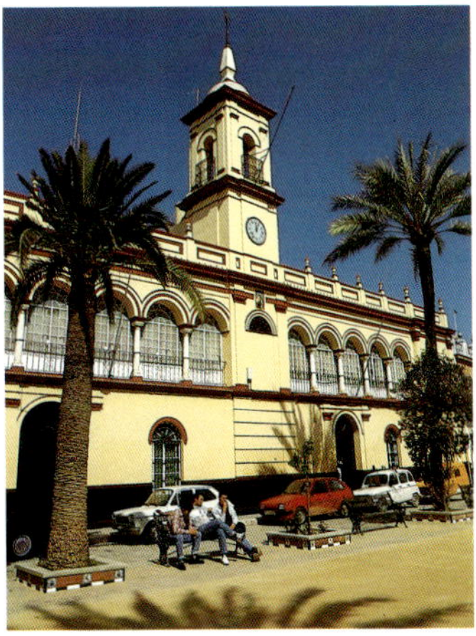

Town Hall.

divided into two sections, each with five arches on double pillars, a terrace roof with balustrade and decorative vases of lilies, and a two-stage clock tower, the lower one with the clock, and the upper one with bells, crowned by a spire consisting of a tiny cupola and needle.

In several streets there are typical miradores or low, closed balconies at street level, and also old mansions now used as headquarters of the Civil Guard and various schools.

Other religious buildings

The chapel of the Vera Cruz is also interesting, with an 18th-century Baroque portal flanked by Solomonic columns, and a lovely belfry on top, as well as the convent of the Dominican nuns, a large, severe building with a very characteristic cropped bell-tower.

After visiting El Arahal, we continue on the same road and bit further, on the left, we find road 333, which will take us to Marchena.

THE TOWN OF MARCHENA

This town was founded by the Romans and known as Colonia Marcia in Roman times. After the Reconquest, it was given by King Ferdinand IV to Fernando Ponce de León in 1309, and his descendants took the title of Dukes of Arcos. Thus, Marchena is known as «the capital of the estates of the Duke of Arcos».

The Walls of Marchena

Marchena was a walled town, and a large part of the walls are still in relatively good condition. Although Roman in origin they were restored and strengthened by the Arabs in the Almohad era, and later by the Duke of Arcos during a very private war fought in the 15th century between the feudal houses of Arcos and of Medina Sidonia, which affected Seville and the whole of its province as well.

These walls have two interesting gateways, the arco de la Rosa (arch of the Rose), formerly the Seville Gate, flanked by two towers with battlements, and also the arco de Santa María.

The total walled perimeter is 2400 meters (7874 ft.) long, and has been declared a National Historical Monument. Pope Martin V granted indulgence to those donating towards the restoration of the walls when faced with the danger of new Moslem invasions, as an inscription inside informs us.

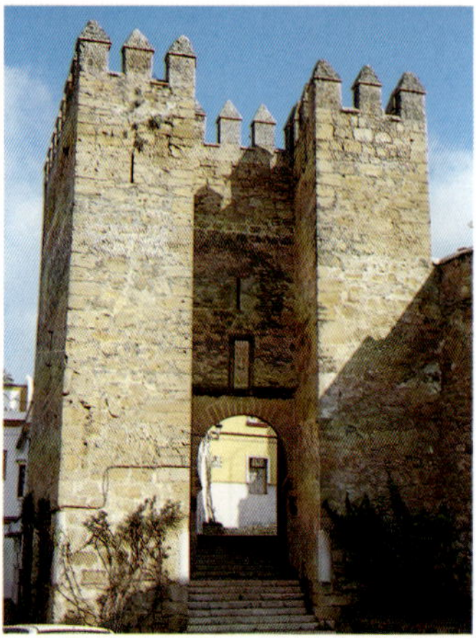

Arch of the Rose.

The Palacio Ducal

Until a century ago, the ducal palace stood here, although today it has disappeared and all that remains is the so called plaza de Arriba, where tournaments or equestrian festivals were held in Renaissance times. On this same square stands the building of the old Casas Consistoriales dating from the 18th century, two stories high, with a splendid portal flanked by Tuscan pillars and a balcony with a coat of arms.

There are many stately houses with stone portals and coats of arms spread out over the rest of the town. In the building of the Cabildo granary next to the Church of San Juan, grain collected as tithe by the church was stored.

The Church of Santiago.

Even if not the wealthiest, it deserves to be visited in the first place because here is the pantheon of the Dukes of Arcos. This is in the chancel, next to the main altar. Here are the tombs of Rodrigo Ponce de León and his descendants, in black marble and red veined marble, as was customary for aristocratic houses. This pantheon dates from the 17th century. The chancel is decorated with the coats of arms of the Ponce de Léon family and the Order of Saint Dominic. The main altarpiece has images of several saints of the same order and paintings representing the Immaculate Conception, Saint Catherine, Saint Teresa, and Saint Francis.

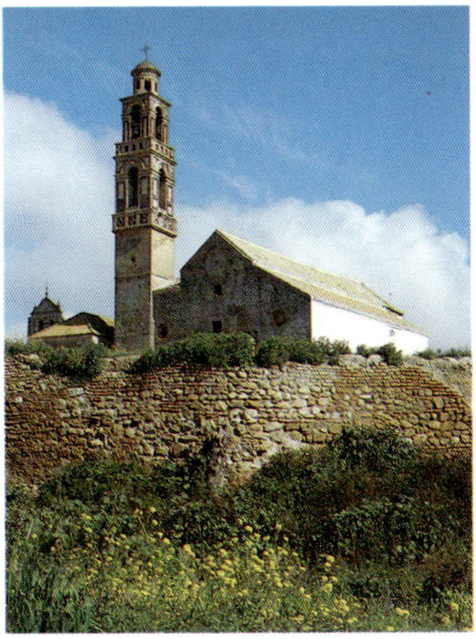

Santa María de la Mota.

The remaining altars have fine 18th century paintings, and there is a processional figure of Our Lady of Sorrows, from the 19th century by Gabriel Astorga.

The church building has a single aisle in Gothic style, dating from the 16th century with some Renaissance decoration: a wooden trellis screen is a splendid sample of Mudejar style.

The Church of Santa María de la Mota

The church of Santa María de la Mota shows a series of styles on the outside, which leads us to think that it was a Mosque in the Middle Ages, over which a military church was constructed in the 13th century, in a transitional Romanesque to Gothic style, and that later in the 15th century, it was re-built once again, maintaining the lower section of the tower. The portal is Gothic with a magnificent pointed arch, maybe too large for the proportions of the façade.

The first stage of the tower is square, without decoration nor windows, and over this, a belfry was added with two bell stories, also square and in Renaissance style, and this is crowned by, a small circular section with a little cupola.

Inside we find three aisles, with Mudejar wooden ceilings, over plain arches on pillars. The chancel has a Gothic vault.

In the main altar, in good Baroque style, there is a 16th century image of Nuestra Señora de la Mota, the patron saint, accompanied by others of Saint Joachim, Saint Joseph, Saint Millan and Saint Anthony.

In the left hand chapel there is a Dead Christ, by Jerónimo Fernández. In the right hand chapel there are good images of Christ Crucified, the Virgin Mary and Saint John the Evangelist, from the 16th century. The rest of the statuary in the church, as well as the paintings in the presbytery, date from the 17th and 18th centuries.

The Church of San Juan

This is the largest church in Marchena, cathedral-like in size. Built in the 15th century, it combines Gothic and Mudejar styles. It has five aisles, the three center ones with vaulted ceilings and the two lateral ones with Mudejar wooden ceiling work.

The main altarpiece is one of the richest in Spain, with paintings by Alejo Fernández from the early16th century and polychromed reliefs alternating with sculptures.

The next altarpiece on the left is magnificent, with a large relief of the Last Supper from the 16th century, profuse Renaissance decoration and images. The one on the right dates from the 18th century, like the rest and the choirstalls.

In the sacristy, there is a painting of the Flemish school of the 16th century, by Juan Bautista de Amiens.

But the most important pictorial work in this church of San Juan is a series of Apostles by Zurbarán, which is kept in the church museum, especially set up for this collection.

Convent of San Agustín

The rival to the Church of San Juan is the convent of San Agustín, since for the order of Augustinian friars it was of the utmost importance to maintain its artistic supremacy. Its size is also cathedral-like, which makes the residents of the Marchena say that their town has two cathedrals but no bishop.

A Mexican architect and friar participated in the construction of the Church of San Agustín, and his presence is apparent in the decoration, with mestizo-faced angels, possibly the only example of Mexican art in Spain. The whole is 18th century Baroque, slightly overdecorated.

The sculptures in the altarpieces date from various centuries, mainly from the 18th century. There is a good Baroque organ from this same century. Curiously, one of the Dukes of Arcos, Manuel Ponce de León was buried in this church, in the presbytery, in the mid-17th century.

This convent has next to it a cloister with a colonnade and an arcade holding up the second story, in the Renaissance style.

Nuns' Convents

Marchena has several well-endowed convents, which were under the protection of the Dukes of Arcos.

Convento de San Andrés, of the Order of La Merced.– The building dates from the 18th century, although the convent was founded by Doña Mercedes Benjumea, who is buried in this church, and whose tombstone says she died in 1530. It houses good sculptures from the 18th century, when the present altarpieces were made, although the image of the saint is the original from the 16th century.

Convento de la Inmaculada Concepción. – Founded in the 17th century, it has a lovely altarpiece in the Churrigueresque style of the 18th century, with sculpted images, except for that of the Virgin in the central niche, which is a clothed figure.

Convent of Santa Clara. – This church is nowadays the chapel of the Brotherhood of Humility and Patience and Our Lady of Sorrows. From the time when it was a convent of Clarist nuns, there is a fine altarpiece of the 17th century and a wrought iron pulpit in the typical Sevillian style of the 17th century.

Having finished the visit to Marchena, we return to Seville by the same road.

Convent of San Agustín

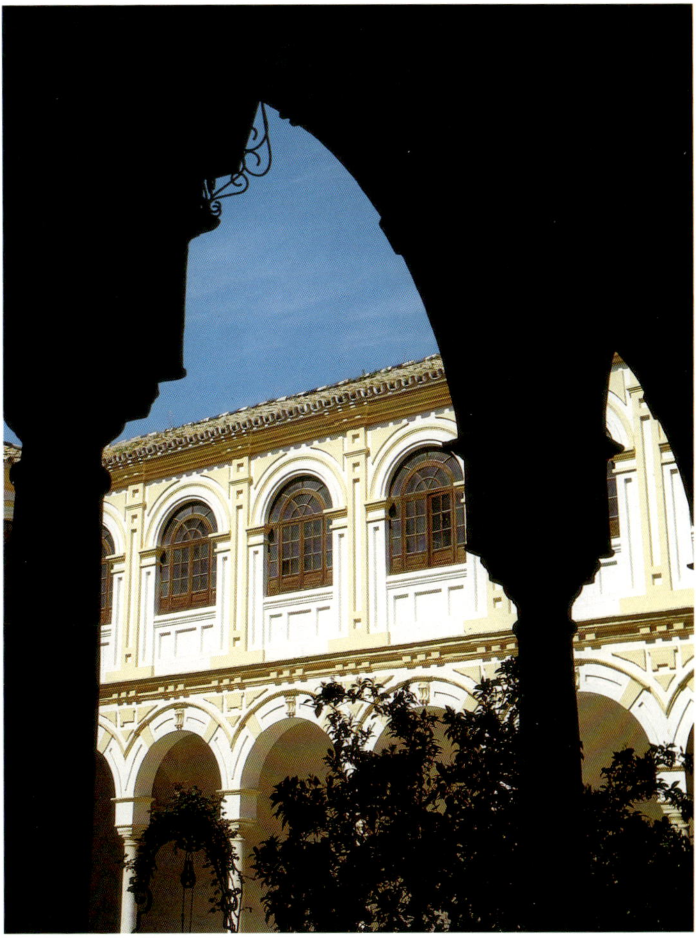

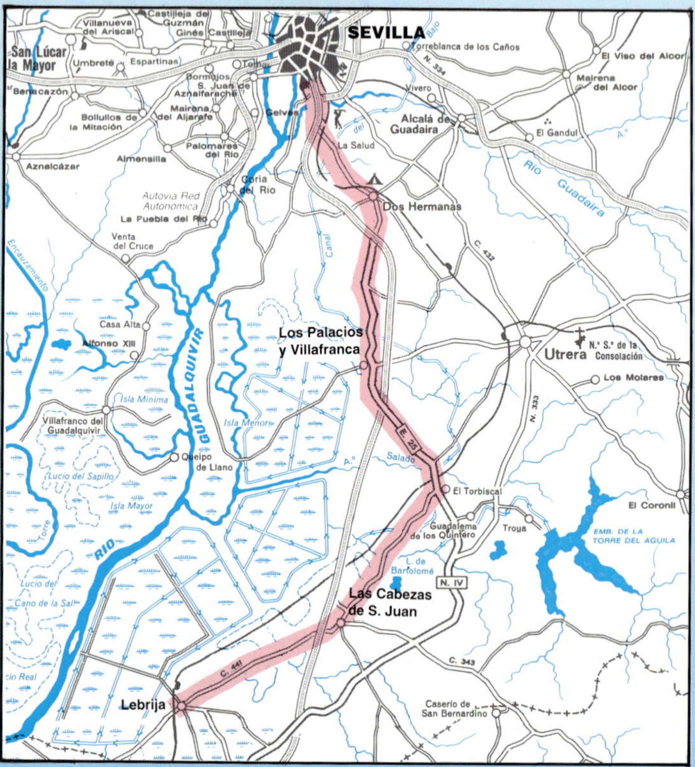

ROUTE 4:
SEVILLE • LOS PALACIOS
LAS CABEZAS DE SAN JUAN-LEBRIJA

PLACES OF INTEREST

- **Los Palacios and Villafranca:**
  Church of Santa María
  Chapel of Nuestra Señora de los Remedios
  Ermita de la Aurora
- **Las Cabezas de San Juan:**
  Constitution Square
  Church of San Juan
- **Lebrija:**
  Church of Santa María la Mayor
  Church of Santa María de Jesús
  Convent of las Concepcionistas
  Convent of San Francisco
  Chapel of Belén

ACCESS	Take road N-IV towards Cádiz. 79 km away from Seville
END OF ROUTE	Take the same road back to Seville

ROUTE 4: SEVILLE · LOS PALACIOS LAS CABEZAS DE SAN JUAN · LEBRIJA

We leave Seville on N-IV heading south (towards Cádiz), and after about 30 kilometers (19 miles) we find Los Palacios.

LOS PALACIOS AND VILLAFRANCA

This is a historical place which already existed over 3,000 years ago in Tartessian times. It developed under Roman rule to the point that the Roman Senate granted it the privilege of minting its own coins. At the time of the Moslems, it was reduced to a small village known as *Almudaina*, which in Arab means «the wall», as there were remains of fortifications from the last stage of the Roman occupation, when the Romans had to fortify it against the Vandals and the Alani.

After the Reconquest in 1250, two villages were founded upon this abandoned territory, on both sides of the road leading from Seville to the Port of Santa María, where King Alfonso X the Wise tried unsuccessfully to create a great religious center dedicated to Saint Mary, to rival Santiago de Compostela in pilgrimages. One of the two villages was called Villafranca del Salado, Villafranca meaning «free town», as exemptions from certain duties and taxes were granted to this village so as to attract new residents capable of defending the territory from new raids by the Moors. The other village was founded a bit later, in the 14th century, and was known as Los Palacios (The Palaces), as King Pedro I built a number of recreational palaces here so as to use this place for big game hunting, mainly bears, which abounded in this land of salt sea marshes.

The two villages were joined in the 19th century, as can be seen in its municipal coat of arms from the word «union».

The Church of Santa María

Unfortunately nothing remains of those royal palaces and hunting grounds, as they were abandoned after the death of King Pedro I and later destroyed by the Inquisition, who took the stones for its buildings in Seville during the 16th century. It is interesting to visit the church of Santa María La Blanca. The church has three aisles, Mudejar in style although reformed in the 17th century. The tower has three stages decreasing in size, the upper two in Renaissance style, topped by a pyramidal spire. The portal is made of stone and has a plain round arch flanked by pillars, the transept has a semiscircular vault while the aisles have barrel vaulting.

The main altarpiece shows notable paintings representing the *Adoration of the Shepherds* and the two *Saint Johns*, made by Pablo Legot in the 17th century. In the center is Our Lady of the Snows, a clothed image sculp-

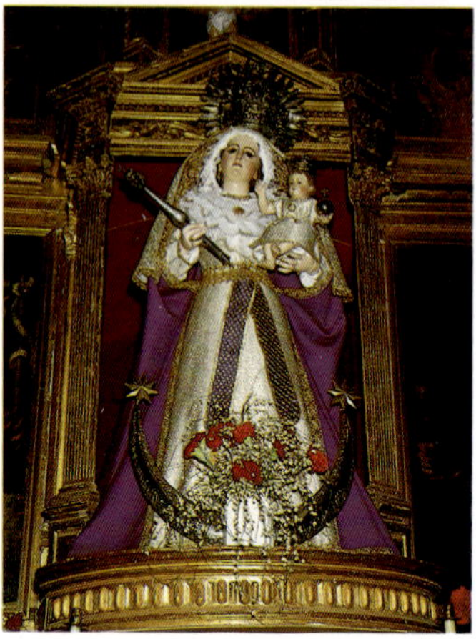

Altarpiece in the Church of Santa María. Our Lady of the Snows.

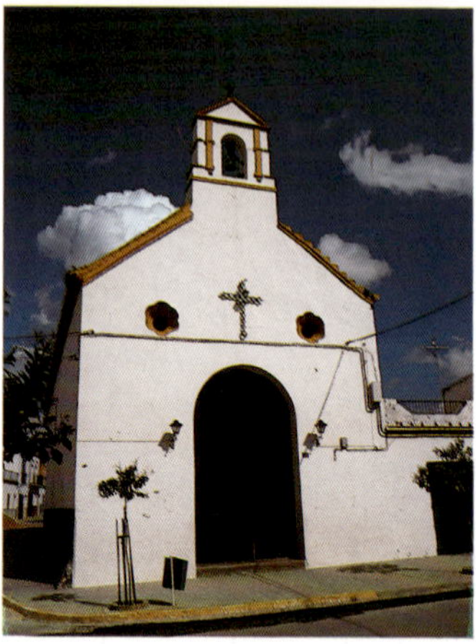

Chapel of Our Lady of the Snows.

ted in the 18th century by an anonymous artist of the Sevillian school.

On the other altars magnificent sculptures and reliefs of several saints dating from the 17th and 18th centuries can be admired, all of them fine works from the school of Seville. The Baroque style organ is worth observing. It was made by a famous organ builder, Juan Ortegaz.

Chapel of Our Lady of Remedies

Also worth visiting is the Chapel of Nuestra Señora de los Remedios, formerly dedicated to Saint Sebastian. This is a small building from the 17th century, in popular architectural style, with plain walls, roofing of curved Spanish tiles and with a simple belfry on top of the façade, all of it whitewashed in the manner of country shrines, although it is located inside the town.

It is small, with a single nave, and a wooden ceiling, but in spite of its size it houses works of artistic value, such as an image of Saint Michael killing the dragon, a magnificent work by Pedro Roldán, in which his daughter «La Roldana» probably collaborated.

Also worth seeing is the main altarpiece, with a crucified Christ and a Saint Sebastian from the 17th century, and Our Lady of Remedies, a clothed image from the 18th century.

The Ermita de la Aurora

The Ermita de la Aurora (Shrine) is also interesting. Dating from the 18th century, it has images of Franciscan saints, such as Saint Anthony of Padua, Saint Dominic and Saint Raphael.

There are two paintings attributed to Murillo or his circle, representing the *Betrothal of the Virgin and the Adoration of the Shepherds*, and a Crucified Christ and a Saint Nicholas of Bari both from the 18th century, in polychromed sculpture.

LAS CABEZAS DE SAN JUAN

Continuing on the same road, about 30 kilometers from Palacios (19 miles), that is, 60 kilometers (37 miles) from Seville, we reach the town of Las Cabezas de San Juan. It is located in the middle of an area of distinct undulations, hence the name of cabezas or heads, meaning rounded hills. There was already a settlement on this site in times of the Iberians, with the name of *Ugía*, and remains have been found of this civilization, as well as from the Roman settlement, which today are kept in the Museum in Seville. Some Roman pillars can be seen today in the porch of the parish church.

Constitution Square

The historical interest of Las Cabezas resides in the fact that here the uprising of General Riego on January 1, 1820 took place.

This revolt is one of the important pages in Spanish history of the 19th century. In this region numerous regiments were encamped in the towns of Arcos, Villamartín, Bornos, Alcalá de los Gazules, Medina Sidonia and others, waiting to embark for the colonies to suppress the rebellions in Mexico and Colombia. Rafael Riego, who was in command of the Battalion of Asturias in Las Cabezas

Constitución Square

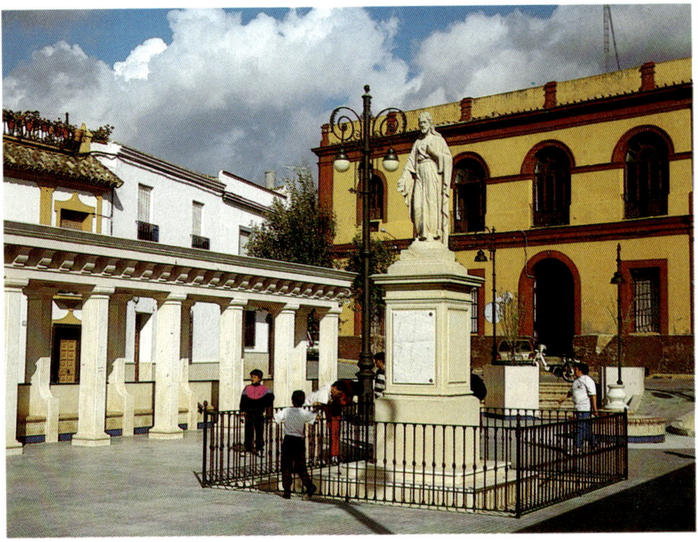

de San Juan, in agreement with Colonels Quiroga, Arco Agüero and López Baños, rose in instruction with his battalion at dawn on January 1st, 1820, proclaiming the Liberal Constitution of 1812, which had been abolished by Ferdinand VII.

For this purpose, he had the battalion form in what is now called plaza de la Constitución and from a balcony he read his proclamation, which was received with enthusiasm by the soldiers and townsfolk.

The house from whose balcony Rafael Riego rallied his troops on behalf of the Constitution is number 26, and has a commemorative plaque.

Church of San Juan

Although as we have said, the name Las Cabezas comes from the topography of the place, de San Juan (of Saint John) was soon added in remembrance of the head of Saint John the Baptist. For this reason this saint was declared the patron saint of the village, today a town. The church of Saint John rises on the highest part of town, which it dominates with its lovely skyline, visible from everywhere. The church was built in 1792, with the participation of the famous architects of the Figueroa family, who also left fine religious and civil Baroque works in Seville: Ambrosio and Antonio Matías Figueroa.

The façade is very beautiful, flanked by two towers: one with a graceful belfry and the other one smaller and without bells. The upper part of the façade consists of a large semicircular blind arch and underneath there is a Baroque portal, with Tuscan pillars on either side supporting a niche, all very handsome.

Inside, it has three vaulted aisles and the transept has a cupola on eight ribs. The main altarpiece is dedicated to Saint John the Baptist, with paintings representing the life of the saint, by Francisco Agustín, court painter to King Charles IV. In the center of the main altar is an image of the Immaculate Conception in the typical Sevillian style of the 18th century.

Another altar has in its center an image of Saint John by the famous sculptor Juan de Mesa, probably dating from the same time as the Saint Christopher he made for the Church of the Salvador in Seville, towards 1620. This and the images of the Vera Cruz, Saint Ferdinand and Saint Hermenegild are from before the construction of the church, from the end of the 17th century. Still older are two paintings of Saint Telmo and Saint Matthew, which are from the early 16th century, and were brought here from other churches. The same can be said of the sacrarium altarpiece, whose images appear to come from different convents which disappeared during the French invasion.

Some of the paintings kept in this church are attributed to Goya, Zurbarán and Valdés Leal, while several sculptures are believed to have been carved by «La Roldana», although there are no documents to confirm this. Since this town was always agriculturally rich and enjoyed a flourishing economic situation, it would be logical for this church and others no longer in existence to have had valuable works of art.

LEBRIJA

From Las Cabezas de San Juan, we continue our excursion, turning right onto road C-441, which takes us to the town of Lebrija, the center of a region known as Las Marismas (The Marshes). As a historical foot-note we could mention that these fields we are crossing was where corn brought from America was first planted in the 18th century, by way of a grant from Charles III. Horses were raised on this plain for the army and for transportation and until then, they were fed with all sorts of wild plants: «the horses are drunk from eating chives, and the mares miscarry when they eat mallows»; for this reason, the planting of corn was authorized to provide less harmful fodder for the horses.

The town of Lebrija is of Turdetan origin and was known as *Nebrissa* already in Roman times, as confirmed by Pliny and Antonius' *Itinerary*. Due to its proximity to the mouth of the Guadalquivir, it was always a strategic location, and thus a powerful castle was built here, which was first Roman, later a Moslem fortress or *Al-Calat*, strengthened in the 9th century by the governor of Sidonia, Suleyman Ben Mohammed. Some ruins of this castle are still left.

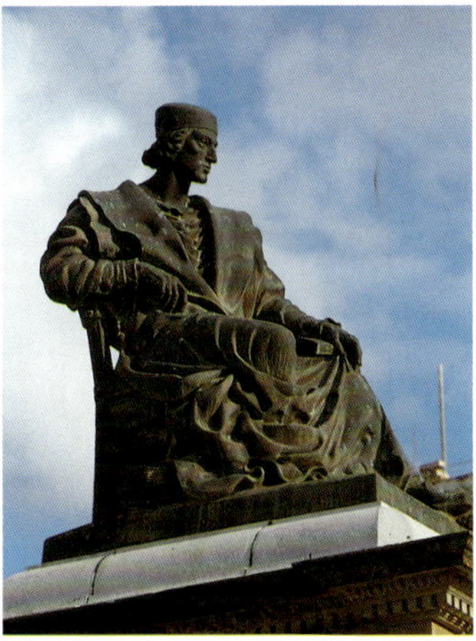

E. A. de Nebrija.

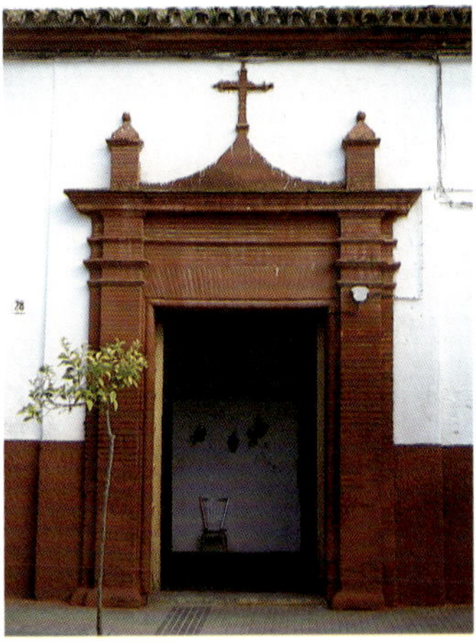

Hospital of Mercy.

El Caserío

The houses of Nebrija reveal great architectural harmony: white houses with fine wrought-iron balconies and barred balconies at street level. Some streets are steep, other have steps.

There are mansions with coats of arms, convents and chapels. Everything bears evidence of a very flourishing economy in times past.

In the main square we come across a beautiful monument to the most famous son of this town: the grammarian Elio Antonio de Nebrija, who in 1492 published the first grammar of the Spanish language and a Latin-Spanish dictionary, so that, as some historians have said, Nebrija was responsible for giving Spain a language capable of being transmitted to the Empire that was born that same year following the discovery of America.

Among the most noteworthy civil buildings are the Cilla del Cabildo (16th century Chapter House Granary), with an artistic Renaissance portal; the once magnificent Hospital de la Misericordia, with an 18th century entranceway.

The Church of Santa María la Mayor

This 15th-century church was built over the site of a 12th-century Arab mosque and the adjoining cloister was probably the ablutions court of the mosque. However, it is likely that there was previously a proto-Christian and Visigothic church or basilica on this spot, as can be deduced from an inscription over the lintel of a side entrance of the original church, where we can read the following text:

«Alexandra, clarissima foemina, vixit annos plus minus XXV, recessit in pace, X Kal.Ianuar. Era DIII. Probus filius Vixit Anos duos mensem unum.»

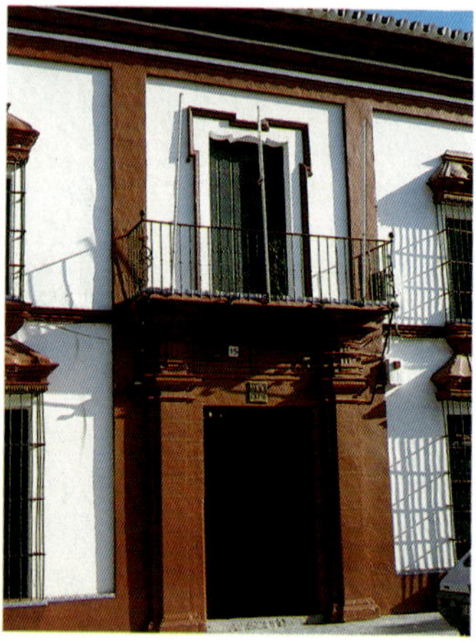

La Cilla del Cabildo. (Chapter House Granary).

Which could be translated as follows: «Alexandra, a very honest woman, lived twenty five years more or less, died in peace on the tenth day of the calends of January of the year 465 (the slab means the Hispanic Era which has 38 years less than the Christian Era) and her son Probus, who lived two years and one month».

The present church contains parts from the 13th century, transitional from Romanesque to Gothic, with alterations and extensions from the 15th century and the first half of the 16th century, in which the great architect Hernán Ruiz, who made the belfry of La Giralda participated, followed by other architects, among them, his son of the same name.

The church tower is made of brick and is reminiscent of La Giralda, specially in the distribution of its balconies in the first section. The interior con-

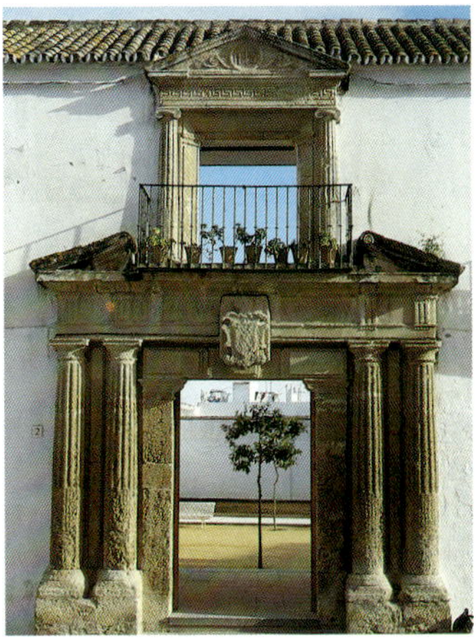

The Chapter House.

sists of three aisles with vaulted ceilings on piers with pilasters adjoined. The ceiling is quite unusual with eleven half cupolas, unique in Andalusia and possibly even in Spain.

The great altarpiece by Alonso Cano

The main altarpiece in this church is the work of the famous sculptor Alonso Cano, who in his time earned himself the title «the Spanish Michelangelo». Alonso Cano was born in Granada and learned sculpture first from his father. He moved to Seville at an early age and was apprentice to the workshop of Pacheco, where he learned to paint alongside Velázquez. However, once he became an excellent painter, he also worked as an architect and did not wish to give up sculpture, the branch in which he had started his artistic career. He led an irregular life and was even accused of assassinating his wife, for which he was imprisoned and tortured to make him confess. However, King Philip IV wrote to the Court ordering them to avoid forms of torture that could harm his fingers, so that such an important artist would not be maimed.

The altarpiece of Lebrija was his first great sculptural and at the same time architectural work. It includes the Virgin of the Olive and a grand Christ Crucified. On the sides there are two sculptures of Saint Peter and Saint Paul and in the sacrarium, four small images of the four Evangelists. Although both the architecture and sculpture are by Alonso Cano, the central niche is by Juan Santamaría, in the 18th century. The paintings of the altarpiece are by Pablo Legot and represent *Saint John the Baptist, The Adoration of the Kings, The Adoration of the Shepherds, and The Ascension.* Alonso Cano started work in 1629 and probably finished it two years later.

Other altarpieces in the church

The first chapel to the left is dedicated to Saint Anne, and the altar has a sculpture of Saint Anne with the Virgin, by Ignacio López, from the end of the 17th century, and paintings by Juan Antonio Sánchez Barahona.

In this same aisle is the chapel of the Vela family, with an image of the Virgen de la Piña , by the great master Juan Bautista Vázquez the Elder in the

16th century. In the upper part of the altarpiece, there is a relief of the Eternal Father by the same artist. There are also fine historical paintings in this chapel, including the *Battle of Clavijo*, with the Apostle Saint James on horseback, and *The Last Communion of Saint Isidore*, from the 17th century.

The right hand aisle is dedicated to the souls, with a great relief on this subject in the center, an 18th-century work by Matías Navarro.

This church also has a baptismal font brought from Flanders, which was probably carved in the 17th century, when Flanders was still a Spanish province. As far as forged iron work is concerned, the screen of the Chapel of the Souls is to be admired, as well as the pulpit, both from the 18th century, by the great wrought iron master Salvador Rodríguez, who was probably also responsible for the baptismal chapel. The choir has lovely choirstalls carved with figures by Juan Santamaría. The church has a large number of gold and silver pieces, liturgical garments, choir books and other ornaments.

The church is known indistinctly as Santa María la Mayor or Santa María de la Oliva as it is the seat of Our Lady of the Olive, patron of the town.

Church of Santa María de Jesús

This Franciscan church belonged to the convent of the Tertiaries, built at the end of the 16th century, and has a single aisle. The portal is not very large, flat and with a curved pediment which holds a small figure in relief of the Virgin Mother.

The altarpieces and images date from the 17th and 18th centuries, the best being the Christ of the Good Death, possibly by Juan Bautista Vázquez the Elder, and a Virgin with Saint Anne in the Sevillian Baroque style of the end of the 16th century.

Convent of las Concepcionistas

The Renaissance portal dating from the 15th century presents a round arch and two fluted pillars with Corinthian capitals on each side, and between both of them niches containing stone statues of Saint Peter and Saint Paul. Over all this there is a curved pediment, broken in the middle by a niche with an image of the Virgin and Child, above the niche a triangular pediment, adorned with small figures also in stone. The church has a single aisle and barrel vaulted ceilings.

And we find ourselves in front of the main altarpiece which is a truly amazing piece of Baroque work, from the best of the 18th century. It was made by Juan Santamaría and Matías José Navarro in 1729. There is not a single centimeter of surface space which is not profusely carved with all types of ornamental reliefs, in the open spaces as well as on the columns framing five rows of niches.

In the center, at the top, an

image of the Eternal Father half emerges from the clouds. Beneath Him there is a Christ Crucified still lower down a Saint Sebastian, and, in the central niche presiding over the altar, a Virgin and Child, standing on a half moon.

The side lanes have niches holding Saint Michael, Saint Augustine, Saint Francis, and Saint Dominic. The outside lanes are exclusively ornamental, with foliage, grotesques and two large lamps bearing angels. The altarpiece is an authentic marvel which the visitor does not grow tired of contemplating.

On the right there is another altarpiece by the same artists, with Saint Anne and the Virgin, an Ecce Homo, Saint Isabel with Saint John as a child and Saint Joachim.

On the left there are two altarpieces with Saint Joseph, Saint John Nepomucene, Saint Lucia, Saint Francis, Saint Bernardine and the Blessed Beatriz de Silva, as well as a relief of the Baptism of Christ, all from the end of the 17th and 18th centuries.

Other Churches in Lebrija

Equally interesting is the 16th century monastery of San Francisco, whose patron was a noble family named Portugal, as can be seen from their coat of arms here. There are good sculptures from the 16th to 18th centuries, and several Passion angels from the 17th century, possibly by «la Roldana».

On the portal at the foot of the church there is a curious Via Crucis (Way of the Cross) with fine sculptures from the 16th and 17th centuries, the most important being the Christ of the Vera Cruz or True Cross, patron of this church.

Worthy of a visit also are the Capilla de Belén with a magnificent altarpiece, at the center of which there is a painting of Our Lady of Bethlehem with the Child, flanked by magnificent Solomonic pillars, images of Saint Thomas and Saint Bonaventure, and the Eucharistic allegories of the pelican and the phoenix bird. This is an exquisite Rococo altarpiece.

Having finished the visit, it is recommended to visit some of the typical taverns in the center of town, to try the typical caracoles (snails) of Lebrija with manzanilla sherry.

We will return using the same road as we came on.

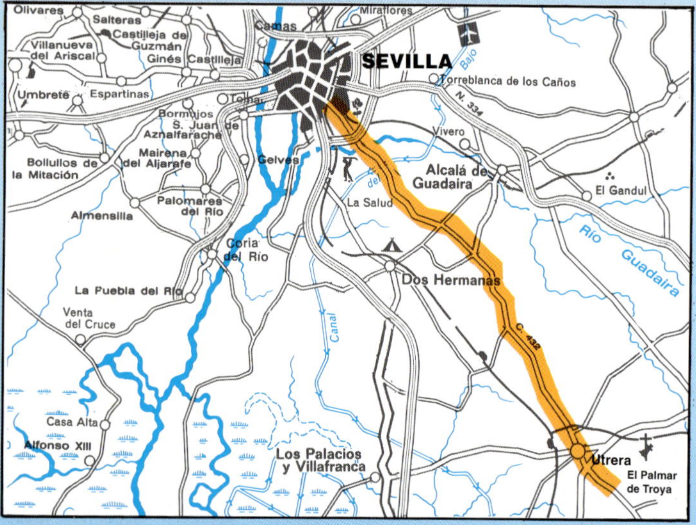

ROUTE 5: SEVILLE • UTRERA EL PALMAR DE TROYA	
PLACES OF INTEREST • **Utrera:** Old city walls Church of Santa María de la Mesa	Church of Santiago Church of San Francisco The mills of Utrera The Shrine of La Consolación • **El Palmar de Troya**
ACCESS	Take road C-432. 40 km away from Seville
PRACTICAL INFORMATION ALONG THE ROUTE	
Utrera: *Useful addresses and telephones:* • Town Hall. Tel 486 00 50 • Local Police. Tel: 486 00 58	• Red Cross. Tel: 470 57 11 • Rural Police. Tel: 486 11 48
END OF ROUTE	Take the same route back to Seville from Marchena.

ROUTE 5: SEVILLA · UTRERA · EL PALMAR DE TROYA

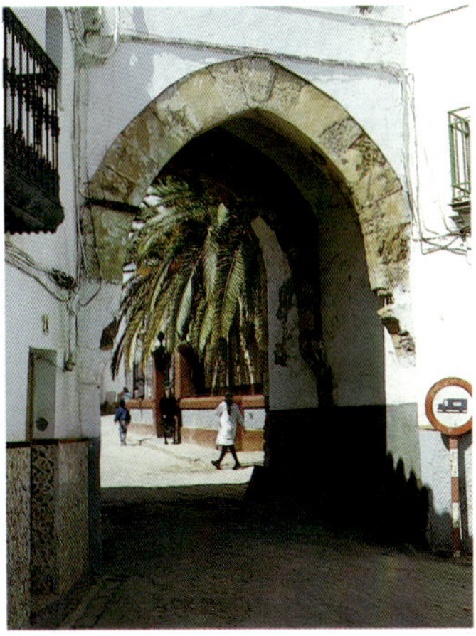

The Town Arch.

UTRERA
The town

Even before entering the town, seen at a distance, we are struck by the sight of its buildings, imagining that we are about to find noble constructions and estately mansions, with church and monastery towers, rising above them. On entering the town this first impression is confirmed.

Utrera was founded at the time of the Tartessians and Caesar mentioned its original name, *Betis*. In Roman times it was called *Utrícula*, from which in Visigothic times its present name of Utrera was derived. After the Reconquest by Saint Ferdinand in the 13th century, it became a bastion against the Moors to protect Seville.

Segments of the wall which embraced the town still remain, including the Town Arch or Gate, built in Mudejar style in the 13th century.

The old town center extended around the castle, and this will be where we start our visit.

The castle dates from the 13th century, was restored in the 15th century, and is a good example of the military architecture of the times. It has now been restored once more, in order to use its installations for cultural activities, which include an outdoor theater. The Torre del Homenaje is impressive, although without battlements.

At the end of the Middle Ages and later, this town has been the residence of noble families, among them the Pacheco, Sanabria, Fernández de Abaunza, Ulloa, Bécquer, Anaya and Bohorquez and a branch of the Ponce de León family. Almost all of them have left stately ancestral homes which we will come across throughout the town center.

Church of Santa María de la Mesa

Although its proper name is Santa María de la Asunción, it is known as Santa María de la Mesa as this church is on top of a small meseta or plateau. The church was built in the 15th century and was extended in the 16th century. First of all, its tower catches our attention:

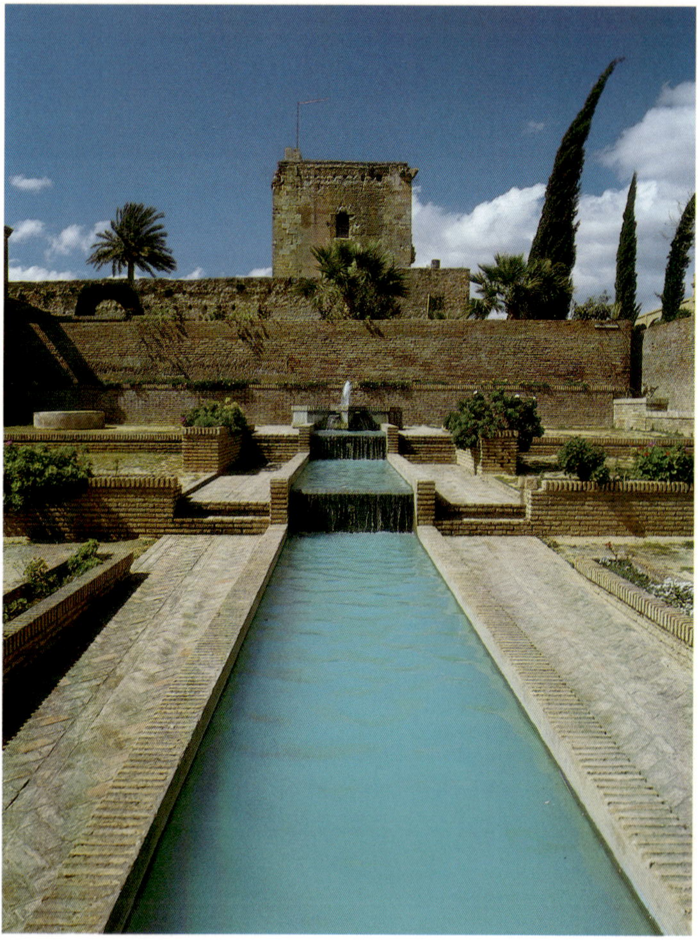

Homage Tower in the Castle.

a unique structure formed by a lower section in the shape of a triumphal arch, built by the architect Martín de Gainza (who built the grand Hospital of the Five Wounds in Seville). The triumphal arch is made of brick with Renaissance-style columns in the same material, forming decorative patterns, and over the tympanum there is an image of the Assumption of Our Lady, while the pendentives bear busts of saints in medallions.

Over this first section there are four more, decreasing in size, the lower two by Hernán Ruiz with a certain influence from La Giralda in Seville, whose belfry was made by the same architect. The upper two stages date from the 18th century, and finish off in a little spire. Apart from the grandiose portal which is the base of

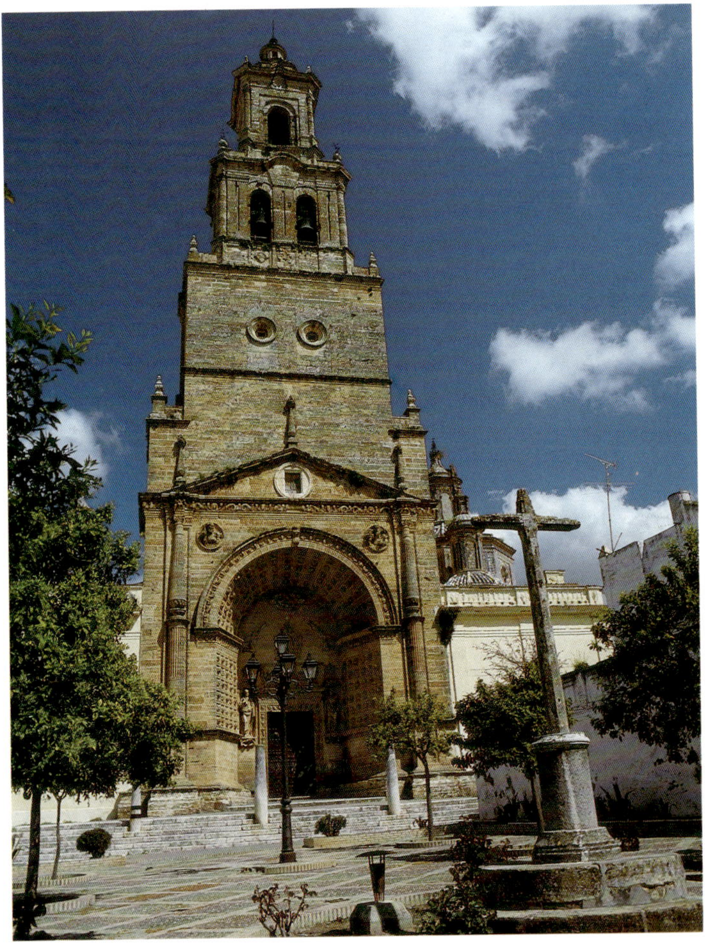

Santa María de la Mesa.

the tower, there is another side entrance from the 18th century in Neoclassical style.

Inside the church has five aisles with Gothic ribbed vaultings resting on clustered pillars. The outside aisles are shorter, so that the transept is formed only by the central nave and the two interior aisles. The choir occupies almost half of the central nave, reducing the perspective of this church, as happens in all churches with low choirs. However, this one is an artistic jewel with 61 choir-stalls carved with figures of saints, made by Felipe del Castillo and Diego Castillejo in the 18th century.

The main altarpiece is from the 17th century, by Martín Moreno, a carved relief with scenes from the life of Our Lady and the martyrdom of saints.

On the right is the chapel of Our Lady of the Rosary, with an altarpiece showing the *Entry of Jesus in Jerusalem*, the *Imposition of the Chasuble to Saint Ildephonse* and the *Burial of Christ*. In this chapel the tomb of Diego Ponce de León is to be seen, with a magnificent praying statue in which he appears dressed in armor and rich robes, with a flag in his hand and accompanied by a page or squire. It is an extraordinarily beautiful tomb.

On the left hand altar we can see a sculpture of Our Lady of the Sweet Name, with several saints and a lovely 17th century painting on the subject of Christ, *Fountain of Life*.

On the right hand aisle is the altar of Our Lord at the Column, a work by Duque Cornejo.

In this church there are two interesting pieces of Colonial art: a candelabrum of guilded wood with silver disks, a present from the governor of Huancavelica, Manuel Saldaña, which are valuable examples of Peruvian art from the 18th century and a silver Mexican tray from the same century, kept in the church treasury.

In one of the niches located on the outer side of the choir is an image of Our Lady of the Paths which could date from the 15th century, since it is recorded that before this church was erected, it was in a country shrine from where it took the name of our Lady of the Paths, whose feast day is celebrated on August 15.

Also worth mentioning in this church is a magnificent processional monstrance in silver, in 18th-century Baroque style, in three stages, with Solomonic pillars, profusely decorated with little silver figures on the four corners of each section and crowned by a small statue representing the triumph of Faith.

The Church of Santiago

Returning to the castle, and next to it we will find the church of Santiago, in Gothic style from the 15th century, with a lovely cupola over the transept, while the rest of the ceilings in the three aisles have pure Gothic fan vaulting.

The tower rises over a lovely portal with a basket-handle arch from the times of the Catholic Kings. The rich decoration of this portal softens the severity of the brick tower with its double belfry.

The sculptures of the main altarpiece, as well as Saint James the Apostle next to it, are good, from the 17th century. Specially notable in this church is the image in the chapel of the Christ of Saint James, from the 16th century, as well as a figure of Mary Magdalene on an altar next to this same chapel, made in the 18th century by Duque Cornejo.

Church of San Francisco

This church was built in the 16th century by the Dukes of

Arcos, of the Ponce de León family, before they decided to build their family pantheon in Marchena. This is why several members of this family are buried here.

The church has a single aisle and transept in Greco-Roman style, with carved and ornate wood ceilings and a fine cupola over the transept.

According to some authors, this is the best church of the Franciscan Order in the whole province of Seville.

The main altarpiece is from the 18th century and dedicated to Our Lady of Sorrows, who occupies the central niche. Also from the 18th century is the altarpiece of Saint Diego de Alcalá.

Special attention should be paid to the frescoes on the transept cupola, representing the *Triumph of the Company of Jesus*, in which figures of various Jesuit saints, surging heavenwards in an apotheosis of angels can be seen. This painting is from the Sevillian school of the 18th century.

The mills of Utrera

After this visit to the main churches, we will turn our attention to the olive-oil mills, one of the most important features of the architecture of Utrera.

The oil mills used to grind the olives from a tower to which a beam was attached that put pressure on the press. The towers of these mills can still be seen in several old houses. Famous were those of Mujeres street, Tetuán street, Preciosa street, Arroyo street, Ponce de León street, Lorenzano Sánchez street and Antón Quebrado street, although in past years some of them have disappeared or are about to do so.

The Shrine of La Consolación

One kilometer away (about half a mile) from the town center of Utrera lies the shrine of Nuestra Señora de la Consolación (Our Lady of Consolation). Regarding popular devotion, the favorite shrines in the province of Seville are those of the Consolation in Utrera, Grace in Carmona, and Setefilla in Lora del Rio.

Nuestra Señora de la Consolación has not only inspired mystic sentiments, but its figure is so beautiful that in order to compare women with the height of beauty, a popular saying goes: Mira qué bonita era que se parecía a la Virgen de Consolación de Utrera (She was so beautiful that she resembled Our Lady of Consolation of Utrera).

Although there was a sanctuary or a shrine here earlier, this present one was built in the 17th century. The church has a single aisle, with Mudejar ceilings in well carved wood. The architecture, as a whole, is very Andalusian with whitewashed outside walls, as benefits a country shrine. It has a small square tower with a belfry and is covered by a pyramidal roof.

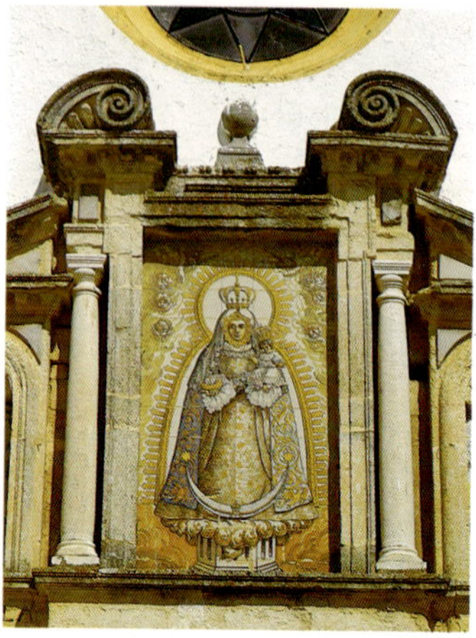

Shrine of Our Lady of the Snows.

The 17th century stone portal has two columns on each side on a single pedestal and between them a niche with a sculptured saint. Over the lintel, a pediment is divided into three spaces separated by marble columns, with the Virgin and two saints.

The main altarpiece has in its center a small chamber showing Our Lady of Consolation, from the 15th century, and to the sides, there are paintings of Saint Joachim and Saint Anne, of the Sevillian school of the 17th century. Also on this altar are two reliefs of the Annunciation and the Visitation, and several sculptures of saints of the Order of the Minims, who built the sanctuary.

On the side walls of the main chapel are two large paintings from the 18th century, representing The Death of the Virgin and The Assumption. On the side altar are saints venerated by this Order, such as Saint Francis of Paola, a Crucified Christ, Saint Anthony, Saint Paul, Saint Raphael and others. On the side walls are paintings by the school of Murillo, and possibly the design is by the master himself. The choir is raised and has good 18th century choirstalls.

Before leaving Utrera, we would be well advised to buy the traditional «mostachones de Utrera », whose recipe dates back to the Middle Ages and which are usually eaten for breakfast or in mid afternoon, as they are like small sponge cakes.

PALMAR DE TROYA

A little over 13 kilometers from Utrera (43 miles) is El Palmar de Troya, which until twenty years ago was little more than a village, and has now become a place of strange and intense religious life.

The origin of the religious phenomenon of El Palmar de Troya dates back to 1968, when on March 30th several people claimed to have seen the Virgin over a mastic bush in the fields.

Soon after, an ex-novice who had left the Order of the Brothers of Saint John of God in Seville, came here and joined those who claimed that the Virgin had appeared to them, becoming the spiritual leader of a small group of followers.

The Catholic Church turned down the alleged apparitions

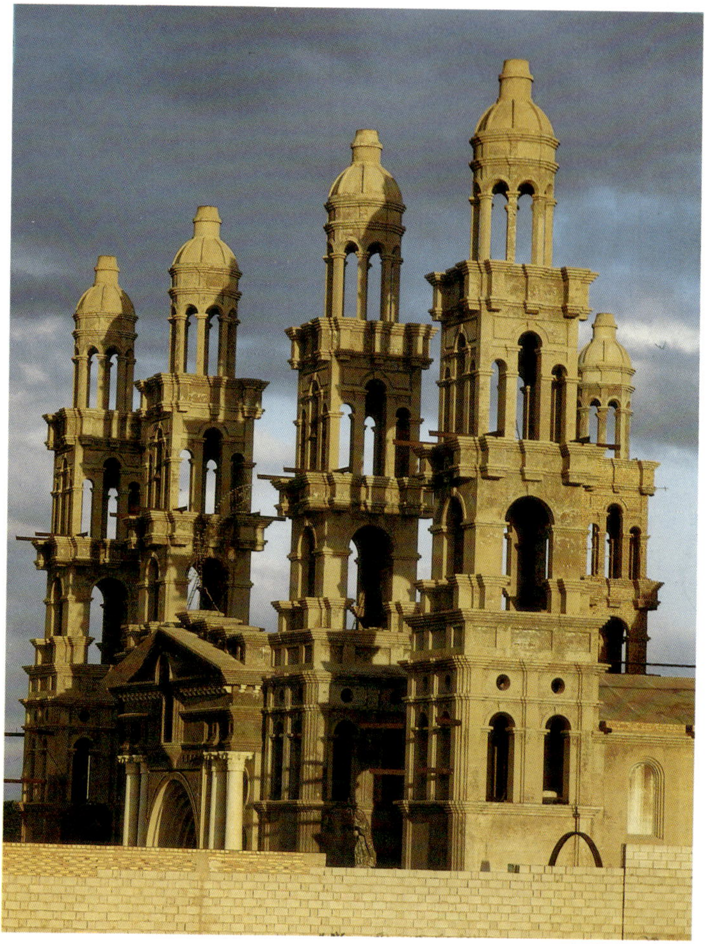

El Palmar de Troya.

but the former novice, Clemente Domínguez, insisted on his spiritual leadership and gradually gathered about him a large number of followers, setting up an association which was rejected as illegitimate by the Catholic hierarchy.

This association has members from Canada and United States, mainly young people who come to register in its two branches: male and female.

On January 1st, 1976, the Archbishop of Vietnam, Monsignor Pedro Martín Ngo-Dinh Tuc, who had just escaped from his diocese due to the Vietnam war and Communist occupation of the territory, ordained Clemente Domínguez as a priest. This ordination was not legitimate, as Holy Orders must be administered by the archbishop of the diocese, in this case Seville, and not by a visiting bishop. Nevertheless, this ordination is valid, because since Saint Peter transmission of priesthood is always valid if administered by a bishop. Thus, Clemente became a priest, although outside the obedience to Catholic hierarchy. The Church condemned his ordination, but eleven days later the same Archbishop of Vietnam invested Clemente Domínguez as a bishop.

After this, events gained momentum. Clemente Domínguez started to build a cathedral at El Palmar de Troya, at the same time acquiring houses in Seville, and he himself started to ordain priests and bishops.

On May 29, 1976, Clemente Domínguez was involved in an automobile accident returning from France, where he had created a religious group, and was on his way to Bilbao. In the crash, Clemente Domínguez's broken glass damaged his eyes and he was permanently blinded.

The unfortunate incident did not make him reduce his activities, and in 1977, a year after he was consacrated as a bishop, he transmitted the same order to 47 of his priests, so that he now has a large body of bishops.

With these bishops he organized communities in several European and American countries. On August 2, 1978, Pope Paul VI died in Rome and Clemente, who was in Bogotá, called a synod of his bishops and had them proclaim him pope.

From this moment we can speak of a genuine schism, comparable to those of Constantinople, Avignon and Peñíscola, situations in which in opposition to the Pope in Rome another pontiff was elected by dissident bishops. Clemente took the name of Gregory XVII.

This is the present situation of Clemente Domínguez's church, which he calls the Holy Apostolic Palmarian Catholic Church. It has its headquarters in Seville and the foundational church, which he calls Patriarchate of El Palmar de Troya, of the Order of the Carmelites of the Holy Face, is the building we have in front of us in El Palmar de Troya. Its grandiose proportions, larger than those of a cathedral can be seen from afar. It is a huge church, and inside, various saints are venerated, presided over by a figure of the Crowned Virgin of El Palmar, a clothed image with the Child on her left arm and a scepter in the right hand, holding a scapulary of Our Lady of Mount Carmel and another of the Holy Face.

The inside of the temple was made according to the liturgy prior to the Second Vatican Council, that is, altars are placed so that the celebrant faces the altarpiece, there is a pulpit for preaching and all ceremonies and prayers are in Latin. Apparently, the church of Clemente Domínguez is quite similar to that of the French dissident bishop Lefebvre.

A characteristic note of this church is that a great profusion of green plants is used in its day-to-day decoration.

It is convenient to visit during the afternoon, which is the only time the temple of El Palmar de Troya is open. Women in slacks are not admitted and they must cover their heads with a veil in addition.

We return to Seville on the same route as we came.

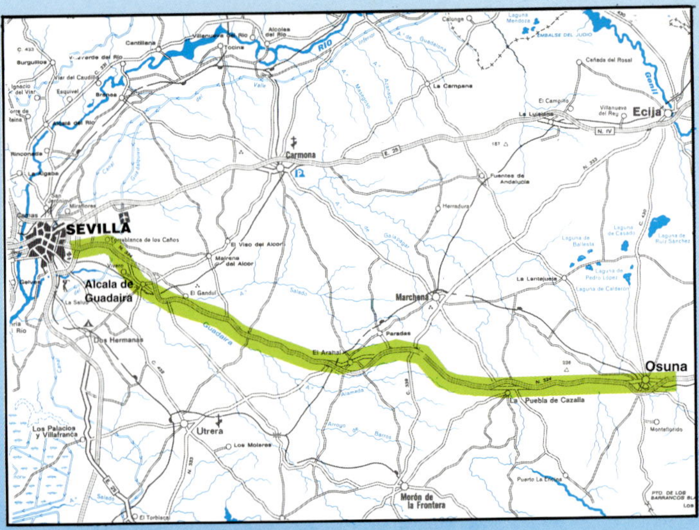

ROUTE 6: OSUNA

PLACES OF INTEREST

- **Osuna:**

Remain of the city walls
Cilla del Cabildo
Palace of the Count Gomera
The Colegiata and the Panteón de los Duques de Osuna
University Chapel
Convent of La Encarnación
Parish Church of Nuestra Señora de la Victoria
Church of Santo Domingo
Church of Nuestra Señora del Carmen

ACCESS

Take road C-334. 82 km away from Seville

PRACTICAL INFORMATION ALONG THE ROUTE

Useful addresses and telephones:

- Town Hall. Tel: 81 00 50
- Local Police. Tel: 81 00 50
- Rural Police. Tel: 81 09 13
- Tourist information office. Tel: 81 16 17. Calle Sepulcro Ducal (outside the walls)
- Archeological Museum. Plaza de la Duquesa.
- Museum of the Collegiate Church. Colegiata de Osuna.
- Museum of la Encarnación. Monastery.

Restaurants:

- Mesón del Duque, Plaza de la Duquesa, 2. Tel 481 13 01. Home-made food.

END OF ROUTE

Take the same road back to Seville.

ROUTE 6: SEVILLA · OSUNA

Osuna is a city of Roman origin whose Latin name was Ursaona, which indicates that at the time bears abounded in this region.

As an autonomous colony of the Roman Empire, it had the privilege of minting its own money from the times of Augustus.

Osuna, a Renaissance Court.

After Moslem rule, it was reconquered by King Ferdinand, who established in this city the Great Commandership of the knights of Calatrava, but in 1445, it passed into the hands of the Girón family, at a time when Pedro Girón was Master of the Order. The fourth Count of Ureña turned Osuna into a kind of border area against the Moors of Granada, founding a university and obtaining from the Pope elevation of the parish church to the category of collegiate church. The fifth Count of Ureña was promoted by King Philip II to the rank of Duke of Osuna and the town became a Renaissance city with nobles of lesser rank, forming a proper court around the Duke of Osuna.

It was at this time is when Osuna was enhanced with numerous buildings of great architectural beauty, palaces, stately houses, monasteries, churches, even buildings related to commercial activities were constructed with a palace-like appearance. Our tour of Osuna will reveal a large number of façades with artistic portals, coats of arms, etc.: what could at the time be a city rivaling with small European courts.

Remains of the walls

Some parts of the walls remain, bearing evidence to the importance of this fortress in Medieval times. The arch known as the Arco de la Pastora (Shepherdess' Gate) was built in the 18th century to embellish the precincts.

The historical center

The historical and artistic center of the city is located around San Pedro, Sevilla, Asistente Arjona and adjoining streets. On San Pedro street we find, at the beginning, the magnificent building of the Chapter House by the architect Alonso Ruiz Florindo, bearing a great resemblance to the Archbishop's Palace in Seville. The façade shows a great portal with two pillars on bulbous pedestals flanking the door and supporting the lintel. Over these rise the Giralda tower in relief, Saint Justa and Saint Rufina, and two jars with lilies, the emblems of the cathedral chapter of Seville, who owned this building.

On this same San Pedro street is the palace of the Count of Gomera, with a façade adorned with gargoyles imitating artillery cannons. The edge of the roof has a curving cornice with volutes. The entrance is monumental, with three large columns on each side supporting a stone balcony with balustrade. The opening is flanked by four Solomonic pillars topped by a carved, broken pediment and over it a coat of arms. On the right of the façade there is a covered tower.

The mansions of the Soto, De la Puerta Cepeda and Govantes families, and many others have very handsome 17th and 18th century façades with coats of arms. The three streets we have mentioned are a pleasure to the visitor's eye and convey the impression of a city where time has stood still.

Of course, we must visit the old university, its artistic façade contrasting with its uniquely severe courtyards.

The Colegiata and the Panteón de los Duques de Osuna

The most important church in Osuna is the collegiate church of the Assumption, which houses the pantheon of the Dukes of Osuna. The main portal dates from the 17th century and is known as the Puerta del Sol, or Door of the Sun, with numerous medallions and modillions in Renaissance style, flanked by two sealed up doors with Baroque decoration.

The inside of the church has three aisles in hewn stone, with vaults, and a transept with cupola.

The main altarpiece dates from the 18th century made by Juan Bautista Pinache, who carved the sculpted groups of the Calvary, Assumption of the Virgin and several saints. The paintings in the same altarpiece are from the Sevillian school, possibly from the circle of Espinal.

The first chapel in the left hand aisle has an altarpiece with Our Lady of Victory from the 16th century, with paintings by Juan Bautista de Amiens. In the following chapel there is a marble altar with a painting of Our Lady of La Antigua and a Calvary on one side painted by José Rivera, which is one of the best works by this artist and one of the finest paintings existing in Spain.

The first chapel to the right has an altarpiece with a crucified Christ made by Juan de Mesa in 1623, whose similarity with the Cristo de la Carretería in Seville, could serve to identify this work, which is at present attributed to Ocampo.

The pantheon of the Dukes of Osuna adjoins the collegiate church and is really another church with three stories. At the level of the collegiate church is the court of the Holy Sepulcher, which is a 16th century cloister with a Renaissance arcade. From the cloister we enter the chapel, whose altarpiece has a relief of the *Entombment of Christ*, an anonymous work from the 16th century, and next to it, an original painting by Gerard Wytwel of Utrecht representing the *Annunciation*, dating from the same time. To the other side there is a painting by Hernando de Sturmio representing the *Immaculate Conception.*

From the chapel, we enter the Ducal pantheon, which on each of its underground levels and on the stairway contains sarcopha-

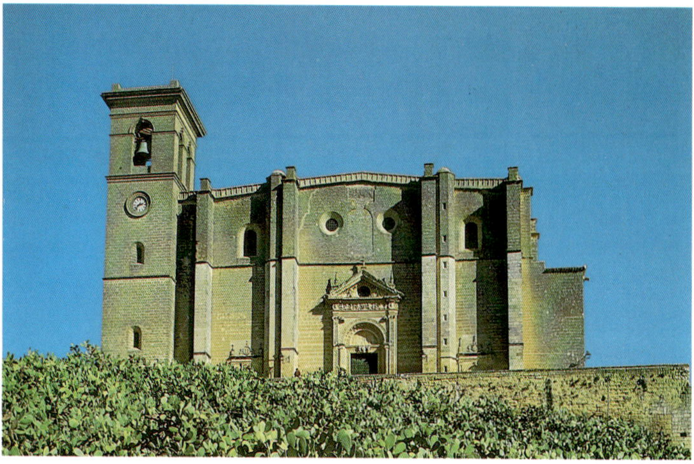

Collegiate church of Osuna.

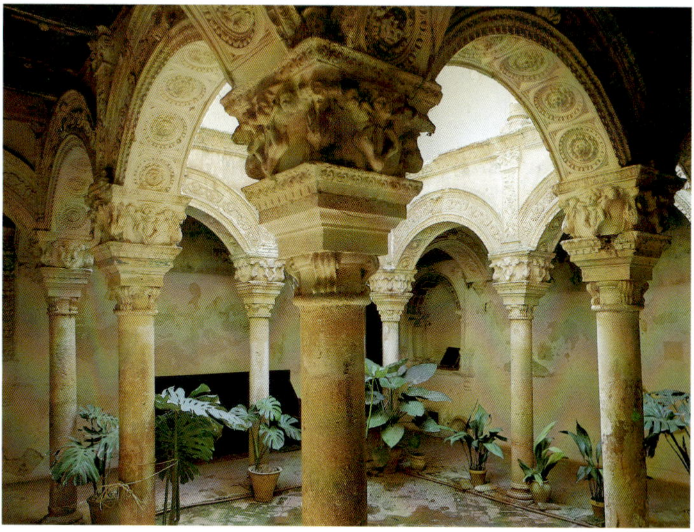

Pantheon of the Dukes of Osuna. Cloister.

gui containing the remains of the Dukes of Alba and the Counts of Ureña, from the 16th century to the beginning of the 20th century. This pantheon is considered to be a «second Escorial».

The same building of the collegiate church houses, in what used to be the principal sacristy, a museum with paintings by José Ribera «Lo Spagnoletto» painted in Naples for the Duke of Osuna, who was at the time viceroy of Spain in the Spanish provinces of Naples and the Two Sicilies during the second decade of the 17th century; these paintings are included in art books and known worldwide.

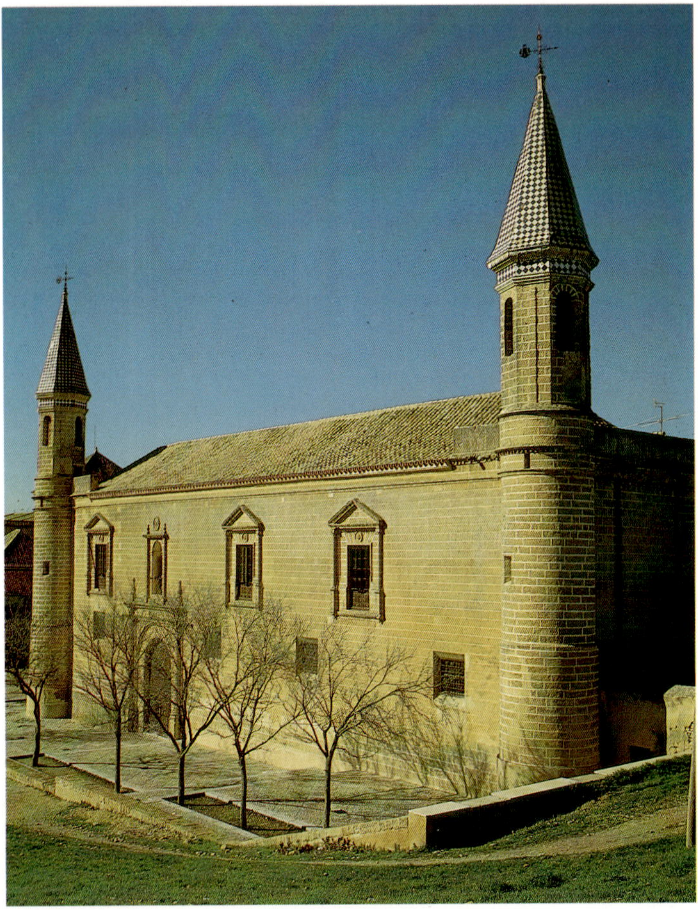

The old University.

Also shown in this museum are jewels, church plate, liturgical vestiments, etc.

University Chapel

In the afore-mentioned University, which dates from the mid 16th century, apart from the courtyard, we can visit the chapel with paintings from the same time by Hernando de Sturmio, representing *The Annunciation*, *The Nativity*, *The Adoration of the Magi* and four saints.

Other churches in Osuna

The *convent of la Encarnación* with a Baroque altarpiece representing Our Lady of Mercy, Saint Peter Nolasco, and Saint Ramón Nonato, is worth visiting. It is a convent of nuns of the Order of Mercy.

The principal cloister has been turned into a museum and here we can see interesting glazed tiles painted with hunting scenes, popular characters and a view of the Alameda de Hercules in Seville, all from the 18th century.

The parish church of Nuestra Señora de la Victoria, a former monastery of the Order of Saint Francis of Paola, has a grand main altarpiece in Baroque Churrigueresque style dating from the 18th century, with Our Lady of Victory, the four Evangelists and other saints venerated by this Order, such as Saint Francis of Paola, Saint Raphael, etc.

The church of San Dominico, from the 16th century, has an altarpiece by Jerónimo Hernández and Diego Velasco, with a Saint Dominic and other saints of his Order such as Saint Thomas, Saint John Nepomucene, etc. since this was formerly a Dominican monastery and later became a parish church.

The choir has outstanding choirstalls from the 17th century and a Baroque organ from the 18th century.

The church of *Nuestra Señora del Monte Carmelo* This church has a main altarpiece by Juan de Oviedo and sculptures by Juan Bautista Vázquez the Elder.

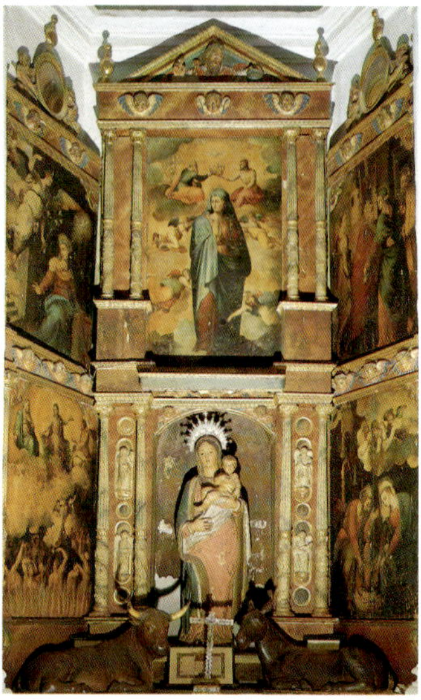

Church of Saint Dominic. Altarpiece.

Having finished the visit to Osuna, we will return to Seville by the same road, C-334.

PRACTICAL INFORMATION ON SEVILLE

HOW TO GET THERE

By air:

- San Pablo National Airport. ☎ 451 25 78
- IBERIA. Almirante Lobo, 2 ☎ 422 26 93

By railroad:

- Santa Justa Station. ☎ 441 41 11
- RENFE. Zaragoza, 29 ☎ 422 26 93

By bus:

- Prado de San Sebastian Bus Station. Calle Manuel Vazquez Sagastizabal. ☎ 441 71 11

By road:

- *North:* A-4 Highway, Madrid-Cordoba
- *South:* Tollroad to Cadiz-Jerez
- *East:* National Road 334 Granada-Malaga
- *Northwest:* National Road 630 to Extremadura
- *Distance in Kilometers from Seville to:* Huelva, 94 km; Cádiz, 149 km; Córdoba, 140 km; Granada, 250 km; Jaén, 244 km; Amería, 412 km; Málaga, 214 km; Madrid, 538 km.
- Assistance to Motorists: ☎ (91) 742 12 13
- Teleruta: ☎ (91) 535 22 22
- RACE, Royal Automobile Club of Spain.
- ADA

- ***Automobile assistance:***

CITRÖEN: Polígono Industrial Carretera Amarilla (Road to Málaga). ☎ 451 45 11

FORD: Luis Montoto, 157. ☎ 457 68 80

LAND ROVER SANTANA: Road to Cadiz (Bellavista) ☎: 469 04 00

MECEDES BENZ: Avenida Kansas City. ☎: 435 92 00

OPEL: Suauto. Avenida Montes Sierra, 30. ☎ 451 53 44

RENAULT: Syrsa. Autopista San Pablo, (Road to Madrid). ☎ 436 01 00

SYTASA: Santo Domingo de la Calzada, 5. ☎ 450 04 00

SEAT-AUDI-VOLKSWAGEN: Carretera de Su Eminencia. ☎ 464 47 50 – 464 47 66

TALBOT-DODGE-PEUGEOT-SIMCA: Autopista de San Pablo, km 537 (Road to Madrid). ☎ 435 04 50

- TOW SERVICE: María Auxiliadora, 18. ☎ 435 05 85 – 435 30 00 Gorrión, 4. ☎ 452 90 16 – 463 96 43 Torneo, 7. ☎ 433 27 37 – 433 64 70
- **Local transportation:**

Radio Teléfono Taxi: ☎ 435 98 35

Tele Taxi: ☎ 462 22 22
Radio Taxi: 458 00 00

- **Car rental:**

ATASA: Calle Almirante Lobo, Edificio Cristina. ☎ 422 09 57 / 422 09 58

AUTOS MARINA: Arjona, 5. ☎ 422 64 49

HISPALCAR: Calle San Francisco Javier. Edificio Sevilla Nº 2. ☎ 465 48 07 / 465 07 03

SEVILLA CAR: Calle Almirante Lobo, Edificio Cristina. ☎ 422 25 87

ATESA: Plaza Carmen Benítez, 7. ☎ 441 97 12 At the Airport: ☎ 451 47 35

AVIS: Avenida de la Constitución, 15. ☎ 412 65 49 / 422 15 12; Telex: 72242 At the Airport: ☎ 451 43 14

EUROPCAR: Airport. ☎ 467 38 39, Ext. 131 Recaredo, 32 ☎ 441 95 06; Telex: 72455

HERTZ: Avenida República Argentina, 3. ☎ 427 88 87 – 427 07 98; Telex: 72602 At the Airport. ☎ 451 47 20

ITAL: Avenida República Argentina, 9. ☎ 427 75 51 – 427 75 52

AUTOS MIGUEZ: Padre Marchena, 13. ☎ 421 26 14 – 412 66 93

REGENTE CAR: Paseo de Las Delicias. ☎ 421 18 58 – 421 24 01/18 – Telex: 72403

RENTALAUTO: Fernando IV, 3 ☎ 427 81 84

AUTOS TAVARES: Bécquer, 17 ☎ 437 12 92 6 437 87 27

- **Horse-drawn Carriages:**

These depart from Adolfo Rodríguez Jurado Street, near the Cathedral, or in María Luisa Park, next to Plaza de España. Rides through the principal sightseeing areas of the city.

- **River Boats Cruises:**

Boarding piers in Paseo Marqués de Contadero, next to Torre del Oro.

Barco Lola. Offices: ☎ 462 74 48; Ship: ☎ 908 15 51 51 Sevillana de Cruceros. Offices: ☎ 421 13 96;
Ship: ☎ 908 15 0051

WHERE TO STAY

Hotels:

Príncipe de Asturias ***** Isla de la Cartuja. ☎ 446 23 83
Alfonso XIII ***** San Fernando, 2. ☎ 422 28 50
Colón ***** Canalejas, 1. ☎ 422 29 00
Armendariz **** Pº de su Eminencia, 15. ☎ 423 29 60
Doña María**** Don Remondo, 19. ☎ 422 49 90

Gran Hotel Lar **** Plaza Carmen Benítez, 3. ☎ 411 03 61
Hispalis **** Avenida de Andalucía, 52. ☎ 452 94 33
HUSA Sevilla**** Pagés del Corro, 90. ☎ 434 27 07
Inglaterra. Plaza Nueva, 7. ☎ 422 49 70
Los Lebreros Sol**** Luis de Morales, 2. ☎ 457 94 00
Macarena**** San Juan de Ribera, 2. ☎ 437 57 00
Meliá Sevilla**** Dr.Pedro de Castro, 1. ☎ 442 2611
Pasarela**** Avenida de la Borbolla, 11. ☎ 442 07 27
Porta Coeli**** Avenida Eduardo Dato. ☎ 457 00 40
Alcazar*** Menédez Pelayo, 10. ☎ 442 20 11
América*** Jesús del Gran Poder, 2. ☎ 422 09 51
Bécquer*** Reyes Católicos, 4. ☎ 422 89 00
Cervantes*** Cervantes, 10. ☎ 490 02 80
Corregidor*** Morgado, 17. ☎ 438 51 11
Don Paco*** Plaza Jerónimo de Córdoba, 4. ☎ 422 49 31
Fernando III*** San José, 21. ☎ 421 73 07
Giralda*** Sierra Nevada, 3. ☎ 441 66 61
Monte Carmelo*** Turia, 9. ☎ 427 90 00
Monte Triana*** Clara de Jesús Montero, 24. ☎ 434 31 11
Reyes Católicos*** Gravina, 57. ☎ 421 12 00
Venecia*** Trajano, 31. ☎ 438 11 61
Virgen de los Reyes*** Luis Montoto, 131. ☎ 457 6815

Camping Sites:

Camping Sevilla. 1st Class. 10 kms on the road to the Airport.
Club de Campo. 2nd. Class. Avenida de la Libertad, 13.
Villsom. 2nd. Class. Road from Seville to Cadiz, km 554.8

Youth hostels:

- Isaac Peral, 2. ☎ 461 31 50

Cultural life

- ***Archives and Libraries:***

Public Library. Alfonso XII, 19. ☎ 422 90 80

Biblioteca General de la Universidad de Sevilla (General Library of the University of Seville). Old Tobaco Factory Building. Calle San Fernando. ☎ 421 84 88

Central Library of Spanish-American Studies. Alfonso XII

Columbian Chapter Library. Orange Tree Courtyard

Circle of Peasants Library (Círculo de Labradores). Pedro Caravaca, 1.

Mercantile Circle Library (Círculo Mercantil). Sierpes, 71.

General Archives of Indies. Only for research scholars.
Municipal Archives & Newspaper Library. Calle Almirante Apodaca

- *Art Galleries:*

Anima. Miguel Cid, 80. ☎ 438 67 08
Fausto Velazquez. San Isidoro, 4. ☎ 421 51 64
Rafael Ortiz. Mármoles, 12. ☎ 412 48 74
Roldán. Sierpes, 32. ☎ 422 63 09
Sala del Pasaje Villasis. Pasaje Villasis. ☎ 422 66 68
Sala del Molviedro. Plaza Molviedro 4. ☎ 421 37 44
Chicarreros. Calle Chicarreros. ☎ 422 88 90
Imagen. Imagen, 2. ☎ 421 57 05
Oriente. Luis Montoto, 112. ☎ 457 86 64
Promoarte. Mariano de Cavia, 4.☎ 422 73 41
Mercantil & Indurial Circle. Sierpes, 65. ☎ 422 29 80
Royal Circle of Peasants. Pedro Caravaca, 1. ☎ 422 66 25
Museum of Contemporary Art. Santo Tomás, 5.
Alvaro. Gloria, 9. ☎ 421 37 96
Juana Aizpuru. Zaragoza, 26. ☎ 422 85 01
Sadartys. Virgen de Luján, 39. ☎ 445 62 33
Marta Moore. Velarde, 9. ☎ 42192 89

Museums

- **Casa de la Condesa de Lebrija (Countess of Lebrija's House).**
  Cuna, 18. ☎ 422 78 02
  Closed Saturdays and Sundays.
- **Casa de Pilatos**
  Plaza de Pilatos,1. ☎ 422 52 98
- **Palace of Las Dueñas.**
  Dueñas,5. ☎ 422 09 56
  Appointment necessary.
- **Museum-Hospital de la Caridad**
  Temprado, 3. ☎ 422 32 32
- **Museum-Treasury of the Hermandad de Jesús del Gran Poder**
  Plaza de San Lorenzo. ☎ 438 45 58
- **Museum-Treasury of the Brotherhood of Our Lady of La Esperanza Macarena.**
  Basílica de la Macarena.
  Calle Resolana. ☎ 437 01 95
- **Museum of the Convent of Santa Paula.**
  Calle Santa Paula. ☎ 442 13 07
- **Museum of the Real Maestranza de Caballeria.**
  At the Bullring.
  Paseo de Colón, 2. ☎ 422 45 77.

- **Naval Museum at the Torre del Oro.**
  Paseo de Colón. ☎ 422 24 19
  Closed Mondays.
- **Museum and Ruins of Itálica.**
  Santiponce, Road N-630 to Mérida (8 km. from Seville) Closed Mondays.
- **Museo Arqueológico (Archeological Museum).**
  Plaza de América. ☎ 423 24 01
  Closed Mondays
- **Museo de Artes Populares (Museum of Folklore and Arts)**
  Plaza de América. ☎ 423 25 76.
  Closed Mondays.
- **Museo de Arte Contemporáneo (Museum of Contemporary Art).**
  Santo Tomás, 5. ☎ 421 58 30
  Closed Mondays.
- **Museo de Bellas Artes (Museum of Fine Arts)**
  Plaza del Museo, 9. ☎ 422 07 90.
  Closed Mondays

Theaters:

- **Apolo** (Headquarters of Seville Symphony Orchestra)
  Gerona, 26. ☎ 421 75 79
- **Imperial Theater** Sierpes, 25. ☎ 422 68 78
- **Lope de Vega National Theater**
  Avenida de Maria Luisa. ☎ 423 45 46.
- **La Maestranza Theater**
  Paseo Colón. ☎ 456 06 42

Movie Theaters:

- **Alameda Multicines.**
  Alameda de Hércules 9 y 10. ☎ 438 01 56.
- **Avenida Multicines.**
  Marqués de la Parada, 15. ☎ 422 15 48.
- **Azul Multicines.**
  La Florida, 15. ☎ 441 53 09
- **Bécquer.**
  Bécqer, 19. ☎ 437 07 85
- **Cervantes.**
  Amor de Dios, 33. ☎ 438 58 10.
- **Corona Center.**
  Pagés del Corro y Salado. (inside shopping gallery).
  ☎ 427 80 64.
- **Cristina Multicines.**
  General Sanjurjo. ☎ 422 66 80.
- **Delicias.**
  Albaida. ☎ 435 27 36.

- **Fantasio.**
  Pagés del Corro, 100. ☎ 433 72 00
- **Florida Multicines.**
  Menedez Pelayo, 31. ☎ 441 35 53.
- **Regina.**
  Jerónimo Hernandez, 19. ☎ 421 42 19.
- **Rialto Multicines.**
  Plaza Jerónimo de Córdoba, 7. ☎ 421 39 83.

SPORTS

- Stadium of La Cartuja. Inside Expo' 92.
- Municipal Sports Arena. San Pablo Highway
- ***Private Clubs:***

Antares. Genaro Parladé, 7.

Circle of Peasants (Círculos de Labradores). Juan Sebastián Elcano,1.

Mercantile Circle (Círculo Mercantil).

Presidente Carrero Blanco, 1.

Seville Swimming Club. Trastámara, 9.

Pineda Royal Club. Avenida de Jerez.

- **Municipal Swimming Pool Virgen de los Reyes.** Avenida del Doctor Fechiani.
- **Riding Club Puerta Príncipe.** On the Road from Seville to Utrera, km 11.5. ☎ 486 08 15.
- **El Carambolo** Shooting Club
- **Benito Villamarín' Soccer Stadium.**
- **Sánchez Pizjuán Soccer Stadium.**

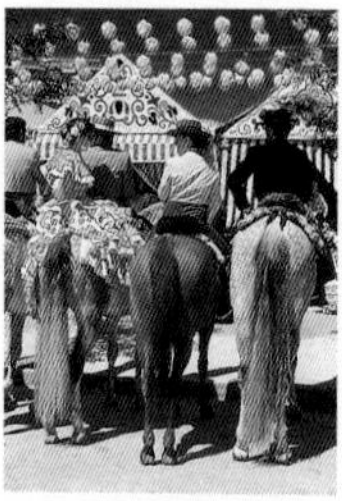

ENTERTAINMENT

In Seville the main event are bullfights, which are held in spring, summer and autumn. The most famous bullfights are held during the April Fair, and take place daily into the month of May. In spring there are bullfights on Sundays and on some days in Summer, as well as during the San Miguel Fair in September.

There are also novilladas, with and without picadores. Tickets are available at authorized offices on calle Sierpes and Velazquez, 12. Here you can also purchase theater tickets.

Shows:

- Florida Show. Menéndez Pelayo, 42. ☎ 441 86 56
- El Cairo Cabaret. Amador de los Ríos, 38. ☎ 442 17 02
- Buque El Patio. Paseo Marqués de Contadero. ☎ 421 38 36

Flamenco Shows:

- Arenal. Rodó, 7. ☎ 421 64 92/ 30 75
- Puerta de Triana. Castilla, 137. ☎ 434 25 07/ 22 04
- El Patio Sevillano. Paseo Colón, 11. ☎ 421 41 20
- El Semáforo. Road to Bormujo. Castilleja de la Cuesta (Seville)
- Los Gallos. Plaza Santa Cruz,11. ☎ 421 69 81

Pubs & Discos:

- Tres. Julio Cesar, 3.
- Antenna. Marqués de Parada, 53.
- Sasayá. Julio Cesar, 3. Salsa
- Lamentable. Perez Galdós, 28. It is also an Art Gallery.
- Groucho. Federico Sánchez Bedoya, 20.
- Sal de Sevilla. Castilla, 165. Open only on weekends.
- Rio. Betis, 67. Live music occasionally.
- Bestiario. Calle Zaragoza.

Ventas (Typical Andalusian Country Inns):

- Vázquez Gabino. At La Pañoleta, 2 km. from Seville.
- Ventorrillo Canario. At Santiponce, 5 km. from Seville, at Avenida de Extremadura, 56
- Pepe Cubero. At Castilleja, 4 km. from Seville. Bar Real, 156. ☎ 416 00 10.
- Las 4 Esquinas. At Valencina, 4.5 km. from Seville. Fray Luis, 2. ☎ 411 77 65
- Sidrería Arias. At Tomares, 8 km. from Seville. On the Road from Tomares to Bormujos. ☎ 476 35 25
- Venta Los Tarantos. At Tomares, 8 km. from Seville.
- Casa Machoca. At Espartinas, 10 km. from Seville. General Franco, 26.
- Casa Pedro. At Espartinas, 10 km. from Seville.
- Casa Pascual. At Coria del Río, 12 km. from Seville. Plaza Sagunto, 11.
- Casa Marqués. At Coria del Río. Avenida de Andalucía.
- Casa Pinichi. At Alcalá de Guadaira, 15 km. from Seville. Orellana, 35.
- Venta El Sombrero. At Utrera, 29 km. from Seville. On the Road from Utrera to Llerena.
- Venta Pazo. At Sanlúcar la Mayor, 19 km. from Seville, Avenida de Colón, 51.
- Venta La Maestranza. At Sanlúcar la Mayor.
- Bar la Isla. At Villafranca, 34 km. from Seville.

SHOPPING

- ***Typical Andalusian Hats:***
  Calle Sierpes on the corner to Rioja.
  Campana, 6.
  Alcaicería, 25.
  Constitución Ave, 21

- ***Bullfighters' Outfits:***
  Pedro Algaba. Virgen de Loreto, 21.

- ***Sevillian Ceramics:***
  Ruiz. San Jorge, 27.
  Sevillarte. Sierpes, 66.
  Macarena. Fray Isidoro de Sevilla, 50.
  Santa Isabel. Antillano Campos, 9 y Alafarería, 10.

- ***Flamenco Costumes:***
  At Sierpes, Cerrajería, Gallegos ,San Angostillo streets, Plaza del Pan, etc.

- ***Manila Shawls:***
  Alvarez Quintero, 52.
  Tetuán, 28.
  Argote de Molina, 18.
  Virgen de Luján, 1.

- ***Fans:***
  Casa Rubio. Sierpes, 56. Typical Sevillian fans, Spanish classical fans, in sandalwood and ivory.

- ***Mantillas:***
  Federico Sanchez Bedoya, 12.
  García de Vinuesa, 33

- ***Holy Week Penitents' Habits:***
  San Esteban, 35.

- ***Antiques:***
  Sierpes, 89.
  Avenida de la Constitucion, 20 y 30.
  Rodrigo Caro, 7.
  Zaragoza, 48.
  Cabeza del Rey Don Pedro, 19.
  Muñoz y Pabón, 4.
  Acetres, 10.
  Plaza del Cabildo,4.

- ***Department Stores:***
  El Corte Inglés. Plaza del Duque, 10.
  Luis Montoto, 122.
  Galerias Preciados. San Pablo, 1.
  Plaza de la Magdalena (annex)
  Ronda de Capuchinos, 36.
  Vilima. Lagar, 2

USEFUL ADDRESSES AND TELEPHONES

Communications:

- Post & Telegraph Offices. Avenida de la Constitución, 32. ☎ 422 88 80
- Telegrams by ☎: – national. ☎ 422 20 00
  – international: ☎ 422 68 60
- Telephone Booths of the Telephone Company: Plaza Nueva, 3 and Plaza de Gavidia.

Emergencies:

- Virgen de la Macarena University Hospital Avenida del Doctor Fleming. ☎ 431 84 00
- Virgen del Rocío Hospital Avenida Manuel Siurot. ☎ 461 21 00
- Valme Hospital On the Road Madrid-Cadiz, km 548. ☎ 461 21 00
- Private Clinics: Sagrado Corazón Clinic, Avenida Manuel Siurot, 49. ☎ 462 44 11
  Santa Isabel Clinic, Luis Montoto, 100. ☎ 457 09
- **Red Cross:** Avenida de la Cruz Roja,1. ☎s 435 12 42 / 0135
- **First Aid Stations:** Jesus del Gran Poder, 34. ☎ 438 2461
  San Jacinto, 25-27. ☎ 433 38 44
  Marqués de Nervión, 63. ☎ 463 56 92
  Juan XXII. w/n. ☎ 463 71 92
- **National and City Police:**
- The Central Police Station is at Concordia Sq. Besides, there are other District Police Stations in the following neighborhoods: Triana: Calle Betis.

Macarena: Lopez de Azmi, 7.
Nervión: Avenida de Cruz Campo 32.
Torreblanca: Calle Ebano.
National Police: ☎ 091
City Police: ☎ 092

- Civil Guard: ☎ 462 81 11
- Civil Defense: ☎ 423 40 40
- Fire Brigade: 442 00 80
- Lost & Found Property: Calle Almansa. ☎ 421 56 94

Tourism:

- Tourist Information Office. Avenida de la Constitución, 21. ☎ 422 14 04
- Tourist Provincial Authority. Adolfo Rodriguez Jurado, 2. ☎ 421 10 91 / 422 56 53
- Municipal Tourist Office. Paseo de Las Delicias. ☎ 423 44 65
- Expo' 92 Office Island of La Cartuja. ☎ 433 30 12
- Expo'92 – General Commissioners' Office. Paseo de La Palmera, 41. ☎ 462 93 11.

CONTENTS

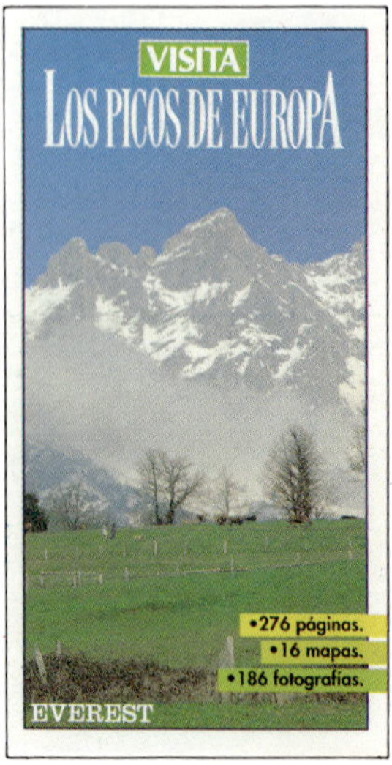

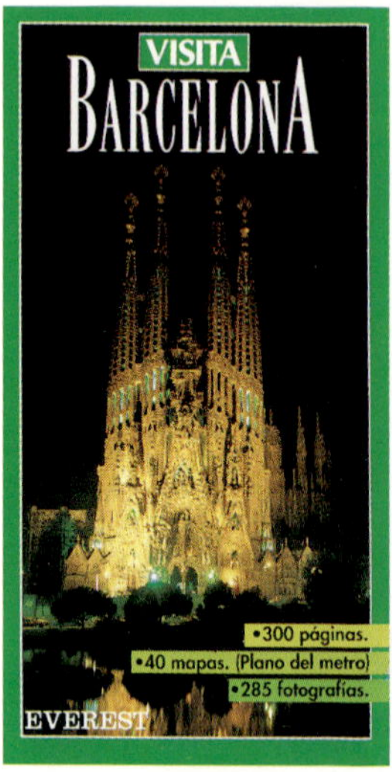

EVEREST SERIES

VISIT

The vast experience accumulated by Everest in the production of its tourist guides, together with full coverage of the whole of Spain, are the best guarantee of quality for this new series, conceived with modern criteria in both lay-out and content.
Special attention has been given to gastronomy, folklore and local craftsmanship, as well as to practical information. Each guide is divided into fully detailed routes, with abundant plans and maps so as to make the most of each visit.

- Ávila
- Barcelona
- La Coruña
- Girona and Costa Brava
- Segovia
- Seville
- Valladolid
- Monastic Hospices in Spain
- The High Alpujarras and Sierra Nevada
- National Park of Cazorla, Segura y las Villas
- National Park of Doñana
- The Picos de Europa Mountains